THE LIVING THREENESS OF SOCIAL LIFE

The
LIVING THREE-NESS
of
SOCIAL LIFE

Discovering and Embodying
in Present Time
the Impulses of Which Rudolf Steiner
Spoke and Wrote

MARC CLIFTON

EPIGRAPH BOOKS
RHINEBECK, NEW YORK

Paperback ISBN 978-1-960090-24-9
Hardcover ISBN 978-1-960090-25-6

Library of Congress Control Number 2023912862

Book design by Colin Rolfe

Epigraph Books
22 East Market Street, Suite 304
Rhinebeck, New York 12572
(845) 876-4861
epigraphps.com

CONTENTS

ABOUT THE AUTHOR AND CONTRIBUTOR

PRELIMINARY NOTES

The 'GA' NUMBERS

Steiner's books, lectures and essays have been cataloged and assigned a 'GA number' where 'GA' comes from the German word 'Gesamtausgabe' meaning 'complete edition.' There is also a corresponding 'CW' abbreviation (with the same numbering) in English for 'Collected Works.' This book will refer to Steiner's works by their 'GA' number.

> The Gesamtausgabe (GA) - or in English, Collected Works (CW) - of Rudolf Steiner's foundational contribution to spiritual science encompasses some 100.000 pages and consists of over 350 volumes that are hopefully nearing completion by 2025. The majority of the content are the 4550 lectures with notes, from the 6200 lectures given in over 120 cities and 13 countries in the period between 1904 and 1924.[1]

An excellent history of how this numbering came into being can be further read about in the footnote for the above citation.

ACKNOWLEDGMENTS

This book arose through conversation and collaboration between myself and Kate Reese Hurd. Though she does not wish to be named as a co-author, I would like to acknowledge the significant amount of work she did for the book. Kate provided an introduction to the material herein and wrote the section, "Free and Ethical Action," which brings Steiner's book, *The Philosophy of Spiritual Activity* (GA 4) to life as part of the foundation for Rudolf Steiner's approach to the social organism. She contributed greatly to the Preface because of her inquiries into Steiner's original texts and lectures in German on the social organism and its three domains. These inquiries facilitated a stronger grasp of the concepts and led to the helpful amendment of the quotes chosen for the book. Kate spurred my

---

[1] https://anthroposophy.eu/Rudolf_Steiner%27s_Gesamtausgabe_(GA)

thinking on a number of chapters and contributed text for many of the earlier chapters. She was generous in offering her editing skills. For all of her work I am deeply grateful.

CONCERNING THE FOOTNOTES

Citations to online articles will have the link to the web page in the footnote. Please note that online content may change or be removed at the discretion of the article publisher or website administrator. Please contact Marc Clifton if the online content cannot be found.

Works by Rudolf Steiner will be referenced by their GA number (GA Gesamtausgabe, or CW, Collected Works.) The full citation will be found in the bibliography. When the original German text has appeared in different translations, the bibliography will cite the translations used in this book. In the case of Steiner's book, *Basic Issues of the Social Question*, it is always referred to as 'GA 23'; and the translation by T.F. Smith will always be cited for reference unless otherwise stated in our text and footnotes.

ON THE WEB

Please visit the website "thelivingthreeness.com" for errata on this book, continuing articles on the three-membered organization of the social organism, updates on current events in relation to the three domains, and an opportunity for discussion and feedback.

PREFACE

Besides illuminating the richness and complexity of Steiner's concepts themselves, developing this book and directly studying Rudolf Steiner's books, articles and lectures on 'the social organism' has also revealed the necessity of striving for clarity in understanding the concepts he originally presented, a clarity born out of seeking to adhere closely to the German. Only then is it possible to begin to grapple with interpreting them with sufficient success, in order to apply them.

One of the first things to note is that while the term, 'the social order,' has been widely adopted in our English translations and writings about the topic (it was coined by early translators), Steiner spoke and wrote of it most often as "the social organism" – the living, evolving organization of human social relationships. Far less often did he use the word, 'order' ("Ordnung" in German). As a living organism, the social organization is not a fixed or arbitrary ordering of our affairs as yet another program to be imposed upon our common social life. In this book, the question of how to express this livingness adequately has had to be grappled with again and again.

Steiner called this organism (italics added) "die *Dreigliederung* des soziales Organismus": 'the three-membering' or 'three member-ness' or 'three-member organization of the social organism.' 'Drei' is three; 'Glied' refers to a member or limb, as of the body; 'Gliederung' refers to an arrangement of the members, their organization, how these members are joined and articulated to move in relation to each other, just as in the body – not a mere 'ordering' of parts. These three members arise out of three different relationship-impulses between human beings within our shared social life: a spiritual-cultural impulse, a rights impulse and an economic impulse (an impulse of exchange.)

It became apparent that translating this concept as 'the threefold social order,' as is so commonly done, is inadequate and rather misleading. To say that something is 'threefold' summons an image of a simple triplicate, a multiplication by three of a single attribute or thing, such as a trifold brochure – 'trifold' and 'threefold' are semantically related and often exchangeable. It does not directly bring to mind the image of a living structuring of human social activity that is composed of three *members*, each bearing within it its own characteristics. And then, when we make a verb out of this simplification in order to say that we will 'threefold' social life, what is this that we do? The image is that we do something *to* the social life; we order it into three parts. This is quite different from the process of recognizing and cooperating with what is there within it but functioning poorly. This abstract verb is therefore not a help. It has felt much better to follow Steiner's lead and simply use the whole concept, just as he repeatedly did, 'the three-member organization.' Not at all did he appear to coin a verb that corresponds to 'threefolding.' On just a few occasions, Steiner can be found to resort to the term, 'dreifach' or 'dreiteilig' – 'three-fold' or 'three-part' – in reference to the three members; but that is the extent of his use. At times (but much less often) he substituted the adjective, "dreigliedert" – 'three-membered' – and with this also, he time and again reinforced the image of a 'membering' (a member of) of an organic whole.

The term 'order' can also lead one to think that Steiner intended that the three-membered social organism that he wrote and lectured about should in some way have a political agenda – it should replace the 'order' of governance, economics, and cultural life that currently exists in society. Any political agenda was absolutely not the purpose of Steiner's work on the three-membered organization (or any of his works for that matter.) Steiner spoke of this misconception when presenting the Statutes of the Anthroposophical Society at the Christmas Conference (please note again the translator's term 'threefold'):

> [The statute:] 'The Anthroposophical Society rejects any kind of sectarian activity. Party politics it considers not to be within its task.'
> [Steiner's explanation:] We need this sentence because numerous misunderstandings were brought about during the year when we were promoting the idea of the threefold social order. The misunderstandings arose out of a lack of clarity in the attitude of many of our members. The impression was frequently given that Anthroposophy wanted to become involved in the political affairs of the world – something that has never been and never can be the case – because many of our friends approached the political parties

regarding the threefold idea. This was an error on their part right from the start.[1]

Those who are acquainted with Steiner's work on the subject of the social organism will notice that the word 'sphere' in reference to these three members of our social life will not be used. This book moves away from this term and instead uses the word 'domain' ('realm' would also work) except when 'sphere' appears in quoted material. There are three reasons for this. First, for this context the Collins Dictionary gives : "A sphere of activity or interest is a particular area of activity or interest." Contrast this with the Collins Dictionary gives for 'domain' (with italics added and an addition in brackets): "A domain is a particular field of thought, activity, or interest, *especially one over which someone* [or something – as shall be seen in this book] has control, influence, or rights." This definition of 'domain,' at least from the perspective of the Collins Dictionary, is far more encompassing of the concepts that pertain to what manifests within the members of the social organism. Second, the German noun that Steiner actually used is, "Gebiet." In the 1910 Muret-Sanders dictionary, this word translates more directly to the word, 'domain' . And the verb form to which 'Gebiet' is related is 'gebieten' – to order, command, dictate, rule over, govern, control. As an image, one could say that in the social life, a domain is characterized by that which holds sway within it. Thirdly, when we imagine a sphere (German, 'Sphäre'), what usually comes to mind is a three-dimensional object with a clearly-defined boundary equidistant to a physical center. By contrast, 'domain' generates an imagination that is more nebulous, possessing the character of interacting with and having its own particular influence upon and within other 'domains.' This is very much the imagination we need relative to the three-member organization of the social organism. In GA 23, Steiner also used the word, 'Leben' – 'life' – freely, routinely and interchangeably with 'Gebiet' when discussing any of the three domains, for instance referring to the rights domain as "das Rechtsleben" – the rights-life. And he also called these three members (Glieder), 'systems.' These are living systems.

With regard to interpreting, it is important to try to avoid construing concepts in a way that takes leave of Steiner's use or that generalizes and mingles them with other ideas, for instance, reframing 'free disposition,'

---

[1] *The Christmas Conference for the Foundation of the General Anthroposophical Society 1923/1924,* Anthroposophic Press, 1990, p 59

'freie Verfügung,' to mean 'free access.' In Chapter 3 of Steiner's book, GA 23, *Basic Issues of the Social Question*, F T. Smith's translation, he wrote (Steiner's italics): "At this present stage, a fertile activation of individual abilities *cannot* be introduced into the economic process without free disposition over [freie Verfügung über] capital. If production is to be fruitful, this disposition must be possible...."[2] The proper disposition of capital is in fact one of the core points in GA 23. Two pages earlier, Steiner had stated: "Capital is the means by which [individual] abilities are made effective for wide areas of the social organism."[3] The verb, 'verfügen' is a rich concept. It means to arrange, prescribe, order, decide, decree, ordain. And the verb expression, 'verfügen über' means to dispose of, as when we tell someone, 'I am at your disposal,' or 'I am at your command.' This image is more complex than simply making 'use' of something (in German, 'benutzen'). But in the F.C. Heckel translation, this 'free disposition over' capital became "free access" rather than *being given the capital by merit*. With this reversal in meaning, It is then an easy step to characterize this 'free access' to capital as 'free of charge' – as we find in literature about the three-membered organization (aka 'threefold social order'). This then brings to the fore pay-to-play arrangements in the reader's mind, where this new arrangement would basically mean no longer having to pay to get capital, that one can freely get it and that it's free for the asking. But that is not the point. With Steiner's use and discussion of the concept, 'free disposition,' our thinking is opened to four questions: how can capital – which includes means of production – be used appropriately on behalf of the entire social organism; who is to be granted the right of disposition over it (i.e., the right to have it at their free disposal and command); how is this right of disposition to be determined; and under what conditions is this right of disposition revoked, reassigned and transferred? The three-membered organism very much allows for private ownership and use of property rather than putting all property into the public domain; but this property right is newly-framed, bounded. To this point, Steiner wrote (Kate's translation):

> The rights-state state will not have to prevent the formation and management of private ownership of capital as long as individual capabilities remain so connected to the capital base that the management represents a service to the whole of the social organism. And it [the rights-state] will remain a rights-state over against [facing, in

---

[2] GA 23, translated by F.T. Smith, about 1/3 into Ch. 3 (p. 98)
[3] GA 23, about 1/3 into Ch. 3 (p. 96)

contrast with] private property. It will never take private property into its own possession, but instead, at the right point in time will cause it to pass over into the right of disposition [Verfügungsrecht] of a person or group of people who can again develop a relationship to the property that is conditional upon their individual circumstances. Through this, from two completely different starting points it will be possible for the social organism to be served. From the democratic subsoil of the rights-state, which has to do with what affects everyone in the same way, it will be possible to be wakeful, that property rights do not turn into property wrongs. Through this, that this [rights-]state does not manage property itself, but takes care of leading [it] over to individual human capabilities, these capabilities will unfold their fruitful power for the entire social organism. So long as it seems expedient, through such an organization the ownership rights or the disposition over them will be able to persist in the personal element. One can imagine that the representatives of the rights-state will at different times make very different laws about the transfer of ownership from one person or group of people to another. In the present, in which a great mistrust of all private property has developed in wide circles, a radical conversion of private property into common property is contemplated. If one were to go far in this way, one would see the possibility of life for the social organism drained thereby.[4]

Correct disposition of capital and individual ability are to be determined by the spiritual-cultural domain, not by the economic domain; and once these determinations are made and the rights domain "cause[s]" the property to pass over to a different person or group of people, the disposition of the capital is considered 'private.' Steiner also went into considerable detail concerning the transfer of capital when deemed necessary to ensure the benefit of the community.

The reader is encouraged to compare the published translations of what Steiner had actually written or had said in lectures with each other and with what others have later interpreted concerning given terms, phrases or sentences. This book is no exception! Of course, studying the original German text is ideal if one can do this.

Working with translations regularly presents difficulties. There are words in German that challenge us to enlarge our English usage (indeed

---

[4] GA 23, Smith translation for reference in relation to K. Reese Hurd's translation, about 2/5 into Ch. 3 (pp. 101-102), "The rights-state will not have to prevent...."

this is what Steiner also did <u>in</u> German!); but are these challenges being well met? In 1919, Steiner published his book, GA 23, with the title *Die Kernpunkte der Sozialen Frage in den Lebensnotwendigkeiten der Gegenwart und Zukunft.* Consulting the large, dense, two-volume 1910 Muret-Sanders German-English and English-German dictionary (abridged encyclopedic) to better understand the meaning of the words that Steiner used in his early 20th century context, Kate renders this title as 'The Core Points of the Social Question in the Necessities of Life of the Present and Future.' In contrast to this, the book was published in English in 1920 as *The Threefold State,* and then in 1923 as *The Threefold Commonwealth,* in 1966 as *The Threefold Social Order,* then also as *Basic Issues of the Social Question* (date unclear), in 1977 as *Towards Social Renewal: Basic Issues of the Social Question,* and in 2019 as *Toward a Threefold Society: Basic Issues of the Social Question.* This is why the book will be referred to simply as 'GA 23'. Also, one can realize that to translate, 'Die Kernpunkte,' as, 'Basic Issues,' is to mute the *truly germinal power* ('Kern') and significance of the points Steiner aimed to present. 'Basic' – especially here without the definite article, 'the' – is more broadly foundational and would be 'grundlich' in German – whereas 'Kern' signifies the kernel, the core of the matter. And 'issues' has a vague, diffusing quality, quite unlike Steiner's focussed word, 'Punkte' – 'points.' To render the subject of the book as "The Threefold State," or "Commonwealth," is to inject concepts into Steiner's title that are not present there. As mentioned earlier, he was not advocating setting up a new kind of political-state entity that is split into three different domains of social life.

Another problem is that the complexities in the meaning of words are narrowed to just one aspect. One example of this is the adjective, 'tüchtig,' which Steiner used in characterization of the proper production of commodities. It has a range of meanings: 'fit, qualified, suitable, strong, vigorous, skilled, efficient, clever, excellent.' What do we usually get in English? 'Efficient.' A dry and impoverished image of the process is all we get. This is especially misleading in the US where we have the term 'quick and dirty' – 'dirty' meaning without care or quality. This is prevalent around the world now, too; and it is most certainly not what Steiner meant with the word, 'tüchtig'!

With another word – an especially important word for us – our narrowed translations routinely impoverish Steiner's entire discussion of the living three-ness of social life. He used the German noun, 'Empfindung,' a great deal. It translates to 'feeling,' 'sensing,' 'perceiving' – *three different meanings*, each one denoting a distinct act of human perception yet being taken together. The verb form is, 'empfinden.' Its closeness to the verb, 'finden,' is clear; and so it bears in it the quality of *finding* something by means of feeling-sensing perception. There is no corresponding word in English that encompasses all three of these rather divergent meanings at once; so, quite oddly, translators usually limit the reader to receiving just one of the aspects, such as 'feeling' or 'sensing.' However, there is a noun in German for just feeling. So if that is solely what is meant, then 'Gefühl' will surely do. And Steiner used this noun, but far less often than he did the nouns, 'die Empfindung' or 'das Empfinden.' And in particular, in reference to the soul faculties that we typically call, "thinking and feeling," in his GA 23 text these are "Denken und Empfinden"; i.e., thinking and feeling-sensing-perceiving, not narrowed in scope to solely a matter of feeling, stripped of these more objective aspects of the soul's activity.

Steiner's manner of using this noun and its related verb, 'empfinden' (to feel-sense-perceive), so repeatedly, suggests to us that he was strongly urging our development of this faculty of the soul, our *Empfindung*, as a *conscious* activity. In light of this urging, it is also unfortunate that in the translations provided by Heckel and by Barton, a merely instinctive sense replaces or is added into the meaning of *Empfindung*. Through this, Steiner is construed to advocate instinctive activity. For example in the following translation, F.C. Heckel inserted the word 'instinctive' (note: the word that is translated as 'sense' here is the word, *Empfindung*, in the German):

> People must acquire an instinctive sense that enables them to distinguish between these two [the rights and economic members] in life. This is essential so that in practice they will be kept as distinct as the work of the lungs is distinct, in the body, from what goes on in the nerves and sensory life.[5]

Here is Smith's faithful translation, which inserts nothing and therefore preserves the *Empfindung*-sensibility as something quite different from instinct, although he narrowed *Empfinden* to its 'sense' aspect:

> It is necessary to sense [empfinden] this difference [between the rights system and the economic system] in life in order that, as a consequence of this sensibility [Empfindung], the economy be separate from the rights member, as in the human natural organism the

---

[5] GA 23, F.C. Heckel translation, about 1/6 into Ch. 2

activity of the lungs in processing the outside air is separate from the processes of the nervous-sensory system.[6]

After reading all of what Steiner wrote about needing to awaken *out of* instinctive social arrangements, Heckel's addition leads the reader to confusion. What Steiner had to say about this urgently-needed awakening culminated in the following (Smith's translation):

> The task of our times is to ... [find], in the primal thoughts, the direction to be taken in order that events be consciously guided. For the time has passed in which humanity can be satisfied with what instinctive guidance is able to bring about.[7]

In his original German, Steiner italicized the word, 'consciously': *'bewusst.'* By contrast, to be 'bewusst<u>los</u>' is to be <u>un</u>conscious, instinctive. The book version of the Smith translation preserves the italics.

Steiner pointed out that in school, one is helped to develop this ability to transcend what moves in us as mere instinct, in order that we may move toward achieving the necessary social sensitivity ('soziale Empfindung'). This is a top priority for the health of the social organism (Kate's translation):

> The anti-social conditions are brought about by the fact that due to their upbringing and education, people enter social life who are not socially sensitive [sozial empfindende]. Socially sensitive people can only emerge from a method of education that is directed and administered by those who are socially sensitive.[8]

Not to belabor the point regarding translations, but there is yet another concept of importance for us. In Steiner's statements concerning "primal thoughts," as referred to in one of the quotes above, the word he used for "primal thoughts" is "Urgedanken" – 'Ur'-thoughts. 'Ur': first, original, primal, archetypal (referring to the original from which other manifestations or expressions are unfolded or copied); and 'Gedanken': thoughts, conceptions, ideas. Here is one of Steiner's statements (Kate's translation, his italics):

> Today, however, it is necessary to see that one can reach a judgment

---

[6] GA 23, Smith translation, about 1/6 into Ch. 2 (p. 59)
[7] GA 23, Smith translation, about 3 pages into Ch. 3 (p. 85)
[8] GA 23, Smith translation for reference in relation to K. Reese Hurd's translation, about 3/7 into the "Preface for the 4th edition, 1920" (p. 14), "The current anti-social state of affairs…"

that grows out of the facts in no other way than through going back
to the *primal thoughts* that underlie all social institutions.[9]

Several translators have inserted an additional concept into their render-
ing of the word, 'Urgedanken,' to make it read, "primal creative thought,"
for example, Heckel's 1966/1972 translation (also note that Steiner's reference to "the facts" is left out by Heckel, replaced by the concept of 'ade-
quacy' in judgment):

> Today, however, we need to see that no adequate judgment can be
> formed without going back to those primal creative thoughts that
> underlie all social institutions.[10]

The injection of 'creative' into the concept of primal or original
thoughts can lead the English reader toward whatever their personal view
is, of what 'creative' means. Two paragraphs later Steiner wrote of "the life
of the impulses carried by these thoughts in human souls" – the life, "das
Leben," of these impulses. Life, yes, but he still did not characterize them
more specifically than that.

Through our feeling-sensing perception we can begin to know and
cooperate with the three distinct, living impulses that are seeking their
way toward realization in our social life. This is why this book bears the
title book, *The Living Three-ness of Social Life*. It is the call of our time
to discover and embody these impulses. Yet, as Steiner pointed out, it is
an ongoing, uphill endeavor. Rather than "purposeful social thinking, the
old instincts still live on;" this means that "[m]ore thoroughly than many
imagine, the human being of the present time must work their way out of
what is no longer viable."[11] Just as we work our way through to the truth
of the Pythagorean theorem and the "thought connections" that it entails,
so it is here:

> Also in social cognition one wrestles through to it, that certain fun-
> damental cognitions can yield themselves up to consciousness as
> true through their inner nature. And if one then only has a sense
> of reality [Wirklichkeitssninn], then one will find that they are also
> applicable wherever they come into question.[12]

[9] GA 23 in the original German, *Die Kernpunkte der sozialen Frage in den Lebensnotwendigkeiten der Gegenwart und der Zukunft*, http://anthroposophie.byu.edu/schriften/023.pdf, see
'Urgedanken,' 2 pages into Ch. 3 (p. 54)
[10] GA 23, Heckel translation, 2 pages into Ch. 3
[11] GA 23, Preliminary Remarks, next to last page; KRH translation
[12] GA 332a, *The Social Future*, 2 pages into Lect. 2; KRH translation

This book cannot take into account all of Steiner's books, articles, and lectures on the living three-ness of the social organism. Nor can it take into account all the numerous derived works that others have produced. The primary influence upon us in writing this book has been GA 23. As Mark Fisher wrote in a 2017 interview: "PhD work bullies one into the idea that you can't say anything about any subject until you've read every possible authority on it."[13] While this book does not aim to conform to the kind of work a PhD might entail, it takes into consideration the difficulty of writing about a subject which has already been covered in a large body of material. Therefore, rather than being a concluding point, this book means to be a renegotiated starting point for further work and discussion. The historical and current references, issues, and questions presented in this book will hopefully create just such discussions between individuals and groups.

And one final but important note concerning the use of the word, 'man.' In the German of Steiner we encounter two words which refer to humanity in general. The German word, 'man,' means an unspecified person or unspecified persons of any gender, and it often translates as 'one'; e.g., 'man denkt': 'one thinks' or 'somebody thinks,' or 'people think.' And the German word, 'Mensch,' and its plural, 'Menschen,' both refer to human beings without regard to gender. But in English these have often been translated as 'man' or 'men.' In our time, this would be all right if our word, 'man,' had continued to be a gender-free designation, *as it used to be.* Perhaps as we read, we can ourselves restore that gender-free meaning and add in *all* genders back in, each time the word 'man' comes in the passages in translation that are cited in this book. Think of 'man' as 'Man' with a capital M, thereby indicating the most inclusive designation, encompassing all human beings.

Regarding the footnotes: while many of these reference the works of Rudolf Steiner, there are also numerous current events and other contextually-relevant citations. The reader is encouraged to explore these, to supplement their understanding of a particular topic, delve deeper into the topic and even discover counterpoints to the points made in this book.

The process of grappling with the primal thoughts of the three domains, their living workings and their interpenetration with each other is certainly open-ended; so do look for subsequent articles by Marc Clifton (and

---

[13] https://www.versobooks.com/blogs/3051-they-can-be-different-in-the-future-too-mark-fisher-interviewed

possibly by Kate Reese Hurd.) Readers' questions, comments and rumi-
nations in response are welcome, to further the process of our collective
grounding of these ideas in practice.

INTRODUCTION *by*
MARC CLIFTON

The purpose of this book is to revisit Steiner's book, GA 23, *Basic Issues of the Social Question* (*Die Kernpunkte der sozialen Frage*), in the context of the 21st century and in relation to the political, economic, and cultural changes that have occurred in America over the last century. Since Steiner's publication of GA 23 in 1919, we have seen significant changes in agriculture, science, medicine, education, social reform, warfare, and media (to name some of the major ones.) The Nineteenth Amendment,[1] passed by Congress in 1919 and ratified in 1920, finally gave women in the US the right to vote. The transistor, key to all modern computer technologies, was invented in 1947.[2] Important civil rights legislation prohibiting discrimination, protecting people with disabilities and protecting the rights of minorities, was passed in the 1960's.[3] Banking regulations[4] such as the 1980 Monetary Control Act[5] have affected banking and commerce, theoretically for the better. The Internet was 'born' on Jan 1, 1983.[6] Generative AI (the ability for 'Artificial Intelligence' algorithms to create new content, such as artwork, music, and text) has been making a significant impact in our society since early 2023.[7]

While legislation and social, economic, and technological advances have been significant, they have, if anything, created an environment that is even more inflexible and resistant to change now than in 1919, when one considers international interdependencies in production, distribution and consumption and how technological advancements in communication

---

[1] https://www.archives.gov/milestone-documents/19th-amendment
[2] https://www.ericsson.com/en/about-us/history/products/other-products/the-transistor--an-invention-ahead-of-its-time
[3] https://www.adainfo.org/ada-information/history-of-the-ada/
[4] https://www.investopedia.com/articles/investing/011916/brief-history-us-banking-regulation.asp
[5] https://www.investopedia.com/terms/m/monetary-control-act.asp
[6] https://www.usg.edu/galileo/skills/unit07/internet07_02.phtml
[7] https://www.forbes.com/sites/tiriasresearch/2023/04/12/the-dawn-of-creation-2023-rise-of-generative-ai/?sh=1edc92ef1a7f

bring heightened and immediate information of cultural disparities, particularly concerning human dignity. Furthermore, we see many inappropriate influences of one domain on another domain – for example, special
interest groups in the domain of economics lobbying to influence legislation in the domain of rights.

Embodying the significant changes outlined in GA 23 will ultimately
entail global change and that global change can only occur if people willingly call for these changes, or if lacking that they are pressed to demand
them under the duress of a true global crisis.[8] However – barring global
catastrophe – in today's world, attempting to make deep system-wide
changes all at once is the wrong approach. Steiner pointed out:

> One need not do away with state schools and state economic insti-
> tutions overnight; but from out of perhaps small beginnings one
> will see the possibility grow up that a gradual dismantling of the
> state education and economics will take place. Above all, however,
> it would be necessary that those individuals who are able to per-
> meate themselves with conviction concerning the correctness of
> the social ideas presented here, or of similar ones, attend to their
> dissemination.[9]

It is my view that even changes "from out of … small beginnings" are
unlikely to happen unless we begin attending to the practice of the dynamics of the three-membered organization, approaching it in a balanced way,
individually and in small local group activity, which will be elaborated on
in the section "Individual and Group Realization of the Three-Membered
Organization." Steiner wrote (this quote is slightly out of context):

> … people say constantly, 'to realize the threefold order, human
> beings must be different than they are now.' No![10]

While governments and corporations will not pursue changes of
this magnitude on the political-rights, economic, and spiritual-cultural
domains, it is absolutely possible to work locally with the three-membered organization right now. In an article on Sept 9, 2022 posted by *The
Guardian* regarding Kohei Saito's book *Capital in the Anthropocene*, Saito

---

[8] *The Challenge of the Times*, GA 186, Lecture VI, "The Innate Capacities of the Nations of
the World," a bit under 1/3 into the lecture – about the necessity of total exhaustion, such as
wars that would end with no nation as victor.
[9] GA 23, a bit over ½ into Ch. 3 (p. 108); KRH translation
[10] GA 24, "Ability to Work, Will To Work, and the Threefold Social Order" last page (p. 83)

points out how the COVID pandemic has demonstrated that rapid change is actually possible, particularly in the context of the environment:

> The response to Covid-19 had shown that rapid change is not only desirable, but possible, he [Saito] says.
>
> "One thing that we have learned during the pandemic is that we can dramatically change our way of life overnight – look at the way we started working from home, bought fewer things, flew and ate out less. We proved that working less was friendlier to the environment and gave people a better life. But now capitalism is trying to bring us back to a "normal" way of life."[11]

Caution, however, is advised. Ironically, the social, economic and technological advances have enabled a 'giving of voice' to anyone with Internet access: podcasts, blogs, Twitter, YouTube videos – these and more are the modern salon[12] for inundating each other with 'opinion overload,' much of which criticizes the very technologies and infrastructure that enable the individual to even have a voice beyond their local community. As often as we complain that the mainstream media lies to us, on the other hand we can be easily overwhelmed with the task of determining the truth (or not) of *each other's* opinion on a particular topic. Especially with social media, "Confirmation bias occurs, when users encounter information that reinforces their pre-existing beliefs and attitudes."[13] To mitigate this, we must consciously engage in thoughtful discernment, both with regard to our own viewpoints and discerning the viewpoints of others as we explore the three domains of our social life.

---

[11] https://www.theguardian.com/world/2022/sep/09/a-new-way-of-life-the-marxist-post-capitalist-green-manifesto-captivating-japan

[12] https://en.wikipedia.org/wiki/Salon_(gathering)

[13] https://link.springer.com/article/10.1007/s10796-021-10222-9

INTRODUCTION *by*
KATE REESE HURD

It is heartening to realize that the social organization that Rudolf Steiner referred to as a "Dreigliederung" – a 'three-membering' or 'three-member-ness' – within the organization of human social life *is something that is emerging directly from within ourselves, from within human beings in our time.* It has in fact been pushing toward emergence for centuries now. We are unfolding our human faculties and capabilities in yet new ways. Steiner perceived and understood this; and over the course of quite a number of years he was able to elucidate these social impulses that are pressing toward unfoldment.

As Steiner said, the trend of human development is such that we human beings are becoming ever more individual and able to 'stand on our own feet' within the flux of life. Yet one of the aspects of these developments – an overlooked aspect – is that in counterbalance to this increasing need for standing-on-our-own, separate from each other, is also a sense for social life – a sense of our need for this social life and a sense for how to come together in it a healthy way nevertheless of our separateness.

What Steiner characterized as this 'three-member organization' of social life is not an arbitrary formulation, nor was it arbitrary in his time. A sense for the three-ness of the domains that characterize human social relations was very strongly pressing toward consciousness in the working class in his time, and we find this to be the case in the awareness of many today. The mobilization of the people that led to the French Revolution was inspired by this pressing up of not just one social element or ideal, but of three distinct ideals, whose reality in practice was being sought: equality, fellowship ('fraternité') and freedom. We feel the same three deeply-human needs in many of the issues that are brought forth by 'activists' in our time. Steiner wrote and spoke of these three aspects as the domains of rights, economic life and spiritual-cultural life.

We have a sense for this three-ness that emerges from within us in the form of deeply-implanted "primal thoughts" (as mentioned in the Preface here), archetypes of human relatedness and relationships. Steiner urged us to approach what we sense vaguely in this regard as instinct and begin to feel-sense-perceive it consciously, to acquire an *Empfindung*-sensibility (as also discussed in the Preface) for what it means to be human and to develop as human beings. Steiner pointed to this over and over again. When we are able to share this social sensibility on a conscious level, its resonance can give us confidence and can guide and support a living and cooperative organization of our social life in harmony with what holds sway in the three distinct domains of rights, economy and cultural activity. Founded on the reality of these primal ideals, the variations in the flux and flow of social life can be fathomed, and a healthy arrangement of affairs between people can then be developed in each of the three domains, even in the smallest setting.

But are we ready? Yes, we are ready, sufficient to begin. Some ask, but don't we need to overcome egoism first since we do not appear to be ready yet to be altruistic toward our fellow humans? No, we do not. I certainly don't feel ready if that is the requirement; but that is not required. As Steiner explained, the basis of egoism is our experience of need: "In speaking of egoism, we should recognize that it begins with the bodily needs of the human being. ... The needs of the human being proceed from egoism. Now we must believe that it is possible to ennoble egoism."[1] He explained further:

> [The person] who is truly interested in his fellowmen, need not be less egoistic in life than the other; for his egoism may be precisely his desire to serve human beings. It may call forth in him a feeling of inner well-being, of inner bliss, even of ecstasy, to devote himself to the service of his fellowmen. Then, as far as the outer life is concerned, deeds which are absolutely altruistic to all appearance may proceed from egoism; in the life of feeling they cannot be appraised otherwise than as egoism.
>
> ... Much of what we carry out in common with other men is absolutely founded on egoism, and still may be credited to the noblest human virtues. If we contemplate maternal love, we find that it is absolutely founded on the egoism of the mother; yet it manifests itself most nobly in the common life of humanity.[2]

---

[1] GA 332a, Lecture 6, "National and International Life in the Threefold Social Organism," 4th paragraph of lecture (p. 13)
[2] GA 332a, Lecture 6, 4th and 6th paragraphs (pp. 133–34)

Hence, it is not a matter of denying one's needs out of altruism, but of working toward ennobling that egoism to include the needs of others. In his discussion of the growth of the human being from caring for the needs only of the self, to caring for the needs of our family and friends also, and for the needs of our folk and of our nation as well. Yet to include the peoples of other nations something more must arise in us as the ground for our care for them, as Steiner described:

> Whereas we grow into our own nation because we are, so to speak, members of it, we learn to know other nations. They work on us indirectly through our knowledge of them, our understanding of them. We learn little by little to love them with understanding; and in proportion to our learning to love and to understand mankind in its different peoples in their various countries, does our feeling grow for internationalism.[3]

This resonates deeply with what he wrote in his seminal work in epistemology, which concerns how we *know* anything and what foundation we actually have for acting in life and the world, *The Philosophy of Spiritual Activity* (also under other titles such as *The Philosophy of Freedom*):

> The way to the heart is through the head. Love is no exception. Whenever it is not merely the expression of bare sexual instinct, it depends on the representation we form of the loved one. And the more idealistic these representations are, just so much the more blessed is our love. Here too, thought is the father of feeling. It is said: Love makes us blind to the failings of the loved one. But this also holds good the other way round, and it can be said: Love opens the eyes just for the good qualities of the loved one. Many pass by these good qualities without noticing them. One, however, sees them, and just because he does, love awakens in his soul. He has done nothing other than form a representation [mental picture] of something, of which hundreds have none. They have no love because they lack the *representation*.[4]

Opening ourselves to perceive (*empfinden*) and work with the primal thoughts that hold sway in the three domains of the social organism will give us a sense of their living dynamics and structures. Within the healthy spiritual-cultural domain, the areas of education and research call on an

---

[3] GA 332a, Lecture 6, 8th paragraph (pp. 135-36)
[4] GA 4, near end of Chapter 1

intensification of *understanding* of the individual human being[5] and of all of the creatures, plants and substances that make up Earth's community. Within the rights domain, it is the *"feeling-to-feeling"* between human beings standing as equals to each other that underlies and guides the laying down of beneficial legal structures to serve us in all three of the domains.[6] And a healthy economic domain, in and of itself with its division of labor and circulation of the means of production (including capital), weaves the human community together and generates selflessness, with no need to preach about it (italics in the original):

> There is no lack of people nowadays who say: "Our economic life will be good — ever so good — if once you human beings are good; you must become good." Think of the people like Professor Förster and his kind, who go about preaching: "If men will only become selfless, if they will only fulfill the categorical imperative of self-lessness, the economic life will become good." Such judgments are really of no more worth than this one: If my mother-in-law had four wheels and a handle in front, she would be a bus! Truly the premise and the conclusion stand in no better connection than this, except that I have expressed it rather more radically.
>
> What underlies the "core points of the social question" [GA 23] is not this moral acid, which can already play its large role in a different field. Rather, ... it is to be shown from out of the economic matter itself, how purely in the circulation of the economic elements, selflessness must be embedded/stuck inside [drinnenstecken].[7]

In as much as we are caused to turn to each other for the fulfillment of our needs rather than filling them ourselves, when we become more conscious of economic dynamics and structures through our growing social sensibilities, these dynamics and structures can support us in the ennobling process that Steiner pointed to.

This book is brought forth in the hope that the text will elaborate on many aspects of the three domains well and bring to light the interconnections between them helpfully, so that with feelings of assurance and optimism we may begin, personally and together, to unfold the domains however this can be done, livingly.

---

[5] GA 332a, *The Social Future*, 1/2 into Lect. 3
[6] GA 332a, about 1/3 into Lect. 3
[7] See GA 340, *Rethinking Economics* (also under the title, *World Economy*), near end of Lecture 10

Chapter 1

WHAT *is the* SOCIAL ORGANISM?

The concept, 'the social organism' encompasses three domains of human activity. Why? How so? Here everything begins and centers on the nature and development of the human being. In human life as a *social* phenomenon, if we ask ourselves about the ways in which we are related to the other human beings around us, we can gradually recognize three different dynamics in our shared social life. There are matters in life which involve entering into exchange with others, to provide and receive goods and services in order to get our needs met. In certain other matters, we will find that we expect to be on an equal footing with other people, to be heard, to be treated with respect and to be recipients of the same rights as others. In yet other matters our relationship to others is such that what we do is solely our own business, where we feel that our personal choices, intentions and desires are to hold sway without the interference of others.

Here, then, are the domains of our economic life, our rights life and our cultural life, which acting together permeate our shared social organism. To this third member of the social organism, Steiner gave the name: "geistige Leben" or "geistige Kultur,"[1] and also "Geistesleben." The adjective, "geistig," refers not only to that which is spiritual, immaterial, but also to capacities which are mental, intellectual; so in English this domain in fuller measure could be referred to as the 'spiritual-intellectual-cultural' domain. It pertains to everything which can be developed out of the natural gifts, aptitudes and capacities of each individual, including those endowments which are physical. Every day, in every setting, these three domains can be found to function in our interpersonal relationships – for better or for worse, well or badly – as one organism.

Currently and historically, human social life has been understood as having an 'order.' A 'social order' is generally said to exist when individuals, communities, groups, businesses, and governments abide by a shared social contract. As Nicki Lisa Cole, Ph.D wrote: "Social order is present when individuals agree to a shared social contract that states that certain

---
[1] GA 23, about 6 pages into Ch. 2 (p. 59)

rules and laws must be abided and certain standards, values, and norms maintained."[2]

Care must be taken with the term "social contract":

> Social contract arguments typically are that individuals have consented, either explicitly or tacitly, to surrender some of their freedoms and submit to the authority (of the ruler, or to the decision of a majority) in exchange for protection of their remaining rights or maintenance of the social order.[3]

Such is the concept of social order and social contract throughout history, including our times. This is in contrast to the three-membered organization of social life, in which there can be no surrender of the freedom of individuals to develop the potentials within them and where the matter of rights is determined by people with the sole purpose of ensuring human rights, human dignity and a what Steiner called "decent human existence."[4] The tension between human rights that are *universal* to all and the freedom that belongs to each person *as an individual* cannot be glossed over. These are deeply challenging differentiations to make; and each of us is affected by the laws (or lack of laws) that are passed in our attempts to address the issues of rights and freedom within our social life. In our current circumstances, three very charged issues can be mentioned: gun ownership, vaccination and abortion. It is not for this book or the author to take a position on these and other issues, but rather to point out that a deeper, more fundamental thinking that is required: a conscious recognition of the tension between us regarding our personal views of human rights and individual freedom, and concerning how and in what setting that individual freedom affects others and therefore requires those others be considered as well.

SOCIAL AND ANTISOCIAL

Broadly speaking, one could say then that a social person is one who abides by the contracts (including laws) of the society and that an antisocial person is one who does not. What it means to be social vs. antisocial could

---

[2] *What Is Social Order in Sociology?* Nicki Lisa Cole, Ph.D, https://www.thoughtco.com/social-order-definition-4138213, updated 9/30/2019

[3] https://en.wikipedia.org/wiki/Social_contract

[4] GA 23, about 2/3 into Chapter 2 (p. 72)

also be viewed as selfless vs. selfish. "Social forces are the result of taking an interest in the thoughts and situations of others. Antisocial forces arise from self-interest and a disregard for the thoughts and feelings of others."[5] Whether a person takes an interest in another person is not a legal mandate, but it is worthwhile to consider that 'social' can be both a matter of adhering to the law *and* of how we interact with each other.

Anti-social behavior actually plays a useful and necessary role in our individuation as human beings. Steiner wrote:

> Both social and anti-social impulses exist in him [people] and must come to expression regardless of what social structure exists and what social ideas are brought to realization. And as we have seen, the anti-social impulses, especially in our epoch of the consciousness soul, play a special role. In a certain way they have an educational mission in the evolution of humanity in that they cause men to stand on their own feet. They [the anti-social impulses] will be overcome by the reason of the fact that after the epoch of the consciousness soul, there will follow the epoch of the spirit-self, already in course of preparation, whose essential mission will be to bring humanity into social unity.[6]

While it is not the place of this book to describe Steiner's seven cultural epochs, we can understand that for the time being and in the future of our 'epoch', the antisocial impulses in us enable us to challenge existing laws, economic systems and social norms. Of course, the extremes of criminal conduct are not what is meant here and is not condoned. Gandhi's hunger strikes, Martin Luther King's speeches, the anti-Vietnam War protests are examples of what is meant here as antisocial impulses – activities that challenge the current laws, military activity, economic activity, and social disparity. And yes, the challenge is that at times these antisocial impulses can in fact have a destructive element to them, for example the Boston Tea Party or the aforementioned anti-Vietnam War protests.

Antisocial impulses also provide us with a necessary counterweight in our interpersonal activities, for example group work. As Steiner wrote:

We live in [an age] in which human beings must become independent. But on what does this depend? It depends on people's ability ... to become self-assertive, to not allow themselves to be put to sleep. It is the antisocial

---

[5] *Steinerian Economics, A Compendium*, edited by Gary Lamb and Sarah Hearn, Adonis Social Science Series, 2014, p. 2
[6] GA 186, Lecture VI, "Innate Capacities of the Nations of the World," first page

forces which require development in this time, for consciousness to be present. It would not be possible for humanity in the present to accomplish its task if just these antisocial forces did not become ever more powerful; they are indeed the pillars on which personal independence rests. At present humanity has no idea how much more powerful antisocial impulses must become.[7]

In the 17th century, Thomas Hobbes argued that without social order, life would be chaos,[8] and therefore there must be social contracts to which we agree. Hobbes' solution, to create a government with absolute power (including oppressive regimes if we have agreed to an oppressive regime), is not the intention of the organization of social life which Steiner brought to our awareness. Instead, each domain – rights, economic, cultural – legislates itself[9] *and* adheres to the laws enacted by the rights domain.

In other words, each of the domains is going to legislate rules and regulations pertaining to its own activities that are separate from the laws enacted by the rights domain, whose primary purpose is to ensure the dignity of the human being and quality of life, as explained in further detail on the chapter on the "Characteristics of the Rights Domain." And if any of those rules or regulations transgress the laws from the rights domain, then the rights domain intervenes to correct the situation. There are people working within each of the domains whose role is to interpret and oversee the application of the laws coming from the rights domain. Although these people work within the economic or cultural domains, they act independently, not influenced by the interests of those domains.

'Legislation' (laws and statutes) laid down by the rights domain and which unfolds within each of the domains (including the rights domain itself) and the 'legislation' (rules and regulations) that each of the domains engage in on their own behalf are different. The laws that each domain enacts and applies to itself are integral to the administration that specifically befits that domain. Within the economic domain, administration oversees how records are maintained and 'legislation' exists to work with charters, licenses, incorporation, security and information access,

---

[7] *Social and Antisocial Forces in the Human Being*, single lecture by Steiner on December 12, 1918 (also GA 186, but not in *The Challenge of Our Times*), translated by Christopher Schaeffer, Mercury Press
[8] Thomas Hobbes, *Leviathan, or The Matter, Forme, and Power of a Commonwealth, Ecclesiastical and Civil*, London 1651; "The First Part, Of Man," Chapter XIII, "Of the Natural Condition of Mankind, as Concerning their Felicity, and Misery" (p. 81)
[9] GA 23, about 2/5 into Ch. 2 (pp.64–65)

minimum liquidity in speculative investments, and so forth. In the cultural domain, 'legislation' might involve how the innate capacities of children in school are to be recognized and fostered, and administration is responsible for scheduling, what supplies make sense and are needed, fostering the development of teachers, where breaks are to be taken, etc. The laws of the rights domain are oriented to the correct, decent treatment of human beings and of nature – for example, the treatment and safety of workers, the equality of people and the proper care and use of natural resources. Administration in the rights domain ensures proper records management, revisions to legislation, procedures and so forth.

Chapter 2

FUNDAMENTAL CONCEPTS *of the* SOCIAL ORGANISM?

One of the core concepts of the social organism is the primal thought that it is essential in our time: that each individual is freely able throughout life to develop the special potentials and capabilities with which they are endowed. Only then will the entire social organism be well-served and benefited in the present and future. The impairment of this impulse from within each individual was a driving force in the unrest of the working class in Steiner's time (and since); but as he explained in GA 23, Chapter 1, the workers themselves did not understand what they actually lacked at the foundation of their grievances, and what would answer their needs. Hence, their demands were off the mark and doomed to bring about renewed or yet other harmful social consequences rather than real solutions and relief. This was also the case at the time of the French Revolution.[1] As Steiner recognized, the three-membered organization would provide in great measure new thinking to what was a keen concern of these workers and of people in many places in his time, a concern which was called 'the social question' (German, 'die soziale Frage'). Hence, his reference to this 'question' was not new. It has also been referred to as the 'social problem' in literature on the subject.

Dr. Andrew Brogan, PhD, who works as a lecturer on the Studium Individuale programme at Leuphana University, Lüneburg, Germany and whose "research interests cross a range of areas including anarchism, education, resistance studies, economics, and political theory,"[2] gave this description: "[T]he social problem as Steiner identified it was that individuals are prevented from fully developing, but the focus here is not on the end-state of a 'developed' individual, but on the process of continual transformation."[3] Relevant also is how John A. Ryan, a writer on many aspects of social reform, characterized it: "A social question is one that

---

[1] GA 23, Chapter 2, last page (p. 82)
[2] https://www.linkedin.com/in/dr-andrew-brogan-b1144a45/
[3] Brogan, A. *Steiner Shorts 3: The Social Problem*

concerns society, or a social group. The social question means certain evils and grievances affecting the wage-earning classes and calling for removal or remedy."[4]

In the deepest sense, the 'social problem' concerns human relationship:

> [P]eople cannot be social if they do not see the human quality in one another, but live entirely within themselves. Human beings can only become social if they really meet one another in life, and something passes between them. This is the root of the social problem.[5]

Within the three-membered social organism, this is a key point: we need to meet each other in all three domains, between worker and manager, in the relationships between parent, teacher and child, and so forth. It is challenging to recognize that we must take an interest in the character of human relatedness that holds sway in each of the three domains, even though our calling or interest might be best expressed in one particular domain – for example, the artist in the cultural domain, the legislator in the rights domain and the entrepreneur in the economic domain.

And:

> Not until we are capable of bringing down onto a material level what we think of as being spiritual shall we be able to grasp the actual nerve of the social question.[6]

This task brings us to another salient point in working with the 'social question.' It requires us to feel-sense-perceive – *empfinden* (verb form of *Empfindung*) – something which we "think of as being spiritual," which we can bring to our work with the issues of rights, human dignity and quality of life, such that we can take steps in our material life towards social renewal, towards becoming whole human beings, together.

Steiner asked (his italics), "Does the *true nature* of the social question agree with what is commonly thought about it – or is a completely different way of thinking necessary?"[7] As Jules Guesde pointed out, Marxism and Socialism were actively trying to answer the social question at that time; and this is what they came to:

The problem that Socialism sets itself to solve is to be found in a fact, of

---

[4] J. A. Ryan and R. A. McGowan, *A Catechism of the Social Question.* Nabu Press, 2011
[5] GA 191, a few paragraphs from end of lecture
[6] GA 191, close to end of lecture
[7] GA 23, Smith translation, 3 pages into Ch.1 (p. 31)

which it can be said as of the sun: he is blind who does not see it. It is the divorce between the means of production and the producers.

> Labour is, on the one hand, more and more furnished by a class; Property or Capital, on the other, held and controlled by another class. Here you have workers without property—the proletariat. There you have property without work—or capital.
>
> It is this separation between the two factors of production which produces all the evils, all the disorders which afflict not only wage-workers but Society as a whole.
>
> The workers without property are excluded from their products, from the riches they create—which accumulate in the hands of the property holders, capitalists and large land-owners.[8]

Certain facts are pointed to here, but the usual way of thinking about them prevents the true impulses from being recognized and worked with to solve the problem. In GA 23, Steiner placed the problem into the deeper context of the primal thoughts of the right to human dignity and the freedom for individual development and unfoldment. And this deeper context reveals that this is not at all just a question of production and producers within the economic domain, but a question that involves the functioning and interaction of all three domains. Steiner made this point in his "Preliminary Remarks Concerning the Purpose of This Book," GA 23: "The 'social question' is spoken of in this book as an economic, a legal rights and a spiritual question"[9] – not a question involving a homogenous and unitary social or political entity. And for example, within the shared economic life (my italics), "The labour question cannot be properly integrated into the social question until it is recognized that the production, distribution and consumption of commodities are determined by interests which should *not* extend to human labour power."[10] In other words, the contribution of labor power, work, productivity, by *human beings* is not to be taken into the economic domain to be handled as a commodity. The fact that we do not see how inappropriate this is, and that we persist with this practice, shows us how very far away we have fallen from a true perception of our world and ourselves as human beings. Steiner made a surprising statement about the underlying and overarching cause of the

---

[8] Jules Guesde, "The Social Problem and Its Solution", Jules Guesde Internet Archive, 1905, https://www.marxists.org/archive/guesde/1905/jan/x01.htm
[9] GA 23, Smith translation, 3 pages into "Preliminary Remarks" (p. 25)
[10] GA 23, 2 pages from end of Ch. 1

social situation (with Kate's addition in brackets): "Contemporary society has become ill due to the impotence of spiritual life – and the illness is aggravated by reluctance to recognize [and acknowledge] its existence."[11]

Steiner outlined a rethinking of the organization of and interaction between the three domains. As Brogan wrote:

> It is these three areas of social life and their guiding concepts which are the grounding of Steiner's suggestions for the threefold social organism as a response to the social problem caused by the unified state. By entering into a process of reconfiguring society with a recognition of the three areas of social life, their distinctions and their roles in human life, society can begin to transform itself and move to rebalance the tripartite division. In this process of rebalancing politics, economics and culture are untangled from one another, breaking down the artificial unity imposed by the unified state and removing the need for each area to compromise. In this untangling politics, economics and culture are not rent asunder, but establish a complex set of interrelationships in which each supports the other where necessary.[12]

For example, in the domain of economics, corporations should not be able to influence politics through lobbyists. The rights domain should not influence the economic domain through means of commodity subsidies, quota limits, price fixing and so forth. And the cultural domain should not inappropriately affect the rights domain[13], such as when religion seeks to dictate the conduct of human beings via the rights/political domain, or to determine the products that are produced in the economic domain. It must be recognized that the implied 'wrong' in the previous sentence for religion to dictate the rights, through laws in the rights domain, and particularly affecting women, is a charged issue and this issue exists with almost all religions, including Christianity.

The three-member organization should not be accepted dogmatically or framed as utopian, but rather worked with as a continually-evolving organism of relationships that must take into account our changing society and human dignity together. Steiner made this point : "The tasks which

---

[11] GA 23, about 5 pages from end of Ch. 1 (pp. 46-47)

[12] Brogan, A. *Steiner Shorts #2 The Threefold Social Organism, An Introduction*

[13] For two striking historical examples from Steiner of the outcome of these unhealthy interferences of the economic and cultural domains on the rights domain, see GA 332a, *The Social Future*, a bit over ½ into Lect. 3

the present-day social life poses must be misconstrued by anyone who approaches them with the thought of some kind of utopia."[14]
These tasks need not and should not be continually put off just because society itself is constantly changing. Rather, as Steiner argued (Steiner's italics):

> Certainly evolution must supply the necessary social adjustments; but in the social organism the human idea-impulses are *realities*. When the times are more advanced and what today can only be *thought* is *realized*, only then will what has been thought be contained in evolution. However, it will then be *too late* to accomplish what is already demanded by *today's* events. It is not possible to consider evolution *objectively* as regards the social organism. One must *activate* evolution.[15]

As human beings, we are responsible for our social evolution, and the question, how do we 'activate evolution' is no longer something we can leave to instinctual feelings. As has been previously mentioned, the complexities of how the three impulses within our social life arise and work together requires conscious activity.

AUTONOMY, INDEPENDENCE AND INTERDEPENDENCE

The three domains must unfold their activities autonomously in relation to each other. As Steiner wrote:

> If this social organism is to function in a healthy way it must methodically cultivate three constituent members. ... This economic life must constitute an autonomous member within the social organism. ... The economy [must] be separate from the rights member. ...[with] [t]he third member, standing autonomous alongside the other two....[16]

As has been noted already, the three domains in our *current* society do not function autonomously. Steiner pointed out that the autonomy of the three domains in a three-membered organization is dependent upon a

---

[14] GA 23, opening of the Preface to the Fourth German Edition1920, KRH translation (p. 9)
[15] GA 23, 3 pages from end of Ch. 3 (p. 124)
[16] GA 23, about 6 pages into Ch. 2 (pp. 58-59)

sufficient growth in awareness among people generally, concerning the need for our cooperation with the three-membering of the social organism, even if only instinctively (italics in two places are Steiner's in the German, with an amendment to the translation in brackets):

> It is often said that 'socialization' is needed for these times. This socialization will not be a curative process for the social organism, but a quack remedy, perhaps even a destructive process, as long as at least an *instinctive* knowledge [die instinktive Erkenntnis] of the necessity for the *[three-member organization] of the social organism* has not been absorbed by human hearts, by human souls. If this social organism is to function in a healthy way it must methodically cultivate three constituent members.[17]

Ideally though, we need to develop a *conscious* knowledge of this necessity. Again, at the heart of this consciousness is the *Empfindung*-sensibility. (Note, because of the importance of the word 'Empfindung,' I will now adopt it and use it.) This is what is needed in order to comprehend *how* the three domains of our social life are "to function in a healthy way."

The three domains are not mere abstractions: they consist of people *engaged* in these domains. It is incorrect to say, for example, that the United States Government funds the Olympic Games[18] – any funding the US Government provides comes from taxes; therefore it is *the people*, not the government, who fund the Olympic Games. In like manner, the three-membered organization is not composed of abstract systems, but rather of domains in which *human beings* are engaged through their work, interest, education and administration. To this end, Steiner wrote about the relationship of each domain to human beings:

> The first system, the economic, is concerned with what must be present in order for man to determine his relation to the outer world. The second system [rights domain] is concerned with what must be present in the social organism in respect to human interrelationships. The third system [cultural domain] is concerned with everything which must blossom forth from each human individuality and be integrated into the social organism.[19]

Thus as individuals we experience three forms of relationship:

[17] GA 23, about 5 pages into Ch. 2 (p. 57)
[18] https://www.gao.gov/products/ggd-00-183
[19] GA 23, Smith translation, about 1/4 into Ch. 2 (p. 59)

1. Relation to the outer world (economic domain)
2. Human interrelationships (rights domain)
3. Our individuality itself in relation to the social organism

Together these three aspects create a vital image of the three domains and our activity within them. The realization of a three-membered organization requires the recognition of the individual *as well* as the relationship that the individual has to the outer world and to other human beings. This image is deeply impactful. We, as individuals, must always be recognized, in our labor, dignity, quality of life, education, adjudication and our different points of view. Our societal trend of removing the individual from 'the equation' must be corrected. It should be acknowledged, though, that this correction – to truly recognize the individual – requires conscious effort on the part of all participants in any endeavor which seeks to bring the three members into conscious functioning. Foremost, to put the human being back into 'the equation', we must not treat human beings generically, in the abstract with rules and regulations (which are present in each of the three domains) that apply universally and in doing so eliminate the recognition of the individual. This can at times seem like a daunting task. And yet, for the human being to experience dignity, this is an absolute requirement. It's much easier to create rules that apply equally to everyone, with the reasoning that one person should not be treated differently from another. This is overly simplistic reasoning that eliminates the individual and their individual needs and desires.

Autonomy does not mean that the three domains do not *inform* each other. For example:

> The economic area will form its legislative and administrative bodies in accordance with economic impulses. The necessary contact between the responsible persons of the legal and economic bodies will ensue in a manner similar to that at present practised by the governments of sovereign states. Through this formation the developments in one body will be able to have the necessary effect on developments in the other. As things are now this effect is hindered by one area trying to develop in itself what should flow toward it from the other.
>
> The economy is subject, on the one hand, to the conditions of the natural base (climate, regional geography, mineral wealth and so forth) and, on the other hand, it is dependent upon the legal

conditions which the state imposes between the persons or groups engaged in economic activity.[20]

Here we see a vital characteristic of the three-membered organization. In specific, the economic domain forms its own legislative and administrative bodies in accordance with its own impulses in keeping with economic activity. These developments inform and will be responded to by the rights domain which defines the legal conditions that must hold sway between persons and groups within the economic domain. Likewise, the cultural domain and its internal legislation and administration inform and will be responded to by the rights domain. The cultural domain is then subject to the legal conditions that the rights domain brings to bear upon the relationships between persons and groups. In a self-reflective way, the rights domain has this inner rights relationship to itself as well.

It is we ourselves who unify the three-membered-ness of our social life, not a single political apparatus (or alternatively, not an economic or cultural apparatus either). Steiner described beautifully this unity which arises from out of ourselves (please note that when Steiner spoke here of 'spiritual life' this refers to the cultural domain and does not imply a *religious* life):

> And the very people who are thus united with that spiritual life and draw their strength from it, those very same people live within the legal and political life, and determine the legal order governing their relations with one another. They establish that legal order by the help of the spiritual impulses which they take in from the spiritual life; and this legal order is the direct result of what has been acquired through contact with the spiritual life. Again, the tie which is developed, binding man to man democratically on the basis of the legal order, the impulse which he receives as the basis of his relationship to other men, he carries into economic life, because there [again] are the same human beings who have a connection with the spiritual life, occupy a legal position, and carry on business. On the one hand, the measures which the human being takes, the manner in which he associates with others, the way in which he transacts business, all that is permeated with what he has developed in his spiritual life, and with the legal order he has established in economic life; for they are the same men who work in the threefold organism and the unity is not effected by any abstract regulation, but by the living human beings themselves. Each member of the community, however, can

---

[20] GA 23, Smith translation, about 2/5 into Ch. 2 (p. 65)

develop his own nature and individuality in independence and can thus work for unity in the most effective manner.[21]

It should also be noted that decisions within the economic and cultural domains are *not* made democratically, but rather are made by those working in their particular domain who possess specific capacities or knowledge, and in addition, an understanding of the interdependencies between their domain and the other domains. As Steiner wrote regarding the economic domain:

> The economic life has its own roots and must be governed in accordance with the conditions of its own nature. The manner in which business is carried on cannot be allowed to be judged democratically by every grown-up person, but only by someone who is engaged in some branch of economic life, who is capable in his branch and knows the links that connect his own branch with others. Special knowledge and special capacity are the only guarantees of fruitful work in economic life. Economic life, therefore, will have to be detached, on the one hand, from the political and, on the other hand, from the cultural body.[22]

This guarantee of fruitful work founded upon special knowledge and special capacities would apply within the cultural and rights domain as well.

THE PREMISES OF THE THREE-MEMBERED ORGANIZATION

An implicit premise of the three-membered organization is that people want to develop themselves. As Brogan wrote:

> ... Steiner draws on a specific vision of humanity which is underpinned by a concept of human nature in which humans are naturally drawn to develop themselves along their own particular and individual paths to the greatest of their capabilities and capacities ... [F]ull human development is not an end-goal in Steiner's work but an ongoing process. It is better approached as a continual becoming or transformation rather than a final condition.[23]

[21] GA 332a, about 3/7 into lecture 5 (p. 115)
[22] GA 332a, about 2/5 into lecture 2 (p. 33)
[23] Brogan, A. *Steiner Shorts #2, The Threefold Social Organism, an Introduction*

A second implicit premise is that people are interested in being engaged in all three domains. Unfortunately, according to a survey in the United Kingdom,[24] less than a third of young people express any interest in politics. And education currently fails those who are interested – for instance, by not equipping them with an understanding of basic economic concepts such as "supply and demand" and "tariffs," etc., with which to even grapple with existing circumstances."[25]

A third implicit premise, that people want to participate by working in the economic domain, can also be challenged. The motivation (or lack thereof) to participate in the economic domain is in many ways directly related to our ability to engage meaningfully in self-development and in the life of all three domains. In recent times, labor as a commodity (where the human being is treated as a labor commodity) is a growing detractor to work. Our participation in work is also directly coupled to our perception that our work has meaning. And a basic expectation is that participating in this domain will mean that people work to actually produce something and that this production both sustains them as a livelihood and benefits society in general. However:

> Over the past two years, young millennials and members of Gen Z have created an abundance of memes and pithy commentary about their generational disillusionment toward work. The jokes, which correspond with the rise of anti-work ideology online, range from shallow and shameless ("Rich housewife is the goal") to candid and pessimistic.[26]

Is this not a symptom of the improper functioning and interaction between the three domains, and most importantly, a sign that human dignity and quality of life are not fundamental features of the three domains as they work today?

The Vox article cited above continues , pointing out that the COVID pandemic has created this shift toward disillusionment with the ideology of work:

> The pandemic changed that for everyone, not just the youngest workers. In addition to reassessing their relationship to work, people

---

[24] https://www.bbc.com/news/uk-politics-26271935
[25] https://www.prnewswire.com/news-releases/teens-think-economics-education-is-im-portant-but-struggle-with-basic-economic-concepts-300953986.html
[26] https://www.vox.com/the-highlight/22977663/gen-z-antiwork-capitalism

are reflecting upon their greater life purpose. One human resources manager called it the 'Great Reflection,' wherein people are 'taking stock of what they want out of a job, what they want out of employment, and what they want out of their life.' More often than not, workers are not content with labor that is unsatisfying, low-paying, and potentially harmful. And Gen Z has not been shy about detailing these expectations to employers and on social media.[27]

Steiner wrote about this in an article entitled, "Ability for Work, Will to Work and the Threefold Social Order," for the Newspaper *The Threefold Social Order*. (See GA 24 for a selection of the many articles he published between 1919 and 1920):

> It should be obvious that a new incentive to work must be created the moment there is any thought of eliminating the old incentive of egotistical gain. An economic management that does not include this profit motive among the forces at work within the economy cannot of itself exert any effect whatever upon the human will to work. And precisely because it cannot do so, it meets a social demand that a large part of humanity has begun to raise in the present stage of development.[28]

And this "social demand" is related directly to the question, 'why am I doing this work?' As Steiner continued:

> This part of humanity no longer wants to be led to work by economic compulsion. They want to work from motives more befitting human dignity. ... If the economic system is to be organized in a way that can have no effect on our will to work, then our will to work must be stimulated in some other way. ... It [the three-membered organization] aims at establishing within an independent, self-sustaining cultural life a realm where one learns in a living way to understand this human society for which one is called upon to work; a realm where one learns to see what each single piece of work means for the combined fabric of the social order, to see it in such a light that one will learn to love it because of its value for the whole. It aims at creating in this free life of spirit the profounder principles that can replace the motive of personal gain. Only in a

---

[27] Ibid.
[28] GA 24, 2nd paragraph of article 6 (pp. 80-81)

free spiritual life can a love for the human social order spring up that is comparable to the love an artist has for the creation of his works.[29]

One might simplify this to the concise question, 'do you love your work and see it as befitting human dignity and society as a whole?'

Particularly relevant to this question (and partly from the shift in thinking about work resulting from the COVID pandemic) is a trend called 'quiet quitting':[30]

The first thing you need to know about quiet quitting is that it's not actually quitting. Instead, the quitter keeps their job and chooses to do only the bare minimum rather than go above and beyond.[31]

This is in response to the implicit assumptions between employer and employee, and also driven by competition in the workforce:

> The implicit contract for employees goes something like this: I will spend as much time and effort as I can in my job in return for a salary, benefits, job satisfaction, and career advancement. Traditionally, career-minded employees chose and were expected to go "above and beyond," giving work 100% of their effort. As a result, they often work more than the assumed 40-hour workweek in a competitive employment marketplace.[32]

The author's view in this ComputerWorld article is that "Quiet quitting happens when an employee feels used by a company and so, in self-defense, chooses to get back at the company." But is this at all an adequate or accurate diagnosis? We need to see that quiet quitting is not an attempt to "'get back at the company," but rather an attempt to achieve a work-life balance, and attempt to regain something of what it means to be human.

What is the current economic system's response to 'quiet quitting'? It is 'quiet firing' – "managers intentionally distance their employees from opportunities to further their career: for example, by obstructing them from participating in special projects, or hindering their chances of a promotion or a raise."[33]

---

[29] GA 24, article 6 (p. 81)

[30] The term quiet quitting was originally coined at a Texas A&M economics symposium on diminishing ambitions in Venezuela in September 2009 by economist Mark Boldger. – https://en.wikipedia.org/wiki/Quiet_quitting

[31] https://www.computerworld.com/article/3673096/its-time-to-quit-quitting-on-the-quiet-quitters.html

[32] Ibid.

[33] https://www.zdnet.com/education/professional-development/move-over-quiet-quitting-quiet-firing-is-the-new-trending-topic-in-the-workplace/

In addition to quiet quitting, the pandemic has spurred a conscious reevaluation of one's labor in the economic domain, which has been called The Great Resignation. The Great Resignation is:

> … an ongoing economic trend in which employees have voluntarily resigned from their jobs en masse, beginning in early 2021 in the wake of the COVID-19 pandemic. Among the most cited reasons for resigning include wage stagnation amid rising cost of living, limited opportunities for career advancement, hostile work environments, lack of benefits, inflexible remote-work policies, and long-lasting job dissatisfaction.[34]

And:

> More than 19 million US workers—and counting—have quit their jobs since April 2021, a record pace disrupting businesses everywhere. Companies are struggling to address the problem, and many will continue to struggle for one simple reason: they don't really understand why their employees are leaving in the first place. Rather than take the time to investigate the true causes of attrition, many companies are jumping to well-intentioned quick fixes that fall flat: for example, they're bumping up pay or financial perks, like offering 'thank you' bonuses without making any effort to strengthen the relational ties people have with their colleagues and their employers. The result? Rather than sensing appreciation, employees sense a transaction. This transactional relationship reminds them that their real needs aren't being met.[35]

Of significance in the quote above is the authors' (Aaron De Smet, Bonnie Dowling, Marino Mugayar-Baldocchi, and Bill Schaninger) use of the words, "the relational ties," "sensing," "transaction," and "real needs." Monetary "quick fixes" fail to meet the individual as a human being who possesses needs for appreciation and respect for dignity.

Similar to this quiet quitting and outright withdrawal from the economic domain is the lack of full engagement in the rights domain, where participation would mean political involvement. Yet sadly, for example, the US presidential election voter turnout has always been under 50%[36] except

---

[34] https://en.wikipedia.org/wiki/Great_Resignation
[35] https://www.mckinsey.com/capabilities/people-and-organizational-performance/our-insights/great-attrition-or-great-attraction-the-choice-is-yours
[36] https://en.wikipedia.org/wiki/Voter_turnout_in_United_States_presidential_elections

for the 2020 presidential election which had a voter turnout of 66.8%.[37] And participating in the cultural domain would predominantly involve education, self-development, religion and the sciences, and engagement with how those activities enliven the economic and political domains. Yet we see much withdrawal from this participation as well.

In our current society, one might conclude that we believe that we are helpless to change anything in a meaningful way and furthermore, we intentionally (or not) suppress this feeling of helplessness via our easy access to various forms of entertainment, so that we are distracted from the otherwise dismaying feeling of helplessness. Obviously not everyone believes this, otherwise we would not have movements such as Black Lives Matter.[38] However, in today's times, we cannot disregard the reality that many of us feel despondent when it comes to the challenge of making real change, either personally, locally, or in society at large. And all of these trends, along with quiet quitting and The Great Resignation, are part of the emergence of our increasingly conscious *Empfindung*-sense that the three domains of our social life are dysfunctional even if we don't phrase it this way or have a conscious understanding of the three domains.

DEVELOPING A HEALTHY SOCIAL LIFE AND SOCIAL ORGANIZATION

Steiner pointed out the interconnectedness between our personal inner well-being and conduct and the three-membering of the social organism:

> Healthy [gesund] thinking and feeling [Empfindung] and healthy willing and desiring with regard to the form of the social organism can only develop when one, even more or less merely instinctively, is clear about it that if this social organism would be healthy it must be three-membered, like the natural organism.[39]

Can we find our way into this awareness? – that to the extent that we can become "clear about it" that our current social organism is itself three-membered, to that extent we will be enabled to develop a healthy engagement with all three domains. So our well-being depends upon

---

[37] https://www.census.gov/newsroom/press-releases/2021/2020-presidential-election-voting-and-registration-tables-now-available.html
[38] https://blacklivesmatter.com/
[39] GA 23, 3 pages into Ch. 2 (pp. 55-56)

waking up to the living three-ness of the social organism. This is contrary to the way we usually approach matters of psychological health and the verdicts we come to about it.

Developing a healthy social life and determining its organization might be fostered by applying our thinking, feeling and sensing to questions such as, how do we:

- move from instinctive needs to conscious needs?
- understand free and ethical action?
- understand the original ideas (primal thoughts) at work in any social movement?
- develop and engage in social life out of our higher sensibilities?

Inquiries such as these would be a continuing process throughout life rather than a destination of total and complete comprehension. Nor need we undertake all of these questions at once. They are intertwined, and the work that we do on one of them informs the others.

From Unconscious to Conscious

Successful engagement with the dynamics of the three-membered organization that presses toward full realization in our time requires that each person is able to bring to clarity what is usually felt more so unconsciously concerning what being human means and what the needs of human beings are. And Steiner did not recommend anything of a passive approach to this! He absolutely equated our need to move from unconscious to conscious in our social sensibilities with all of the other subjects we expect to learn in our formative years:

> The present historical crisis of humanity demands that certain *sensibilities* [*Empfindungen* (plural form)] arise *in every single human being*, that the stimulus for these sensibilities be given/bestowed by rearing and the school system in the same way as that for learning the four types of arithmetic, The old forms of the social organism which up to now have not been consciously absorbed into human soul life will no longer be effective in the future. Among the evolutionary impulses that newly want to enter human life from the present onwards, is that the sensibilities indicated are demanded of the individual in the same way that a certain school education has been demanded for a long time. That one must learn a healthy sensibility

for how the forces of the social organism should work, in order for it to prove viable, is something that is demanded of man from the present onwards. One will have to acquire a feeling that it is unhealthy, antisocial, not to want to place oneself with such sensibilities into this organism.[40]

Not to be overlooked here is that Steiner stated that these sensibilities are to be given or bestowed upon the young not only by the school system but by the *rearing* of the child as well. Family life matters. As a Waldorf parent, Marc has observed that the parent's home can often be quite a contradiction to the tenets of Waldorf education – frequently enough the child's home (particularly for children in Kindergarten through 3rd grade) is pervaded with technology, media, poor nutritional choices, a lack of rhythm, and so forth. How can the child make sense of the contradiction between the Waldorf classroom and their home life? How does this affect the child's development of the *sensibilities* that Steiner described?

This contradiction and disconnect between home and school environments is present in the public school system as well. Teachers and students alike are dismayed by the budget cuts in the arts[41] and the reduction of outdoor play time.[42] The American Academy of Pediatricians (AAP) has recommendations regarding the benefits and risks of media for school-aged children and adolescents.[43] It also guidelines on media exposure[44] for young children (before school age) that often conflict with home media exposures. Not to belabor the point, but in the rearing of our children it is our responsibility as parents to educate ourselves concerning the home life we provide to our children, regardless of the kind of school they go to.

---

[40] GA 23, Smith translation for reference in relation to Kate's translation, 5 pages into Ch. 2 (p. 57). Also for reference: *Die Kernpunkte der sozialen Frage*, (the passage is p.28 in the PDF format)

[41] https://www.denver7.com/news/local-news/pomona-high-school-students-participate-in-walkout-to-protest-cuts-to-arts-classes (one of many citations searching for "teachers protest cut in arts")

[42] https://www.edutopia.org/article/time-play-more-state-laws-require-recess

[43] https://publications.aap.org/pediatrics/article/138/5/e20162592/60321/Media-Use-in-School-Aged-Children-and-Adolescents

[44] https://www.pathwaypeds.com/american-academy-of-pediatrics-announces-new-recommendations-for-childrens-media-use/

In the Context of Mental Health Currently

How do we move toward "healthy thinking, feeling-*Empfindung*, willing and desiring" (as quoted from Steiner here above)? We could start with the question, 'are we healthy?' To this question, Steve Taylor Ph.D blogged:

> We suffer from a basic psychological disorder, which is the source of our dysfunctional behaviour, both as individuals and as a species. We're all slightly mad – only because the madness is so intrinsic to us, we're not aware of it.[45]

And in Taylor's book, *Back to Sanity, Healing the Madness in our Mind*s, he wrote: "We will only be able to live in harmony with our planet, other species and with each other when we are able to live in harmony with ourselves."[46]

The term, 'healthy,' relates not just to our physical health but also to our mental health. In modern parlance, the term 'mental health,' which encompasses the relationship between our thinking, feeling and willing, did not formally exist in 1919.

> Although references to mental health as a state can be found in the English language well before the 20th century, technical references to mental health as a field or discipline are not found before 1946. During that year, the International Health Conference, held in New York, decided to establish the World Health Organization (WHO) and a Mental Health Association was founded in London.[47]

And:

> The APA [American Psychological Association] Committee on Nomenclature and Statistics developed a variant of the ICD–6 that was published in 1952 as the first edition of DSM [Diagnostic and Statistical Manual of Mental Disorders]. DSM contained a glossary of descriptions of the diagnostic categories and was the first official manual of mental disorders to focus on clinical use.[48]

In our cultural trend to categorize, quantify and objectify the world around us, the DSM has become a standard for diagnosis and treatment of

---

[45] https://www.psychologytoday.com/us/blog/out-the-darkness/201205/humania-the-madness-the-human-mind
[46] Taylor, S. *Back to Sanity, Healing the Madness in our Mind*s, Hay House UK Ltd, 2012
[47] https://www.ncbi.nlm.nih.gov/pmc/articles/PMC2408392/
[48] https://www.psychiatry.org/psychiatrists/practice/dsm/history-of-the-dsm

mental health issues and has been co-opted by the insurance industry for standardizing billing, coding and mental health diagnostics,[49] including mandating the amount of therapy an individual can receive. However: "Many critics of the DSM see it as an oversimplification of the vast continuum of human behavior."[50]

This "oversimplification of the vast continuum of human behavior" should be a signpost alerting us that something else is needed to truly comprehend the word that Steiner used in reference to thinking, feeling, willing and desiring: 'gesund.' The word translates as 'healthy,' but also as 'wholesome.' Its importance for the social organism cannot be overstated. We all would do well to ask ourselves, 'how healthy am I?' and 'how does my mental health affect my *sensibilities*?' This question can of course be broadened to include our physical health, as there is an undisputed relationship between physical and mental health[51] as well as between engagement in a spiritual practice and mental health.[52]

In the Context of Spiritual Science

The following will most likely be controversial and stands in opposition to the 'science' of the DSM (The Diagnostic and Statistical Manual of Mental Disorders). Rudolf Steiner began to use the word, 'anthroposophy,' to connote the entire body of the science of the spirit and the human activities and initiatives which are based upon it. One can see that the word, 'anthropo-sophy,' would refer to 'human wisdom.' In this case, what is meant is the *objective* wisdom that each human being has the possibility of seeking and grasping directly, through their development of the inner faculties of higher cognition which lie dormant within them. Through its objective nature, the research that can be done by merit of these higher faculties is scientific, just as the research that is conducted in the material sciences – in each case, of course, the research must be done rigorously and responsibly. Steiner expounded the results of his own spiritual-scientific

---

[49] "Since DSM-5 is completely compatible with the HIPAA-approved ICD-9-CM coding system now in use by insurance companies, the revised criteria for mental disorders can be used immediately for diagnosing mental disorders." https://www.psychiatry.org/File%20Library/Psychiatrists/Practice/DSM/APA_DSM_Insurance-Implications-of-DSM-5.pdf
[50] Nemeroff CB, Weinberger D, Rutter M, et al. DSM-5: a collection of psychiatrist views on the changes, controversies, and future directions. BMC Med. 2013;11:202. doi:10.1186/1741-7015-11-202
[51] https://ontario.cmha.ca/documents/connection-between-mental-and-physical-health/
[52] https://www.webmd.com/balance/how-spirituality-affects-mental-health

research in his many books and lectures. In the November 29, 1918 private lecture given to Anthroposophists in light of the 'social question,' Steiner spoke directly of the necessity for spiritual-scientific knowledge of the human being if these circumstances were (and are) to be met:

> There is no possibility of our reaching an understanding of the demands of our age otherwise than by acquiring the capacity to understand human beings. This can be achieved, of course, only on the basis of those perceptions that a science of the spirit brings to light.[53]

And (my italics):

> ... What really matters most of all is to learn the truth that human beings must not conduct themselves in one way or another in the various parts of the world according to abstract notions, but that, the moment their conduct may have social consequences, they must choose their course according to how they are impelled to act by the impulses existent in the sequence of *cosmic events* into which man himself is integrated.[54]

And:

> ... The social question is not to be solved by cliches, programs or Leninisms, but by an understanding between man and man — such an understanding, however, as can be acquired only when we are able to recognize the human being as an external manifestation of the eternal.[55]

The fact that Steiner did not make these points in his book, GA 23, possibly indicates that he was sensitive to the issue of publicly (i.e., outside the Anthroposophical community) stating the requirement for the broader perceptions and knowledge that spiritual science can give us.

Most of us – even those who believe in a spiritual world – do not have the direct, objective perception into the spiritual world that he spoke of, that would give us "a healthy sense of how the forces of the body social have to work in order for it to live." We are therefore confronted with a question – how do we move forward with the core concepts of the three-membered organization without this? Or more accurately, how

---

[53] GA 186, *The Challenge of the Times*, 6 pages into Lecture 1 (p. 6)
[54] GA 186, 7 pages into Lecture 1 (pp. 7-8)
[55] GA 186, about 5/8 into Lecture 1 (p. 25)

can we nevertheless develop a real understanding of the human being? One answer is that we must consciously bring our *Empfindung*, our feeling-sensing-perceiving, to our understanding of human beings – their individual capacities, needs, human dignity and human rights. One might develop this *Empfindung* through meditative exercises such as the six basic exercises[56] or the Noble Eightfold Path[57] and through setting aside time to study materials of a spiritual nature. How one develops one's *Empfindung* is of course a personal choice. Regardless of the approach, this is not an easy question to answer and bears careful consideration.

Free and Ethical Action

Beginning with ourselves, when each person develops more clearly an *Empfindung*-sensibility for the character and dynamics of fundamental human needs, this sensibility can also grow and be shared among people generally to encompass how everyone's needs must be reflected in the social arrangements between people. This *heightened* sensibility is what will give rise to and support the free and ethical fashioning of social relationships such that human dignity and a decent human existence is ensured for each individual throughout the social organization. As Andrew Brogan wrote:

> At its heart Steiner's [three-membered organization] is an ethical individualism which places the responsibility of free and ethical action squarely on the shoulders of the individual while maintaining sufficient nuance to recognize the difficulty of such action. Indeed, to be free, to act for themselves, individuals must engage in a continual process of reflection and engagement, approaching actions in the context and immediacy of the moment of action. This is not an approach which is present without practice, and while some might display greater intuition regarding these actions than others, all individuals need to make a concerted effort and pay particular attention to their actions.[58]

Steiner examined the basis for this much more conscious individual engagement with the manner in which we take action – in other words

---

[56] https://tomvangelder.antrovista.com/pdf/basic.pdf, "The Six Basic Exercises," by Tom Van Gelder; and *Knowledge of Higher Worlds and its Attainment*, GA10, by Rudolf Steiner (a bit under t 1/3 into "Some Results of Initiation")
[57] https://en.wikipedia.org/wiki/Noble_Eightfold_Path
[58] Brogan, A. *Steiner Shorts 3: The Social Problem*

our moral conduct – in his book, *The Philosophy of Spiritual Activity* – *Die Philosophie der Freiheit* (GA 4). Readers might appreciate knowing that Steiner himself recommended that "Freiheit" be rendered as "spiritual activity," not as "freedom" in the title of the book in English. I believe that he was correct in this, because the freedom that we in the English-speaking world are usually thinking of is *not* the freedom that is pointed to in his book.

In the book, Steiner expounded upon a moral philosophy within which "*ethical individualism*" constitutes the highest most conscious level of human activity. Chapter 9, "The Idea of Freedom,"[59] takes the reader from the lowest level of functioning – unconscious, instinctive or purely personal – to the highest, going through four levels of subjective dispositions and four levels of motives. Our personal, characterological dispositions provide the *driving force* for actually rousing to act, and our motives are the ideas that serve as the *aims* behind our actions, our conduct. These ideas might be in the form of mental pictures, thoughts or envisionings that have "a definite reference to what is perceived," or they might be concepts and imaginations of a general or "pure" nature, that do not have this definite reference to something already in existence.

Here in brief are the four levels of characterological disposition or driving force from lowest to highest (as best as can been summarized here – please do study the chapter in Steiner's book):

1. Our will is stirred without thought or feeling in response to instinct and biological needs and urges (likely including the urge to imitate); on a higher sensing level these responses include established habits and "moral taste" or "moral etiquette" – social exchanges carried out without the intervention of thought or feeling;
2. Our will is stirred by the subjective, personal feelings that we associate with what we perceive – e.g., upon seeing a starving person, the feeling of pity can drive our action (Steiner's example);
3. Our will is stirred by our store of mental images and thoughts about what we and others have done; this level constitutes "*practical experience*" and can gradually entail "purely tactful conduct";
4. Our will is stirred by concepts which are not (or not at first) related to specific perceptions of things or events; there are no automatic sense-and-do or feel-and-do responses, nor is our action governed

---

[59] GA 4, Ch. 9, "The Idea of Freedom," 1/5 or 5 pages into chapter (p. 165ff)

by the template of mental images born of past experiences; this is the level of *"pure thinking," "practical reason."*[60]

Here in brief are the four levels of motives from lowest to highest. *These are always ideas:*

1. Mental images of personal gain through benefit or pleasure or through avoidance of adversity or pain, as *"pure egoism,"* or gain through refraining from harming others when it would endanger oneself as well, as *"morality of prudence"*;
2. A system of principles set by authority (family, church, state, field of activity) and adopted without questioning the source and validity; *"conscience"* is a result;
3. Principles which we have examined to determine the reasons behind them become a base of knowledge that informs our actions; *"moral insight"*;
4. Our motives for acting are determined case-by-case in relation to each perceived circumstance, such that a fresh cognitive grasp of each situation informs each action to be taken; *"conceptual intuition."*[61]

At the level of "conceptual intuition" – the direct grasp of concepts through thinking-intuition – our motive and driving force become synonymous. Steiner described the nature and importance of this thinking-intuition, and pointed out that "intuition is for thinking as observation is to perception."

However, the capacity for thinking-intuition varies from individual to individual (Chapter 5, "The Act of Knowing the World," and Chapter 9, his italics):

> In contrast to the content of perception given to us from outside, the content of thought shines forth in the inner being of man. The manner in which the content of thought first appears, we will call *intuition.* Intuition is for thinking what *observation* is for perception. Intuition and observation are the sources of our knowledge. An observed object or event is foreign to us as long as we do not have in our inner being the corresponding intuition which completes for us that part of reality which is missing in the perception. To

<hr>

[60] GA 4, about 1/3 into Ch. 9 (pp. 167-69)
[61] GA 4, about 1/3 into Ch. 9 (pp. 170-73)

someone who lacks the ability to find intuitions corresponding to things, the full reality remains inaccessible. Just as the color-blind sees only differences of brightness without any color qualities, so the one who lacks intuition can observe only disconnected fragments of perceptions.[62]

Men differ greatly in their capacity for intuition. In one person ideas bubble up easily, while another person has to acquire them with much labor. ... Insofar as this intuitive content is directed toward action, it is the moral content of the individual. To let this content come to expression is the highest moral driving force and also the highest motive for the one who has recognized that ultimately all other moral principles unite in this content. This standpoint can be called *ethical individualism.*

The discovery of the quite individual intuition which corresponds to the situation, is the deciding factor in an intuitively determined action.[63]

This is the basis for Steiner's statement concerning the source of human moral freedom (Chapter 12, "Moral Imagination," his italics):

A free spirit acts according to his impulses; these [impulses] are intuitions chosen by means of thinking from the totality of his world of ideas. ... [A free spirit] makes an absolutely *original* decision. In doing so he worries neither about what others have done in such an instance, nor what commands they have laid down. He has purely ideal reasons which move him to single out from the sum of his concepts a particular one and to transform it into action.[64]

This is where *freedom* in human activity is achieved. And furthermore, in the continual unfolding and renewing of the healthy three-membered organization of social life, it is this 'bubbling up' of intuitive content within individual human beings, retrieved by them from the universality of the idea-world, that provides the fresh supply of insights and ideas for the development of our common life. This is what needs to flow from out of a healthy cultural domain into the other two domains. But at the outset these ideas that bubble up (grasped through thinking-intuition, which Steiner appears to have also called, "*moral ideation,*"[65] are only related to an

[62] GA 4, Ch. 5, "The Act of Knowing the World," about 2/3 into chapter (pp. 112-13)
[63] GA 4, about 1/2 into Ch. 9 (p. 175)
[64] GA 4, Ch. 12, "Moral Imagination," opening paragraph (p. 205)
[65] GA 4, about 2/5 into Ch. 12 (p. 208 and footnote there)

intended event or creation in a general way, just as the general concept, 'lion,' is related to a specific lion (Steiner's example[66]). Two other steps need to be taken if it is to make its journey toward realization, toward fruition as a deed or a creation. Through "*moral imagination*" we inwardly create a mental image or "representation" of it. And to this we must apply "*moral technique*" – knowledge and skill in working with the laws that prevail in the realm of the world to which this deed or creation will relate.[67] It can be the case that those who possess the faculty of moral ideation, in whom ideas bubble up, possess neither the faculty of moral imagination nor the moral technique needed to ground the ideas in earthly reality. But others who do possess these capabilities can receive the ideas and work with them, to envision them and begin to give them form or to take what is envisioned and apply technical expertise. These others might not themselves have the capacity of laying hold of completely new ideas through moral ideation, yet are able to work with them after being given them. A healthy functioning of the cultural domain would no doubt be characterized by this interdependent flow of activity between people, to generate possibilities not only for tangible creations but for all of the deeds and agreements within and between the domains that will continually renew the social organism. Technological advancements are ripe with examples of this, where one person or group of people creates a technology (generative AI, for example) and the ensuing discussions and concerns by others as to the 'deeds and agreements within and between the domains' on the use of a technology: "...there is still no comprehensive federal legislation on AI in the country that takes into account and would address recent concerns on the dangers the technology poses. In view of this, the Senate is taking steps to formulate a plan to control the use of artificial intelligence."[68]

On self-examination we will typically find that our daily life is a mix of the levels of driving forces and motives. But in the rise through the four levels of personal dispositions and of motives we can see the nature of our necessary path socially, too, leading from a merely instinctive sensing of the primal thoughts that inform the three-membered organization of the social organism toward a fully-conscious grasp of these primal thoughts and how they would rightly hold sway in this organism.

---

[66] GA 4, 2nd paragraph of Ch. 12 (p. 206)
[67] GA 4, about 2/5 into Ch. 12 (p. 208)
[68] See: "Is there any legislation regarding AI in the US?" https://en.as.com/latest_news/is-there-any-legislation-regarding-ai-in-the-us-n/

We can begin to recognize that our *Empfindung*-sensibility, our capacity for feeling-sensing perception, is to begin with just *perception*. And as Steiner explained in the earlier chapters of *The Philosophy of Spiritual Activity* and then recapitulated in the first few pages of Chapter 9, just as with all perceptions, in order to grasp of the complete reality that these *Empfindung*-perceptions belong to, we are required to engage our conscious thinking activity, our thinking-intuition. This is because we need to lay hold of the *concepts* that belong to these perceptions. We must unite the two halves that belong together, uniting each percept with its right concept; and thus, in us, the two halves complete each other to make a whole. As he wrote (Chapter. 5 as above), "An observed object or event is foreign to us as long as we do not have in our inner being the corresponding intuition which completes for us that part of reality which is missing in the perception." Here in this innate belonging-ness between a given percept and its specific concept is the basis for truth, for the human capacity to lay hold of truth. This is also the basis for all scientific research, which includes spiritual-scientific research, anthroposophy.

Steiner described the utter incompleteness of percepts by themselves; and he made it clear that feelings, too, are only percepts that exist in us as only one half of full reality and are therefore incomplete. Here is from Chapters 5, 8, "The Factors of Life," and 13, "The Value of Life," (with additions in brackets for further clarity in our context):

> Let us look at this realm of mere perceptions: it appears as a mere juxtaposition in space, a mere succession in time, an aggregate of disconnected entities [or experiences]. None of the things which come and go on the stage of perception have any direct, perceptible connection with any others. From this aspect, the world is a multiplicity of objects [and experiences and feelings] of equal value. ... Without the functioning of thinking, the rudimentary organ of an animal which has no significance in its life appears to us as equal in value to the most important limb.[69]
>
> ... [F]eeling is an incomplete reality which, in the form it is first given to us, does not as yet contain its second factor, the concept or idea. This is why in actual life, feelings, like perceptions, appear before cognition has occurred.[70]
>
> ... For reality is attainable for man not through concept alone,

---

[69] GA 4, nearly 2/3 into Ch. 5 (pp. 111-12)
[70] GA 4, Chapter 8, "The Factors of Life," about 1/3 into chapter (p. 155)

but through the inter-penetration, mediated by thinking, of concept and perception (and a feeling is a perception).[71]

Supposing that we begin to achieve the ability to work at the level of ethical individualism, the question arises: but can we then be in agreement with each other? Steiner answered this in the affirmative, and here is why: the fact that the world of ideas is "coherent" and "undivided" guarantees for us the possibility of "unity" (his italics):

> What appears to our observation as single entities, combines, bit by bit, through the coherent, undivided world of our intuitions, and through thinking we again fit together into a unity everything we had divided through perceiving.[72]
>
> The difference between me and my fellow men is not at all because we live in two quite different spiritual worlds, but because from the world of ideas which we share, he receives different intuitions from mine. He wants to live out *his* intuitions, I *mine*. If we both really draw from the idea, and are not obeying any external impulses (physical or spiritual), then we cannot but meet in the same striving, in having the same intentions.[73]

We might also want to ask: but where does love come into this ethical individualism? – for love would surely seem to be the highest ethical conduct. We can consider three entries by Steiner in answer to this. This first entry concerns the nature of thinking itself (his italics in each of the three entries):

> No other human soul-activity is so easily underestimated as thinking. Will and feeling warm the human soul even when experienced only in recollection. Thinking all too easily leaves the soul cold in recollection; the soul-life then appears to have dried out. But this is only the strong shadow cast by its warm luminous reality, which dives down into the phenomena of the world. This diving down is done by a power that flows within the thinking activity itself, the power of spiritual love. The objection should not be made that to see love in active thinking is to transfer into thinking a feeling, namely love. ... One who is willing to *experience intuitively* in thinking, will also be able to do justice to what is experienced in the realm of feeling and in the element of will, whereas mysticism of feeling and

---

[71] GA 4, Chapter 13, "The Value of Life," about 2/5 into chapter (p. 231)
[72] GA 4, about 2/3 into Ch. 5 (p. 113)
[73] GA 4, about 3/4 into Ch. 9 (p. 180)

metaphysics of will are incapable of doing justice to the activity of permeating existence with intuitive thinking.[74]

A second entry is this:

> While I am acting I am moved to act by the moral principle insofar as it lives in me intuitively; the moral principle is united with my *love* for what I want to accomplish by my deed. I ask no man and no code, Shall I do this? – rather I do it the moment I have grasped the idea of it. This alone makes it *my* action. ... I have found the source of my conduct within myself, namely, my love for the deed. I do not prove intellectually whether my deed is good or bad; I do it out of my *love* for it. My action will be "good" if my intuition, immersed in love, exists in the right way within the relationship between things; this can be experienced intuitively; the action will be "bad" if this is not the case.[75]

And a third entry (Michael Lipson's translation, Steiner's italics, plus Kate's underline to point out the distinction between motives – which are always ideas – and driving force; plus Kate's restoration of part of the description in brackets):

> This is by no means to claim that all our actions flow only from the sober deliberations of our reason. I am far from calling *human*, in the highest sense, only those actions that proceed from abstract judgment alone. ... But as soon as our actions lift themselves above the satisfaction of purely animal desires, our motives are always permeated by thoughts. Love, pity, patriotism are springs of action that cannot be reduced to cold rational concepts. People say that the heart, the sensibility [Gemüt, soul disposition], comes into its own in such matters. No doubt. <u>But heart and sensibility do not create the motives of action.</u> They [heart and soul] presuppose them [die selben, the same, i.e., the motives] and then receive them into their own realm. Pity appears in my heart when the mental image of a person who arouses pity in me enters my consciousness. The way to the heart goes through the head.
>
> Love is no exception here. If it is not a mere expression of the sexual drive, then love is based on mental pictures that we form of the beloved. And the more idealistic these mental pictures are, the more blessed is the love. Here, too, thought is the father of feeling.

---

[74] GA 4, end of Ch. 8 (p. 160)
[75] GA 4, about 1/2 into Ch. 9 (p. 176)

People say that love makes us blind to the beloved's flaws. But we can also turn this around and claim that love opens our eyes to the beloved's strengths [merits]. Many pass by [having no inkling of (ahnunglos)] these good qualities without noticing them. One person sees them and, just for this reason, love awakens in the soul. What else has this person done but make a mental picture of what a hundred others have ignored? Love is not theirs because they lack the *mental picture.*[76]

And if we remain in any doubt about the power and significance of our thinking activity, we can be helped through knowing that an important fact stands behind Steiner's advise that the English title for GA 4 should be "The Philosophy of Spiritual Activity."" He stated that the aim of the philosophical foundation he laid in the book "is to show that a properly understood experience of thinking *is already an experience of spirit*"[77] (Kate's italics). In a lecture he enlarged on just what he meant by this:

Nobody could really develop genuine clairvoyance unless he already possessed a tiny bit of it. ... Ordinary thoughts and ideas have always contained the pearl of clairvoyance. All such thoughts and ideas owe their origin to the very same process that generates the loftiest faculties, and it is of the utmost importance to realize that the first stage of clairvoyance is actually something perfectly commonplace. We just need to recognize the supersensible nature of concepts and ideas to get clear on the fact that they come to us from supersensible worlds. This puts them in the right perspective.[78]

And with gratitude to Rudolf Steiner, and in honor of this powerfully helpful and illuminating work in epistemology, GA 4, I would like to add what he wrote to draw our awareness to an aspect of work of philosophy that is typically not recognized and appreciated (his italics): "All genuine philosophers have truly been *artists in concepts.*"[79]

---

[76] GA 4, end of Ch.r 1 (p.45)
[77] GA 4, "The Consequences of Monism," 5/6 into the section (p. 268}
[78] GA 146, *The Occult Significance of the Bhagavad Gita*, R Steiner, Lecture II, a bit over 1/2 into lecture
[79] GA 4, "2nd Addition to the Revised Edition, 1894," near end (p. 284)

Primal Thoughts

Steiner wrote:

> Even the first step [in unfolding the three-membering of the social organism] will not be taken in a worthwhile manner if it is not known what relation this step should have to the foundations of the healthy social organism. One who knows this will be able to find the appropriate tasks wherever he happens to be, or wherever he decides to go. Acquisition of the insight referred to here has been prevented by what has passed over, during a long period of time, from human will into social institutions. People have become so accustomed to these institutions that they have based on the institutions themselves their views about what should be preserved in them and what should be changed in them. Their thoughts conform to the things, instead of mastering them. It is necessary today to perceive that it is only possible to arrive at factual judgements through a return to the primal thoughts which are the basis for all social institutions.[80]

It is not easy to determine, in our ever more complex world with its almost daily new challenges, how cultural, economic and rights decisions are related to "the foundations of the healthy social organism," with emphasis on 'healthy.' This is particularly difficult because our thinking is framed in existing social structures and it is difficult to think outside of this framing. One might even need to ask: is a given decision actually based on thinking activity at all, or is it merely a primitive reaction? Where or how are primal thoughts able to come in? Consider Article 1, Section 9, Clause 1 of the US Constitution:

> The Migration or Importation of such Persons as any of the States now existing shall think proper to admit, shall not be prohibited by the Congress prior to the Year one thousand eight hundred and eight, but a Tax or duty may be imposed on such Importation, not exceeding ten dollars for each Person.[81]

Besides the ugly use of the euphemism "such persons," in reference to slaves, the clause quoted above imposes an endpoint for when the importation of black people as slaves must be stopped (1808), which was

---

[80] GA 23, 2 pages into Ch. 3 (p. 84)
[81] https://www.heritage.org/constitution/#!/articles/1/essays/60/slave-trade

a concession to "slave-holding interests,"[82] in other words, slave owners. Jefferson, who owned over 600 enslaved people in his lifetime,[83] stated in the first draft of the Declaration of Independence: "the African slave trade [is] an 'execrable commerce' and an affront 'against human nature itself.'"[84] Here we see the conscious recognition of a primal thought – that the slave trade is counter to human dignity and human rights – and at the same time its forced submission and its sacrifice to economic and cultural pressures.

The above exemplifies the complexity of the words 'primal' and 'thoughts.' And in the context of 'healthy,' the challenge is to actively step outside of the framework of institutional thinking, to discern the primal thought, and then to determine whether what we discern is actually primal and a thought. Only then can we find our way. As Steiner wrote: "One who knows this [primal thought] will be able to find the appropriate tasks wherever he happens to be, or wherever he decides to go." This seems rather daunting but it is critical to take up the point made by him in the quote at the start of this section. Furthermore, we are challenged with the fact that many of these institutions have deviated greatly from their original intention. As Steiner wrote, we must "observe" these deviations and keep them in check before they bring harm. He explained (Kate's translation):

> If the right sources are not present from which the forces that lie in these primal thoughts flow ever anew to the social organism, then the institutions take on forms that are not life-promoting, but life-inhibiting. In the instinctive impulses of the human being, however, the original thoughts live on more or less unconsciously, even if the fully conscious thoughts stray into error and create or have already created life-hindering realities, facts. And it is these primal thoughts, which express themselves chaotically in the face of a life-inhibiting world of facts, that are evident or appear veiled in the revolutionary convulsions of the social organism. These convulsions will not occur only then, when the social organism is designed in such a way that there can at all times be present a tendency to observe where there is a deviation from the institutions formed by the original thoughts,

---

[82] https://www.heritage.org/the-constitution/commentary/what-the-constitution-really-says-about-race-and-slavery

[83] https://www.whitehousehistory.org/slavery-in-the-thomas-jefferson-white-house

[84] https://www.heritage.org/the-constitution/commentary/what-the-constitution-really-says-about-race-and-slavery

and where, at the same time, the possibility exists to work against this deviation before it has acquired a fatal strength.[85]

We must become ever more conscious of these matters rather than allowing our sense of a healthy social order to remain merely instinctive. Again, as Steiner wrote: "... we need to learn the direction in which the actual realities must now be consciously guided, for the time has gone by in which the old, instinctive guidance sufficed for mankind."[86]

These primal-thought impulses are always flowing to us. The need of our time is to receive these thoughts consciously, in order to direct our responses to them in health-giving ways within our social life.[87]

These impulses further our understanding of human dignity and human rights and inform all three domains of the corrective action we need to take. And in that way primal thoughts are not absolute; instead, they are related to the social awareness of the time. Consider the evolution of the concept of gender equality. First we have the Declaration of Independence, 1776, that states that all *men* are created equal. In 1923 – but to this day not ratified at the Federal level – the Equal Rights Amendment[88] was proposed, designed to guarantee equal legal rights for all American citizens regardless of gender, which at that time was limited to 'men' and 'women.' In 2022, United Nations Independent Expert on sexual orientation and gender identity, Victor Madrigal-Borloz said that "in access to health, employment, education and housing, the LGBTQ community suffers."[89] Here we see how the sensibility for equality in relation to gender has shifted over time as societal consciousness evolves, bringing a shift in the perception of the primal thought, if one has arrived at the conviction that gender equality is in fact a primal thought.

---

[85] GA 23, 2 pages into Ch. 3 (pp. 84–85), KRH translation

[86] GA 23, 3 pages into Ch. 3 (p. 85)

[87] See Steiner's lecture, "The Work of the Angels in Man's Astral Body," Zurich, Switzerland, October 9, 1918 (in GA182). Here he described the deleterious effects which unfold when these impulses are left to work into social life unconsciously. We can observe these in our present social conditions.

[88] https://en.wikipedia.org/wiki/Equal_Rights_Amendment

[89] https://www.nbcnews.com/nbc-out/out-news/us-sees-progress-lgbtq-rights-equality-lacking-un-expert-says-rcna45622

What is a Healthy Social Organization?

This brings us to the question, what is a healthy social organization? Or more concretely, can the vision of a healthy social organization be considered separately from the context of *the current social organization* of a given place or society? Are activities such as slavery or gender inequality to be considered 'healthy' because these arrangements between people are condoned in a given social structure?

Slavery very much still exists in the 21st century and in varied cultural contexts, far more than many people realize, as pointed out by this CNN article based on a report published on Sept 12, 2022 by the International Labour Organization (ILO), Walk Free and the International Organisation for Migration:

> An estimated 50 million people worldwide are believed to be victims of forced marriage and forced labor. … Modern slavery refers to forced labor and forced marriage, when someone cannot refuse to comply or escape owing to threats, violence and deception … armed conflicts, and the climate crisis caused "unprecedented disruption" to employment and education, leading to an increase in poverty, unsafe migration and gender-based violence – all risks for modern day slavery.[90]

These questions confront us, but points of view vary. We might find that many people think society is generally healthy, but is it in actuality healthy? Conversely, we might find that many people think society is generally unhealthy and are asking, 'how do we make it healthy?' What parts are healthy and what parts are unhealthy?

We see that these questions (and many others) are equally valid depending on the viewpoint of the person asking and the question being asked is influenced by the person's confirmation biases which "indicate why a group of individuals with opposing views on a topic can view the same evidence."[91]

There has always been a lag time between human activities or behaviors and the consideration of whether those activities or behaviors are healthy for society. The issues that face us have multiplied and accelerated exponentially as a result of rapid technological development. Ironically,

---

[90] https://www.cnn.com/2022/09/12/asia/modern-slavery-forced-marriage-climate-health-intl-hnk/index.html
[91] https://link.springer.com/article/10.1007/s10796-021-10222-9

the advent of the Internet has expedited the discussion of the ethics of an activity if for no other reason than that awareness of that activity occurs faster and with broader reach than any time before in our history. The sheer volume of issues to consider and the complexity of those issues can be overwhelming. "People may experience feelings of powerlessness when considering areas where they feel a lack of strength, competence, or skills to overcome realities in life that have no solution or answer."[92] This paints a bleak picture. We can ask ourselves the question: is there really any challenge in life that has no solution or answer? We can explore our personal relationship to our feelings of "lack of strength, competence, or skills" when confronted with situations that seem to have no solution or answer. Are there situations where there is truly no answer? Kate and I believe that with understanding the distinct impulses which are alive in the three domains, we begin to have the opportunity to discuss real solutions with others which will overcome this sense of powerlessness and bewilderment and actually begin to find answers and move toward a healthy social life.

A HEIGHTENED SENSIBILITY

Again, to discern the idea of 'healthy' requires our faculty of feeling-sensing-perceiving, our *Empfindung;* but the fact that the social organism is constantly changing makes this discernment complicated. Steiner pointed out several times that what he presented in GA 23 is not some kind of utopian solution to put in place. It is something which evolves, as it must in order to meet the needs of the society as the society itself evolves. In 1919, the ethics of artificial intelligence and cloning were not within the scope of our concerns because they simply did not exist. LGBTQ rights were shunned/ignored by the social norms of that time. In the face of these modern developments, psychologist Robert Sardello advised that "[p]erhaps the most challenging virtue in this time is discernment, and it may be the one most needed."[93] As humanity as a whole becomes more conscious of its challenges, discernment of matters of human dignity and human rights must become a more conscious process and must advance at a pace that matches the rate of social change.

But how? Even the concept of truth is questioned. Over two thousand

---

[92] http://psychology.iresearchnet.com/papers/power-and-powerlessness/
[93] Robert Sardello, The Power of Soul: Living the Twelve Virtues,Epilogue, Goldenstone Press, 2012

years ago Pilate asked: "What is truth?"[94] The rock opera Jesus Christ Superstar[95] expanded Pilate's question to reflect our modern day thinking: "And what is 'truth'? Is truth unchanging law? We both have truths. Are mine the same as yours?" How can we agree that someone's discernment of 'healthy' is actually an archetypal truth in relation to a healthy social order? – archetypal referring to a concept or idea which all human beings can grasp in common that does not depend upon personal opinion, from which multiple manifestations or expressions can be unfolded. Can we even agree that there are archetypal truths in the various fields of inquiry? Steiner laid the foundation for answering this question in the affirmative in his book on *The Philosophy of Spiritual Activity* (see in the section on "Free and Ethical Action"). And others have also answered this in the affirmative. Amit Goswami, PhD and theoretical quantum physicist wrote:

> One of our most important archetypal values is truth. All our intu-
> itions hint at a truth-value, and that bothers us: Seek and ye shall
> find, and you will be troubled! If we follow up our troubled minds
> and engage creativity, the products will express a transcendent
> truth—this truth is a common aspect of the archetypal themes.[96]

We can only penetrate the primal thoughts and develop our relationship to the concept of a healthy social order through our individual *Empfindung* of what human dignity and human rights mean, as we find our way along the rising inner path to the achievement of moral intuition and ethical individualism – as outlined in the section here on "Free and Ethical Action."

There are two key points here in relation to the task of moving toward a healthy social organization. The first is that we participate consciously rather than instinctively. As Steiner wrote: "Modern times demand the individual's conscious participation in this [social] organism."[97] And he firmly wove our outer life and our inner penetration to the primal thoughts together, for we really must not shy away from the task of discovering these primal thoughts:

> Good will is therefore necessary in order to turn energetically to
> the primal thoughts and not to underestimate how damaging it is,

---

[94] The Book of John 18:38
[95] https://en.wikipedia.org/wiki/Jesus_Christ_Superstar
[96] https://www.amitgoswami.org/2018/09/09/the-archetype-of-truth/
[97] GA 23, 3 pages from end of Ch. 2 (p. 80)

especially today, to banish them from life as 'impractical' generalities. Criticism of what modern times have made of the social organism exists in the life and in the demands of the proletarian population. The task of our times is to counteract the one-sided criticism by finding, in the primal thoughts, the direction to be taken in order that events be consciously guided. For the time has passed in which humanity can be satisfied with what instinctive guidance is able to bring about.[98]

And these primal thoughts *are* the truths in which we can find agreement concerning our social arrangements. As already mentioned, Steiner said: "[It] is necessary to see that one can reach a judgment that grows out of the facts in no other way than through going back to the *primal thoughts* that underlie all social institutions."[99]

The second key point is that exercising our faculty of *Empfindung* is a continual process, not a utopian endpoint from the perspective of a constantly changing society and our own human limitations. This process demands our engagement and conversation, particularly in disagreements over what we individually feel-sense-perceive. Listening is a key element of conversation. As Sardello wrote: "Listening rescues truth from the current degradation of living falsely, living anonymously, and living separate from the listening cosmos and the sacred Earth."[100] Sadly, when we fail to listen, truth has a tendency to walk out the door.

THE CRITICAL ROLE OF ADMINISTRATION IN THE THREE DOMAINS

While taking up the discussions on the three domains that come in the next chapters, we can cultivate our *Empfindung*-sensibility for the distinct impulses that are pressing toward realization in our social life. Hopefully, our sensibilities will guide us in the steps to take, to achieve a healthy functioning of these domains in our endeavors of all kinds – not just the obvious ones like businesses, non-profits, schools, health care centers,

---

[98] GA 23, 3 pages into Ch 3 (p. 85)
[99] GA 23 in the original German, Die Kernpunkte der sozialen Frage in den Lebensnotwendigkeiten der Gegenwart und der Zukunft, http://anthroposophie.byu.edu/schriften/023.pdf, see 'Urgedanken,' 2 pages into Ch. 3 (p. 54)
[100] Robert Sardello, from a description of his book,*Contemplative Listening*, Independently Published, 2020

cultural organizations, professional societies, but also clubs (even hobbies shared between just a few people), family life, community life and political activities. (Note: we will work much more with the task of discerning how the three domains hold sway in endeavors, big or small, in the section on "Individual and Group Realization of the Three-Membered Organization.") One of the things we can begin to understand is how each domain must have its own kind of administration "which emerges from its special powers,"[101] an internal legislation that has dynamics, structures and rules that are specific to the nature of that domain. We point this out now, because the importance of the administrative aspects of each domain cannot be overstated, especially today, when everything has become – or very much seems to have become! – more complicated since 1919.

Within each domain, establishing and maintaining documented procedures, practices, and workflows is critical to the smooth operation of the domain. Having documentation that informs people of how a particular process should work is vital for consistent and safe repeatability of that process. Documentation actually promotes creativity because it serves as a reference point for the suggestion and development of improvements. Having an organized repository of documentation allows one to review the internal policies with regard to the needs of human relationships and dignity. This includes policies such as 'code of conduct' – a simple example being the request to remove one's shoes in a particular venue. This is clearly not a concern of the rights domain but is instead an administrative concern of the venue as part of its participation in the cultural domain. Another example is how the money collected in a donation basket is to be dispersed. By having a clearly-stated policy, the venue, the event speaker/performers and the sponsor of the event all know what the intended standard practice is (established for the sake of all in the present and foreseeable future) and can therefore negotiate adjustments to it consciously.

In our technological society, administration must also take into account the issues of security and data collection at all times. Personal Identifying Information (PII) such as names, physical and email addresses, phone numbers, credit card information, and so forth, is not just a consideration of the domain internally but in our society is often regulated by the rights sphere:

> In the U.S., no single federal law regulates the protection of PII.
> Instead, there is a complex patchwork system of federal and state

---

[101] GA 23, 2 pages from end of the Preface to the Fourth German Edition 1920 (p. 20)

laws, sector-specific regulations, common law principles, and self-regulatory programs developed by industry groups.[102]

Endeavors must have the administration in place such that these endeavors function with cognizance of the laws governing PII, laws which can of course be ever-better guided and crafted by our *Empfindung* concerning the handling of PII.

Administration in any one of the three domains must also consider intellectual property, copyright, patents, trademarks, and confidential information. Even if the work one is providing is 'free' or 'gifted', a copyright notice such as a Creative Commons[103] license gives important information to others as to the extent of use and further distribution of a work. Because such endeavors (whether personal or a group) must interact with people, businesses and governments outside of itself, as part of its administration, it is important to consciously consider the protection of their work.

Administration of 'what was decided' is also important, typically in the form of minutes. Minutes offer legal protection and structure, drive action, act as a measuring stick, and declare ownership of roles and responsibilities.[104] Accurate minutes are useful to newcomers to the endeavor, too (such as new board or executive committee members), enabling them to review what decisions have been taken in the past and how and why they were taken.

Again, the importance of administration within each domain of an endeavor cannot be overstated. This aspect of the life of each domain needs to be seriously considered right at the start, before unfolding any other activity toward the endeavor, asking ourselves, 'how do we administer ourselves in relation to the three domains within our smaller organism and in relation to social organisms beyond ours in the larger society?'

---

[102] https://legal.thomsonreuters.com/en/insights/articles/data-privacy-principles
[103] https://creativecommons.org/
[104] https://www.allbusiness.com/five-reasons-why-meeting-minutes-are-important-4113272-1.html

Chapter 3

CHARACTERISTICS *of the*
SPIRITUAL-CULTURAL DOMAIN

This is the domain in which the individual unfolds their capacities and endowments and potentially practices self-development. It is in this domain where we find the activities of education, religion, the arts, and the sciences. For those who are prepared to see it this way, this is the domain in which the individual grows through the gifts, blessings and challenges they have 'brought with them' into life. Within every human being lies a treasure, no matter how deeply hidden. And in this domain, education plays a large role. We get a feeling for this characteristic through the way Steiner described the role of the teacher: "Everything in education and instruction and in culture in general requires the devotion of the individual human beings. ... It demands, above all, real individual understanding of the human being – special individual capacities in a teacher or educator...."[1]

Rudolf Steiner called this domain of human activity the "Geistesleben' the 'spiritual-intellectual-mental life' of the human being, often referred to in English as simply the 'cultural' life. Hence the word 'cultural' should be thought of as gathering these aspects together. Brogan summarized that the "cultural life aims at the development of the individual which is rooted in the process of freedom and free ethical action."[2] And as a result of this, a fundamental characteristic of the cultural life is that the advancements made by people in education, religion, the arts and the sciences enliven and advance the work of the rights and economic domains. The new ideas coming from the cultural domain continually inform issues of human rights and dignity, and they improve economic activity, for example the kind and quality of products and services and the nature of the production processes. The environment is very much the concern of our time; and it is within the cultural domain that research is carried on, to find ways to reduce the environmental impact of commodity production,

[1] GA 332a, *The Social Future*, 1/2 into Lect. 3
[2] Andrew Brogan, *Steiner Shorts 3: The Social Problem*

including the production and use of energy. Everything to do with inno-vation and human advancement arises out of this 'geistig' or cultural aspect of each human being. This is why individual freedom characterizes the fundamental impulse that holds sway within this domain. The other two domains do not share this same impulse as their fundamental character.

It would be easy to overlook the much less intentional activities of the individual in this domain – leisure time. In Steiner's time, leisure was often seen as decadent and something to be controlled by the political state:

> Those persons who imagine themselves to be 'practical' may object that people would pass their leisure time drinking and that illiteracy would result if the state occupied itself with the right to leisure and if school attendance were left to free human common sense. Let these 'pessimists' wait and see what will happen when the world is no longer under their influence all too often determined by a cer-tain feeling which, whispering in their ear, softly reminds them of how they use their leisure time, what they needed to acquire a little 'learning'. They cannot imagine the power of enthusiasm which a really self-contained spiritual life can have in the social organism, because the fettered one they know cannot exert such an enthusias-tic influence over them.[3]

In other words, leisure time is a right and furthermore, what we in modern parlance call 'down time' actually enhances creativity and pro-ductivity and helps us avoid burn-out. "Downtime replenishes the brain's stores of attention and motivation, encourages productivity and creativity, and is essential to achieve our highest levels of performance and simply form stable memories in everyday life."[4]

EDUCATION

Steiner stated that it is from "[t]he administration of education ... [that] all culture develops...."[5] The entire social order must arise and take form out of a heightened and healthy sense of what it means to be a human being here on earth, as an individual in relation to nature and human activity.

[3] GA 23, about 5/6 into Ch. 2 (p. 78)
[4] https://www.scientificamerican.com/article/mental-downtime/
[5] GA 23, Smith translation , about 1/3 or 4 pages into the "Preface to the Fourth Edition, 1920" (p. 12). (Note: this Fourth Edition preface is different from the "Preface to the New Edition of 1920" in the Heckel translation.)

The assumption is that this can only be realized through changes in our approach to education. While we might agree that society as a whole must develop further as regards what it *means* to be a human being, the challenge is: how can this development be furthered without diverting the responsibility for it onto educational reforms which continue – and will continue in the foreseeable future – to fall short of meeting this goal and merely push the problem yet again[6] onto our children? Can we not as adults gain a deeper relationship to human dignity and begin to put that deeper understanding into practice? If through this our children see their parents and teachers struggle with the important issues of society, does this not provide an excellent role model for them? This would help to harmonize what teachers in Waldorf Schools (and other school systems) are attempting to engender in children as a growing awareness of ethics and morality and what those same children experience in their homes.

Even Waldorf schools are challenged by the social, political, and economic pressures of our times. One only need look at how some Waldorf High Schools have succumbed to the demand for "college prep" curricula,[7] often made in order to meet financial and societal pressures. Parental concern about their children missing out on technology leads to statements being made by schools, such as "In the high school curriculum, Waldorf embraces technology in ways that enhance the learning process, by using it as a tool, rather than replacing the role of the teacher. Students quickly master technology, and many Waldorf graduates have gone on to successful careers in the computer industry."[8] Do college prep-oriented Waldorf Schools actually engender the development of the human being from K–12? Does the introduction of technology in high school actually "enhance the learning process?" Rather, should technology be taught in Waldorf Schools as a subject like any other, or an elective subject? Are there not children who have little or no interest in technology? And should not the moral/ethical implications of the use of technology be directly and actively taught, so that an awareness is raised within high school students regarding the effects of technology on themselves and, with forward thinking, their future children? These are challenging questions that Waldorf Schools really must face and address in light of the

---

[6] https://www.waldorf-100.org/en/waldorf-education/history
[7] Example: "The Waldorf School of Garden City is an independent college preparatory day school for children in Nursery through Twelfth Grade," https://www.waldorfgarden.org/basics/campuses/garden-city-new-york/
[8] https://waldorfpeninsula.org/curriculum/media-technology-philosophy/

expectations that parents feel they should have, that correspond to today's societal expectations. If we all take steps toward a deeper understanding of the human being, we can know better how to address these questions.

The spiritual/cultural domain emphasizes not just K–12 education but *all* education. "Even the schools which directly serve the state and the economy should be administered by the educators: law schools, trade-schools, agriculture and industrial colleges, all should be administered by the representatives of a free spiritual life."[9] As already mentioned, it is from out of the cultural domain, especially out of the educational institutions, that new ideas arise and can then stream into the economic and political domains, as well as, of course, into all areas of the cultural domain itself. While the economic and rights domains do not dictate or control curricula, those who possess the relevant expertise will find their places as teachers in the educational institutions of the cultural domain, thus offering the necessary training, fresh ideas and impulses to these two other domains. This prevents the economic and rights domain from stagnating. For example, technological advancements can improve production and quality. Philosophical advancements bring new awareness to the rights domain regarding human dignity, equality and quality of life. The arts enrich all three domains. Steiner did not place science into the economic domain because it is the *fruits* of scientific inquiry that are taken hold of by the economic domain. Scientific pursuits belong to the unique striving of individuals, and therefore find their place in the cultural domain. Science not only relates directly to our understanding of the world around us but also informs our relationship *with* the world, something that deepens our understanding of ourselves and potentially not just from a material perspective.

Unfortunately our current education systems on all fronts are in many respects failing our young people, and thus failing us all through the loss of what they can bring into our common life:

> In terms of readiness for the future of work, young people were far less positive when asked about the usefulness of school. Approximately 56% of young people know what they want to do for work in the future, however they do not feel supported by their

---

[9] GA 23, 1/3 into the "Preface to the Fourth Edition, 1920" (p.13)

education system, and 44% fear that their skills or knowledge won't be in demand in the future.[10]

Within the scope of the cultural domain is the task of assisting each individual to find their place in the community by unfolding the capabilities that lie in them, whether obviously so or dormant, or in seed form: through education in particular, each one is allowed to develop along a self-directed path (with the help of parents, guardians, mentors and teachers). Each will then be able to find their place the flow of productive life, in whichever domain they feel led to contribute:

> Out of the strength of free spiritual life, education/rearing and school will equip/furnish [ausrüsten] people with impulses which bring them, by strength of this indwelling understanding, to realize for what purpose their individual capabilities impel them.[11]

We see awareness of this in schools, but for many young individuals this worthy outcome is inadequately realized. Together with the capability for a satisfying participation in economic life, the social *Empfindung*-sensibilities must be cultivated in this cultural domain.

THE ETHICAL FOUNDATION OF OUR ACTION

So we see that right along with the active education aspect, the cultural domain encompasses all matters pertaining to philosophical, ethical, spiritual-religious and personal striving and development. Many people who do not have a belief in the spiritual none-the-less act in very moral and ethical ways. Yet from the perspective of many belief systems, this innate sense of morality/ethics is still understood as having its foundation in the spiritual. Through his epistemological writing in particular, Steiner established a concrete relationship between the spiritual and our sense of morality/ethics in *The Philosophy of Spiritual Activity* (GA 4, also as other titles in English), as discussed above in the section on "Free and Ethical Action." He made the point that truths are in fact archetypes, and that if we can correctly sense these archetypes – the archetypal ideas, *Urgedanken*, primal thoughts – these can form the conscious basis for 'free ethical action.' Such

---

[10] https://www.oecd-forum.org/posts/53006-young-people-don-t-feel-ready-for-the-future-of-work
[11] GA 23, about 1/6 into Ch. 3 (p. 87); KRH translation

a statement will be refuted by some, or even by many, even by those with spiritual convictions. And this is not surprising in our time: philosophers and religious figures have struggled with these questions for centuries. It is necessary that we struggle our way toward knowing where our sense of morality/ethics comes from as it pertains to the issues of equality, human dignity, self-development, and our development of human sensibilities generally, which are the foundational building blocks of the three-membered organization. We *can* become more conscious of that 'source' of all of these impulses.

Bias

As human beings we face the whole realm of "personal opinion." Opinion is "a statement that expresses a feeling, an attitude, a value judgment, or a belief. It is a statement that is neither true nor false."[12] This differs from a fact which can be proven through objective observation. Here we are not talking about scientific 'proof' but rather, all that confronts us as the known and learned content of our daily existence that makes our existence possible and to a certain extent predictable. With regard to opinion, Steiner wrote:

> Man as he is born today is necessarily full of prejudices; that is the nature of present-day man. And if we remain as we are born we carry these prejudices with us through life; we live in one-sidedness. We can save ourselves only by having inner tolerance, by being able to enter into the opinions of others even when we think them wrong. If we can bring a deep understanding for the opinions of other souls even when considering them mistaken, if we can take what the other thinks and feels in the same way as we take what we think and feel ourself, if we adopt this faculty of inner tolerance, we may overcome these prejudices due to the human cycle in which we were born.[13]

Unfortunately, nowadays we tend not to discern the difference between objective fact and opinion. We have all heard the reply, concerning an actual fact, that "well, that's your opinion." Or even worse "there are no facts, only interpretations [opinions]" based on Friedrich Nietzsche's (and

---

[12] https://www.palmbeachstate.edu/slc/Documents/fact%20or%20opinion%20hints.pdf
[13] GA 189, Lecture II, February 16, 1919, about 2/3 into lecture

other philosophers) concept of perspectivism, "that perception of and knowledge of something are always bound to the interpretive perspectives of those observing it."[14] (Ironically, this is one of the principles of quantum physics,[15] that the observer affects the outcome, but people are not sub-atomic particles.)

The struggle over personal opinion, even more so today, results from our taking our convictions to the extreme, disregarding other people's viewpoints. As Steiner wrote, "being intolerant in our thoughts and feelings prevents us from engaging in others' viewpoints; and while we bring forth our own ideas 'without reservation,' we need to enter the ideas of others just as fully."[16]

Significant impediments to our ability to penetrate to the primal thought of a matter and grow toward free ethical action are the biases – both conscious and unconscious or implicit– that pervade human interactions. "Implicit bias … refers to attitudes and beliefs that occur outside your conscious awareness and control. Explicit bias, on the other hand, are biases that you are aware of on a conscious level."[17] Our biases concerning race, ethnicity, economic status, physical appearance, are a few examples that affect our social behavior. Harvard University has an online Implicit Association Test[18] that can reveal one's biases across a wide range of biases.

One of the most powerful forms of implicit bias is confirmation bias. Confirmation bias is the tendency for people to seek information that confirms pre-existing beliefs or assumptions. People group around each other with the same or similar views. One's thinking is confirmed by other like-minded individuals, whether it is about politics, medicine, education, technology, or about social issues such as gun rights. In this age of the Internet our own views are very easy to confirm, given the ease of access to other people's like-minded viewpoints. We frequently cite other people's like-minded views to justify our own thinking and convince other people of its correctness. Furthermore, once a bias is formed, it is very persistent[19] and reinforces the propensity for confirming one's bias rather than seeking out opposing viewpoints.

---

[14] https://en.wikipedia.org/wiki/Perspectivism

[15] https://arxiv.org/pdf/1806.08788.pdf

[16] Source (German): Rudolf Steiner – GA 34 – LUCIFER- GNOSIS 1903-1908 GRUNDLEGENDE AUFSÄTZE ZUR ANTHROPOSOPHIE UND BERICHTE – April 1904, translated by Nesta Carsten-Krüger (page 453, "Und die Schattenseite…")

[17] https://www.getimpactly.com/post/implicit-vs-explicit-bias

[18] https://implicit.harvard.edu/implicit/takeatest.html

[19] https://www.newyorker.com/magazine/2017/02/27/why-facts-dont-change-our-minds

It was perhaps not so easy to find confirming views 100 years ago. In 1919 Steiner wrote that people "have based *on the institutions themselves* their views about what should be preserved in them and what should be changed in them" (with my italics for clarity).[20] This has shifted considerably – social, political and economic institutions are no longer trusted as sources from which to take our opinions; and this trust factor is further complicated by economic factors and governance. For example:

> Evidence from opinion surveys shows that levels of institutional trust vary significantly across countries. Higher income countries tend to enjoy higher levels of institutional trust than lower income countries, for instance, while opinion polls also suggest that trust in national Government is higher in countries with authoritarian Governments than in those with established democracies....While data for long-run trends are limited, the data available show a marked decrease in institutional trust in developed countries. In the United States, trust in the national government has declined from 73 per cent in 1958 to 24 per cent in 2021.[21]

Given the easy access in the 21st century to views that confirm our own thinking, we no longer meet individuals with different views in person at pubs or salons, but instead actively seek out the opinions of others on the Internet who share our views. How often does a proponent of 5G 'google' for opposing views? How often does someone claiming 5G is carcinogenic research the positions stating otherwise? We rarely give voice to the views of others when they oppose our own views, and this limits our ability to 'enter into the opinions of others even when we think them wrong.' As Steiner wrote (with a translation clarification/alternative from Kate):

> The shadow side of personal conviction is willfulness, pride in our thoughts. As good as it is to advocate one's own opinion without reservation, from another point of view, it is necessary to assert the ideas of one's fellow human beings as entirely as well [or, allow these ideas to be equally considered]. And how little does this fit the character of those who hold fast to their conviction! They often show

---

[20] GA 23, 2 pages into Ch. 3 (p. 84)
[21] https://www.un.org/development/desa/dspd/2021/07/trust-public-institutions/

intolerance in their feeling and thinking, which makes it impossible for them to engage in the opinions of others.[22]

The term 'confirmation bias' was coined in 1960 by the English Psychologist Peter C. Wason. This term did not exist in 1919, and yet Steiner clearly wrote about the concept, as the quote above implies.

Questions the reader can ask themselves:

1. What are my confirmation biases?
2. What people and groups do I seek out to confirm my viewpoints?
3. What people and groups do I avoid that have opposing viewpoints?
4. Do I represent the viewpoints of others that oppose mine when talking with people about my viewpoints?
5. Do I spend time researching the viewpoints of others that oppose my own?

The reader might be amused to know how easy it was to find numerous references for this book that validate the 'viewpoints' made here. In the cases where this book cites opposing viewpoints, this took conscious effort to rephrase the search criteria to find opposing viewpoints; and of course there were many to find. And that is the point of this section – that in many ways, achieving free ethical action through feeling-sensing-perceiving archetypal truths is not possible unless we consciously identify our biases, and in particular, our confirmation biases, ask others what their biases are, and consciously reframe our views to seek out those with opposing views and understand their position.

SELF-DEVELOPMENT

As Andrew Brogan summarized:

> … Steiner is drawing on a specific vision of humanity which is underpinned by a concept of human nature in which humans are naturally drawn to develop themselves along their own particular and individual paths to the greatest of their capabilities and capacities. This is more than an externally produced and imposed push for

---

[22] Source (German): Rudolf Steiner – GA 34 – LUCIFER- GNOSIS 1903-1908 GRUNDLEGENDE AUFSÄTZE ZUR ANTHROPOSOPHIE UND BERICHTE – April 1904, translated by Nesta Carsten-Krüger (page 453, "Und die Schattenseite…"), http://fvn-archiv.net/PDF/GA/GA034.pdf#page=453

life-long-learning and self-improvement as is currently promoted through neoliberalism, this is an inbuilt desire that all humans possess irrespective of their current social contexts.[23]

As MorningCoach counseled on their website:

> Self-development means taking the necessary steps to make positive changes in our lives. It creates self-awareness of your strengths and weaknesses and what is your personality and attitude towards various things that happen in your life. Getting to know yourself better will allow you to figure out what you can do and what you want to get out of life. Creating new goals is not the only benefit you can get once you develop yourself. There are several other benefits, as we list them down below.[24]

Self-development can be seen as a means of furthering one's awareness of the salient issues of the three-membered organization: human dignity, human rights, and the quality of life. Self-development is not necessarily 'self-ish': "A self-improvement journey has a positive impact on relationships because it conveys a sense of self-awareness and an ability to grow and evolve, says Alex Dimitriu, MD…"[25] The question 'are people still interested in self-development?' is relevant. This question was asked on Quora[26] and some of the answers are informative. Mei Michaels replied:

> I'd say that there are so many people who are not interested in self-development because of the times we live in. The world is trying to make us care about the money, the value of material things. We are forced to lead a life and think only about other's [sic] opinion, being the best in earning money.
>
> Do we have time to make ourselves better? I think it is hard. We have so many things to do. But time passes more slowly when you quit the bustling city and go to a peaceful place.
>
> Being far from the [sic] nature is also the reason. While you are close to the forests, rivers and the miracles of nature, you become more focused.
>
> People think it is too hard to develop yourself, it is easier for them to stay who they are now. Look at the movies, ads, the society. Does anyone care about your development? No. The point is

---

[23] Andrew Brogan, *Steiner Shorts 2, The Threefold Social Organism, An Introduction*
[24] https://www.morningcoach.com/blog/why-is-self-development-important
[25] https://www.fatherly.com/life/self-improvement-benefits-all-relationships
[26] https://www.quora.com/Why-are-so-many-people-not-interested-in-self-development

to be as stupid as possible, to be influenced by the stupid forms of spending time.

And Marjorie Smith replied:

> Depends on what you mean by self-development. If you mean developing things about yourself that make it easier to function in society, there is no real need to. We tell people that they should be who they are and that's its [sic] the other person's problem if they can't cope with you. It's okay now to be boorish, rude, anti-social, sexual [sic] aggressive etc. Why improve when there's nothing wrong with how you behave and its [sic] not your fault that others don't like it.

These two viewpoints are informative because they reveal systemic issues in our current culture resulting in part from materialistic thinking, the distraction of entertainment, the psychology of advertisement, and the general attitude of acceptance. The motivation for self-development (besides being required to do so on account of a crisis in one's behavior) is stimulated by upbringing and education. But it can be difficult particularly for adults to engage in self-development while being mired in the lifestyle circumstances that the commentators above bring up. As Michael Mehlburg wrote:

> Self-improvement requires change. It requires us to do things we're not familiar with, that we're uncomfortable with. But our routines, the expectations we've built for how our life runs, they don't allow for the uncomfortable. And so, they don't allow for growth. Without modifying your expectations, you can't hope to change. And without change, you can't hope to grow.[27]

It is something to consider, that self-development requires doing "things we're not familiar with, that we're uncomfortable with." This requires a certain vigilance, even with meditation, that we continually expand our comfort zone into the unfamiliar and the uncomfortable.

---

[27] https://michaelmehlberg.com/blog/2019/9/13/what-neuroscience-says-on-why-self-improvement-is-so-effing-hard-and-what-to-do-about-it

CARRYING OUT JUSTICE, ADJUDICATION

Everything which holds sway within the cultural domain is in support of the development of human beings as individuals, to bring forth their gifts and capacities of all kinds, including moral capacities. Without honoring individual human freedom this development cannot unfold, nor can the evolution of humanity proceed. In our relationships to each other in this domain, freedom of the individual in their choices and course of life is the dominant ideal.

But what if this were the only relationship aspect that we pursued? Where would there be any consideration of the effects that each individual has on others in the human community *outside of* the fostering of individual capabilities? Can we sense another impulse demanding to be followed in light of our common life, together with each other? This impulse will lead us to a discussion of the rights domain. Here is where laws and regulations are crafted to ensure to each person those aspects of life which are recognized as applying in common, equally, to everyone. However, while the rights domain creates the laws and these apply *to everyone*, when it comes to handling transgressions of these laws, this involves *individual* human beings. Hence, the rights domain will not adjudicate transgressions. Steiner elucidated this:

> The laying down of laws is in the most eminent sense a social concern. The moment that one is obliged to turn to a judge it usually has to do with a super- or anti-social matter, with something which falls out of the social life. Such matters are basically all individual matters of the human being. Such matters are [within] the administrative branches of spiritual-cultural life, and among them also, the administration of the finding of justice [Rechstfindung]. The finding of justice grows out, beyond the boundaries of democracy.[28]

Through our increasing *empfindung*-sensibility for the three domains and their three very different relationship-impulses, we can begin to grasp that adjudication – either civil or criminal – of a matter that "has fallen out of the social life" must be handled within the cultural domain, not the rights domain. In the assignment of consequences for rights violations, the individual's situation in life must be taken into account; and the effect of consequences or punishment must also be evaluated .[29] In light of these

---

[28] GA 332a, 2 pages from end of Lect. 3); KRH translation
[29] GA 23, 2-3 pages from end of Ch. 3 (pp. 124-25)

factors, pre-set and fixed sentences cannot be universally applied. And we already have a sense for this. One simple example is the difference we make between the consequences to be meted out to someone for speeding while intoxicated versus for speeding while taking an injured person to the hospital. Another example of this is in the case of a person suffering from mental illness. US courts consider it unreasonable to apply the same consequences to such a person, in contrast to a person not suffering from mental illness or temporary insanity.[30]

Because of the sensitivity to the individual circumstances, judges are to arise out of the cultural domain – individuals who of course possess understanding of the laws and legal structures of the rights domain. And the nomination to judgeship would not be for political reasons, but for reasons "like those which determine the nomination of the best teacher to a particular post."[31] Defendants are then to be able to avail themselves of a judge who possesses the cultural understanding necessary to judge their circumstances rightly and apply fitting sentences. The sentences applied are then the purview of the rights domain to enforce.

THE FRUITS OF THE CULTURAL DOMAIN

Within the cultural domain, we can recognize that individuals are in fact at work in the service of their fellows in many different capacities. Teachers prepare and give lessons, performances are rehearsed and presented, works of art are created, equipment and physical settings are improved in one way or another, and so on. Does all of this entail only the cultural domain? No; for in the moment that any of these fruits are brought forth and received by others, they become the concern of the economic domain – the domain of exchanges between people in fulfillment of needs of all kinds, also for those needs which have their roots in the spiritual life, such as art, literature and music do. And the answer to the above question about whether these cultural activities entail only the cultural domain, is yet again but for another reason, 'no.' For through our *Empfindung*-sensibility we can discern that weaving into these activities is the human impulse to meet each other on quite a range of issues *not only*

---

[30] https://www.law.cornell.edu/wex/temporary_insanity
[31] GA 332a, 2–3 pages from end of Lect. 3

as unique individuals, but also as human beings who have equal standing with other human beings. And this is the concern of the rights domain, which comes next.

Since a great deal of what is carried out in the cultural domain is not necessarily or immediately of economic value in the form of commodities and services for exchange in the ongoing economic cycle, in order to continue, cultural domain work must be provided the means of support. This would of course be most obviously necessary for education and for adjudication, so that those who are drawn to serve in these areas are afforded a 'decent human existence' (more about this in the next chapter). Steiner pointed to two ways that this can come about in a healthy social organism:

> Technical ideas flow into the economic life which originate in the spiritual-cultural life. They stem from spiritual life, even if they come directly from members of the state or economic domain. All the organizational ideas and forces that fertilize economic and state life come from there. Compensation for this inflow into the two social areas will either come about through the free understanding of those who depend on this inflow, or its arrangement will be found through rights that are developed in the domain of the political state. ... This will develop through a harmonization of the requirements of the rights-consciousness with those of economic life.[32]

And in particular, in the lectures Steiner gave that are collected in GA 340, World Economy (Rudolf Steiner Press, 1990, 3rd edition) Steiner points out how corporate surplus capital, instead of being invested into land, or nowadays commonly through acquisitions of other companies and stock dividends, is instead returned to the cultural domain which achieves "the free understanding of those who depend on this inflow." Aspects of this are discussed further in the chapter on The Characteristics of the Economic Domain.

---

[32] GA 23, about 3 pages from end of Ch. 2 (p. 80); KRH translation

Chapter 4

CHARACTERISTICS *of the* RIGHTS DOMAIN

Steiner often used the word, 'Rechtsleben,' rights-life, in reference to this domain: 'Recht' – right, law. Sometimes he referred instead to the 'Staatsleben' – the political-state-life. The political-state is the means by which laws (Gesetze) pertaining to rights are legislated, laid down and enforced. Translating 'Recht' or 'Staat' as 'justice' or 'equity' gives it a more generalized meaning which tends to suggest that this domain would include adjudication, the seeking of redress from a justice or a judge, through the judicial system, which it does not, as discussed in the previous chapter. For this reason to avoid confusion we want to limit our use of both of these other terms.

In *The Social Future* lectures (GA 332a) Steiner referred to this domain as the 'Recht*sboden*,' the rights-ground. 'Boden' literally meant not only the ground, but the *soil* beneath our feet. With his repeated use of this word, 'Boden' – also when referring to the two other domains – he brought us the image of something that *supports life*.

Pointing out that the human being is the driving force of the social organism, Steiner said:

> Whoever looks impartially into social life will be able to discover that ultimately everything that we have around us as institutions/arrangements comes about through the measures, through the will of human beings.[1]

So, where do the arrangements of our common life of rights come from? How do we 'will' them into existence? In the 1920 Preface to GA 23, he began to set forth their source and differentiated that source from the sources from which the other two domains arise:

> In it [in the true political-state member of the social organism], everything that must depend on the judgment and *Empfindung*-sensibility

---

[1] GA 332a *The Social Future*, first paragraph of Lect. 3); KRH translation

of every adult who has come of age is asserted. In the free spiritual life each one establishes/substantiates themselves according to their special abilities; in economic life everyone fills their place according to their associative context. In the political and legal life of the state, [each] comes into their purely human validity….

… In this [domain], everyone stands facing the other as an equal, because it only negotiates and administers in those areas in which every person is equally capable of making judgments. Human rights and duties/obligations are regulated in this member of the social organism.[2]

It is important to understand what Steiner meant by, in the rights domain, "everything that must depend on the judgment and sensibility of every adult who has come of age is asserted." In an attempt to explain what Steiner meant, we can look at two important points. First, as an adult (one who has come of age), "everyone stands facing the other as an equal" they stand facing each other as equals regardless of age. The second point to be made here is actually a question - does judgment/sensibility develop over time and with experience? Article II of the US Constitution states (among other requirements) that a person must be at least 35 years old to be president of the United States.[3] Is this Article not intended to ensure that someone seeking the presidency has a certain amount of experience? Steiner breaks down the development of the human being into 7 year periods:[4]

0-7: from baby to schoolhood
7-14: schoolhood to adolescence
14-21: puberty to young adulthood
21-28: young adult to adulthood

and continues the seven year cycle further with 'insight', 'unfolding', 'uniqueness', 'overview', 'intuition', and from 63 and on, 'preparation.' Here, while each adult human being "stands facing the other as an equal" in the interest of determining and regulating matters concerning the common life, the question that applies in general, from young to old, is how do we stand as equals in the context of our unique life experiences? Yes, we stand as equals in that each of our 'votes' on a matter is considered equal, but are we truly "equally capable of making judgment?" Not to

[2] GA 23, 2 pages from end of the Preface to the Fourth German Edition 1920 (p. 21)
[3] https://www.loc.gov/classroom-materials/elections/presidential-election-process/requirements-for-the-president-of-the-united-states/
[4] https://waldorfinspiration.com/en/the-seven-year-stages

contradict Steiner, but the view of this author is that the only reasonable answer is 'no' because, whether we are 18 or 118, we bring unique, individual experiences to bear on a matter requiring judgment. We might say that we are equally capable of making a judgment *within the context of* our spiritual and world-experiential development and it is in the context of that development that we stand equal, which points out the importance of engaging in conversation to express our unique experiences when making a judgment. The answer (again the author's view) can only be 'yes' to the above question when we strive to attain the primal thought on a matter requiring judgment. To reiterate an earlier quote:

> The difference between me and my fellow men is not at all because we live in two quite different spiritual worlds, but because from the world of ideas which we share, he receives different intuitions from mine. He wants to live out his intuitions, I mine. If we both really draw from the idea, and are not obeying any external impulses (physical or spiritual), then we cannot but meet in the same striving, in having the same intentions.[5]

To "really draw from the idea, [where we] are not obeying any external impulses" is, in the author's view, the task of determining the primal thought, and when we do so, "we cannot but meet in the same striving, in having the same intentions" and as a logical conclusion, come to deeper understanding in matters of judgment. This gives some guidance on how to concretely work as equals in the rights domain.

Another point that Steiner makes is that, unlike the economic and cultural domains, the respective "associative context" and "specialized abilities" do not require specialized knowledge "in which every person is equally capable of making judgments." Given that "[h]uman rights and duties/obligations are regulated in this member [the rights domain] of the social organism" it is in our times necessary to have specialized knowledge to make appropriate judgment concerning human rights, duties and obligations. We see this when addressing the complexities of today's issues (for example, Artificial Intelligence, medical interventions, cell towers, global warming) in relation to human rights and dignity. The issues confronting the rights domain in the 21st century (and beyond) do in fact require specialized knowledge to even understand why an issue stands before the rights domain.

---

[5] GA 4, about 3/4 into Ch. 9 (p. 180)

Steiner said that "[a]ll such things as are related to the development of human capacity … are excluded from democratic measures" – in other words, things related to the development of human capacity is not something we vote on, it is 'a given.' Steiner elucidates this further: "[W]hat is democratic must be separated from the ground of spiritual life, from the ground of economic life." In these determinations of the rights domain "everyone brings an equal human competence" (see above for the author's view on this); and the determinations are made by majority vote. By contrast, "majority resolutions must be kept out of the domain of economic life," for the reason that special competency *is* needed for this domain. And likewise, such majority resolutions are excluded from that which is strictly spiritual–cultural activity.[6]

Rather than letting the term, 'equality' (Gleichheit), float ungrounded as an abstract ideal, Steiner helped us by conveying the concept descriptively, as above: that the human being 'stands facing' other human beings 'as an equal.' This gives us a picture of the human being *as present* to other human beings, *as real, seen and heard, as completely "valid"* in their humanness. And in his GA 332a, Lecture 3, he asked, "What is the origin of rights? What is the origin of the feeling [Gefühl] that prompts people to say in their dealings with one another that something is just or unjust?" As part of his full discussion of the answer, he said:

> Whoever omits feeling in the study of human nature leaves out all consideration of the real rights-relationships in the social organism. For rights relationships can only develop in the common life of human beings, as feeling-to-feeling [Gefühl an Gefühl] in this common life … is stripped/shed [abstreift], becomes refined/polished/milled [abschleift]. As people feel toward one another mutually, so it follows, what public law is.[7]

The verb 'abstreift' suggests the image of something being sloughed off, like an old skin; but it can also refer to patrolling a plot of land, scouring an area. We begin to build a picture of the growing nature of the human being in this life of rights-relationships that develops within the feelings, and with this the growing and flowing nature of the whole social organism.

Hence, it is a welcome realization that Steiner soon brought when he

---

[6] GA 332a, 1/2 into Lect. 3 (same passages for all of these quotes)
[7] GA 332a, about 1/3 into Lect. 3; KRH translation

spoke of *how* this "feeling in cooperation with the feeling of the other in public life kindles the law [Recht] within public life": it develops in the same way that language does; it "flames up/becomes kindled by other human beings, by the whole human community." And through the mutual feelings and relationships which grow up, people then "anchor, settle these relationships in laws." In this way the longing for democracy emerges from out of the fundamental nature of human relationships, bringing more and more the recognition that what is "valid for others" is what one "feels to be right and best for oneself." Steiner characterized this principle as "an elementary force."[8] And as he had suggested in GA 23, the healthy human being will not want to enter social life without bearing this feeling-sensibility within themselves.[9]

How do we 'strip/shed' this feeling-to-feeling in the common life and instead 'refine/polish' it? The common life of feeling is often little more than sentimentality. As Panu Poutvaara (University of Munich, Ifo Institute, and IZA, Germany) summarized, "Good-looking political candidates win more votes around the world. This holds for both male and female candidates. Candidate appearance may be especially important for uninformed voters, as it is easy to observe."[10] He points out that in Finland, 'beauty' has a 20% effect on the relative success of a candidate, while competence and trustworthiness only have a 5% effect. Again, we come back to the point that, to work with the highly charged issues we face today and develop a grounded feeling-to-feeling relationship, we must determine the primal thoughts of an issue rather than adhere to a feeling-sentimentality and, we must in many situations acquire specialized knowledge on the issues.

In the image he gave of the shedding or scouring and milling-refinement of the impulses of feeling-to-feeling between human beings, we are reminded of what he had said about the importance of rearing and educating children with an awareness of the social *Empfindung*-sensibility.[11] A striking example of the possibility for bringing forth the "elementary force" of this impulse was the work of Janusz Korczak, who established a large orphanage in pre-World War II Poland.

---

[8] GA 332a, about 2/5 to 1/2 into Lect. 3 for these excerpts; KRH translation
[9] GA 23, 5 pages into Ch. 2 (p. 57), as above in the section on "Developing a Healthy Social Life and Social Organization"
[10] https://wol.iza.org/articles/how-do-candidates-looks-affect-their-election-chances/long
[11] GA 23, 5 pages into Ch. 2 (p. 57)

> The orphanage was radically progressive at a time when children
> were beaten and starved in many institutions. Dr. Korczak taught
> the children to trust and rely on adults. He instituted self-govern-
> ment and a court of peers. He taught the children how to work
> together, accept responsibility, and respect themselves and others.[12]

Dr. Korczak watched for the emergence of talents and potentials in
the children and supported their unique development. It is clear that he
consciously engaged in the primal-thought impulses of all three domains
for the good of the whole community. "One of Korczak's orphans later
said, 'If not for the home, I would not know that there are honest people
in the world who never steal. I would not know that one could speak the
truth. I would not know that there are just laws.'"[13] The sense for rights,
the law, flamed alive in the children, kindled by being in community
under his guidance. And thus it was shown that not only grown adults,
but even appropriately-reared children could stand as equals in the task of
self-government.

In the rights domain, each human being – and in this case, each grown
human being able to make judgments – is able to stand facing other human
beings on an equal footing – to be present, to be seen and heard, to participate and have their views carry weight equal to others. This is at least a step
toward affirming the dignity of each one. Grievously, Korczak was denied
equal standing in relation to those who led him and the children to their
death during the Nazi occupation of Poland in World War II.

When, 'feeling-to-feeling,' we can gradually raise ourselves in our
common social life, strip off and surmount our biases and prejudices (see
also the section on this in the chapter on the cultural domain), we can
begin working on the real rights that guarantee human dignity. Steiner
stated that "in truth, all the turmoil in the social organism results from the
feeling that existence is unworthy of human dignity."[14] This is the core;
for our life of rights will only be as wholesome as our feeling-to-feeling
sensibilities are toward our fellow human beings. And out of its fertile
'rights ground,' the rights domain can be brought to function properly to
resolve that turmoil.

What are the rights that we typically agree to as being equally proper

[12] See the brochure, "Janusz Korczak and The Last Journey," from the Korczak Association
of the USA, https://korczakusa.com
[13] Again, see the brochure, "Janusz Korczak and The Last Journey"
[14] GA 23, about 2*3 into Ch. 2 (p. 73); KRH translation

for both ourselves and every other person? As Steiner summarized the equal-to-equal relationship, "[t]he political state must … ensure that each individual is able to assert his opinion. The appreciation or non–appreciation of individual abilities is not one of its functions."[15] The US Declaration of Independence states this concept of standing equal-to-equal succinctly (ignoring that some of the authors of the Declaration were slave owners[16]): "We hold these truths to be self-evident, that all men are created equal, that they are endowed by their Creator with certain unalienable Rights, that among these are Life, Liberty and the pursuit of Happiness."[17] It has been suggested that the word "men" excludes women. The Library of Congress comments on this:

> Although most people have interpreted "all men" to mean human-
> ity, others have argued that Jefferson and the other authors of the
> Declaration meant to exclude women and children. Within the
> context of the times it is clear that 'all men' was a euphemism for
> 'humanity' … [18]

However:

> When Thomas Jefferson and those who helped him draft the
> Declaration of Independence described a new order among the thir-
> teen colonies of the new United States, they did not include women.
> Under the laws of the new United States, women were denied prop-
> erty rights, lacked the ability to vote and could not make or enter
> into a legal contract.[19]

Even now, in the spring 2023, this matter remains unresolved. As mentioned in the section on "Primal Thoughts," one hundred years ago, in 1923, the Equal Rights Amendment[20] (ERA) was proposed. Its federal ratification would guarantee equal legal rights for all American citizens regardless of gender, which at that time was limited to 'men' and 'women': "*Section 1:* Equality of rights under the law shall not be denied or abridged by the United States or by any state on account of sex."[21] In 1982, fifteen

---

[15] GA 23, 4 pages into Ch. 3 (p. 86)

[16] https://www.crf-usa.org/images/t2t/pdf/HowShouldWeJudgeOurNation.pdf

[17] https://billofrightsinstitute.org/primary-sources/declaration-of-independence

[18] https://www.loc.gov/exhibits/creating-the-united-states/interactives/declaration-of-inde-
pendence/equal/index.html

[19] https://electwomen.com/2012/07/did-the-statement-all-men-are-created-equal-include-
women/

[20] https://en.wikipedia.org/wiki/Equal_Rights_Amendment

[21] https://www.equalrightsamendment.org/faq, "ERA: Frequently Asked Questions"

states had still not ratified the ERA, preventing it from becoming federal law. And while now the necessary number of states have ratified the ERA, it is still not law because the 1982 deadline has passed, and the government would probably have to allow each state to review their original vote. Furthermore, in 2023 "Sen. John Kennedy (R-La.) today joined Sen. Cindy Hyde-Smith (R-Miss.) in introducing the Equal Rights Amendment (ERA) Resolution to recognize that Congress does not have the authority to deem the ERA as a ratified amendment to the Constitution."[22] The ERA continues to be a controversial topic as illustrated by an article posted by Caroline Reeves on the Alliance Defending Freedom website:

> First drafted nearly 100 years ago, the Equal Rights Amendment appeared to be nearing ratification in the '70s but was stopped in its tracks, and for good reason.
>
> It was largely American women who campaigned against it and helped others understand the damage it would wreak upon the country.
>
> Thanks in large part to the STOP ERA campaign, lawmakers realized the amendment would have unleashed a cascade of government actions that would harm women.
>
> This included government-financed abortion, the legal dissolution of biological differences between men and women, and restrictions on women's legal rights in matters of divorce.
>
> Today, the Equal Rights Amendment is an even worse idea than it was in the '70s. The ERA centers on the word "sex" at a time when ideologues and activists are aggressively pushing to disassociate the term from biology and reinterpret it to include "gender identity."
>
> That increases the danger that "sex" becomes meaningless, opening the door for men who identify as women to compete in— and dominate—women's sports, and for men to enter into shelters designed to protect women who have suffered domestic abuse, rape, and trafficking.[23]

Here then is a very relevant example of the difficulty of passing legislation on the subject of 'equality of rights' and the difficulty of working feeling-to-feeling when facing each other with very different viewpoints. How can we stand equal-to-equal when we cannot even agree on the

---

[22] https://www.kennedy.senate.gov/public/2023/3/kennedy-hyde-smith-introduce-resolution-to-stop-equal-rights-amendment-from-illegitimate-ratification

[23] https://adflegal.org/article/great-news-equal-rights-amendment-will-remain-dead

terms 'sex' and 'gender', and furthermore, according to the quote cited above, such 'equality' would have profound effects on sports, shelters, and to add, the use of bathrooms? Regardless of one's position on the ERA, there are tangible consequences, and the consequences of any legislation must be considered.

The rights which apply to *all* human beings must of course apply without regard to individual capabilities, skills and position in life. In 1948, the members of the United Nations Assembly adopted the Universal Declaration of Human Rights.[24] Forty-eight voted for it, eight abstained and two did not vote; none voted against it. The United Nations webpage on Human Rights give this summary (their bold):

> "Human rights are rights we have simply because we exist as human beings – they are not granted by any state. These universal rights are **inherent** to us all, regardless of nationality, sex, national or ethnic origin, color, religion, language, or any other status. They range from the most fundamental – the right to life – to those that make life worth living, such as the rights to food, education, work, health, and liberty."

The concerns about the ERA amendment that were brought forward included concern that there would no longer be separate-sex athletic teams, prisons and public restrooms, and that abortion would be legal and on demand. Examining these particular matters can perhaps help us to come to terms with the scope of the rights domain better. We need to ask: in what ways are human beings equal regardless of the gender of their body, and in what ways are they not? It can perhaps be seen that the factor of physical sex is *not so simple.* Male and female hormones bring about sexual traits and functions; but they also have other effects, such as on the muscles. "While men may perform better at strength and speed sports, women certainly have the biological upper hand in endurance activities."[25] Hence, in some cases there is a very real *inequality;* and it would seem that unisex teams cannot be simply mandated or litigated[26], and that in actuality, this difference in capabilities is probably a matter for the cultural domain to take up and clarify before the rights domain can approach it properly.

Equality of people should be self-evident, but it is not, nor are the

---

[24] https://www.ohchr.org/en/what-are-human-rights
[25] https://themusclephd.com/gender-differences-in-training/
[26] https://www.pbs.org/newshour/politics/supreme-court-says-transgender-girl-can-run-track-in-west-virginia-as-lawsuit-proceeds

current laws adhered to. In the domain of economics, Title VII of the Civil Rights Act of 1964[27] prohibits workplace discrimination based on religion, national origin, race, color, or gender. Yet a 2021 study in the UK showed that: "In 2019 – before the pandemic disrupted data collection – women were paid 16% less per hour than men on average. The gap in average annual earnings was even larger, at 37%, since women are much more likely to work part-time."[28] The median black male worker earns 74 percent as much as the median white male worker, while the median Hispanic male worker earns only 63 percent as much.[29] And as reported to the United Nations in 2022, "in access to health, employment, education and housing, the LGBTQ community suffers."[30]

To the extent that the recognized rights of the people are encoded into law, the political-rights domain in many ways lays down restrictions upon the extent of its own activities. thus protecting the rights of the people. For example, the US Bill of Rights Amendments to the US Constitution[31] lay down the following restrictions and rights:

- First Amendment: Congress shall make no law respecting an establishment of religion, or prohibiting the free exercise thereof; or abridging the freedom of speech, or of the press, or the right of the people peaceably to assemble, and to petition the Government for a redress of grievances.
- Second Amendment: A well regulated Militia, being necessary to the security of a free State, the right of the people to keep and bear Arms, shall not be infringed.
- Fourth Amendment: The right of the people to be secure in their persons, houses, papers, and effects, against unreasonable searches and seizures, shall not be violated, …
- Sixth Amendment: In all criminal prosecutions, the accused shall enjoy the right to a speedy and public trial, by an impartial jury of the State and district wherein the crime shall have been committed; …
- Thirteenth Amendment: Neither slavery nor involuntary

---

[27] https://www.eeoc.gov/statutes/title-vii-civil-rights-act-1964
[28] https://ifs.org.uk/publications/15657
[29] http://www.gpoaccess.gov/eop/ca/index.html
[30] https://www.nbcnews.com/nbc-out/out-news/us-sees-progress-lgbtq-rights-equality-lacking-un-expert-says-rcna45622
[31] https://www.aclu.org/other/bill-rights-us-constitution

servitude ... shall exist within the United States, or any place subject to their jurisdiction ...

- Fifteenth Amendment: The right of citizens of the United States to vote shall not be denied or abridged by the United States or by any State on account of race, color, or previous condition of servitude ...
- Nineteenth Amendment: The right of citizens of the United States to vote shall not be denied or abridged by the United States or by any State on account of sex.

In our time, the issues of surveillance are potential violations of the Fourth Amendment, as was determined by the Foreign Intelligence Surveillance Court (FISA Court) ruling in 2019 concerning the FBI's warrantless surveillance of emails.[32] Shocks to the social organism such as the terrorist attacks of 9/11 in the US and the COVID-19 pandemic worldwide can be taken advantage of to violate these rights: "Governments and corporations have historically used crises as opportunities to introduce new policies which would otherwise be impossible to pass, normalizing them in a new status quo – what author Naomi Klein calls the "shock doctrine."ise be impossible to pass, normalizing them in a new status quo—what author Naomi Klein calls the 'shock doctrine.'"[33,34]

Should the backscatter x-ray machines and random body searches at airports be considered a violation of the Fourth Amendment[35]? Who defines what "unreasonable search" means and in what contexts does that meaning change?

In some of the US Bill of Right Amendments, we see that *freedoms* are laid down as rights. We have the right to be free of a state religion, to hold, speak and publish different views, to freely assemble (peacefully) and to seek redress, to be free of enslavement and involuntary servitude.

During the French Revolution, some of those involved felt that there was something of a problem in calling for Freedom, Equality and Fraternity and hoping for realization of all three together. As Steiner pointed out:

[D]uring the course of the nineteenth century, some very clever

---

[32] https://www.brennancenter.org/our-work/analysis-opinion/how-fbi-violated-privacy-rights-tens-thousands-americans
[33] https://www.afsc.org/blogs/news-and-commentary/are-governments-violating-human-rights-and-civil-liberties-coronavirus
[34] https://naomiklein.org/the-shock-doctrine/
[35] https://www.hg.org/legal-articles/the-constitution-and-airport-full-body-scans-7886

thinkers took pains to point out the impossibility of realizing these ideals of fraternity, equality and liberty in a uniform social organism. ...[F]or example, that ... freedom would not be possible if the equality principle were practised.[36]

This impossibility only confronts us if we look – as they did – toward a *unitary government* as administering both or all aspects of the social life. For, as those who have crafted the US Bill of Rights Amendments realized, the domain of equality (the political-state) needs to be explicitly prohibited in certain areas, in order that the freedoms of individuality can be claimed. However, when the primal thoughts which inform the three distinct members of the social organism are brought to consciousness, then we will know better and better which aspects of life are rights (political-state, legislative domain) and which are freedoms (cultural domain), and which aspects involve exchanges between us in the best sense of mutuality (economic domain). What is tricky here is that we have *rights to certain things* equally with others such as to have an equal voice, an equal vote, security in our home, to have possessions, to seek redress for harms; but we also consider ourselves as having *rights to freedoms*, as being equally free as others are free – meaning freedom in a whole range of areas in which we are allowed to have very individualized needs and desires and to unfold very individualized pursuits, to choose our own vocation, our livelihood, etc. It is difficult to find an example more charged and urgent in our society than gun rights, which directly concerns rights to certain things, rights to freedoms, and the right for security in our homes, schools, and public and private events. Another charged and urgent example are the positions of the pro-choice and pro-life groups, challenging the right to freedom and the right to life, and even more profoundly, challenging the meaning and interpretation of the word 'life.' These are indeed challenging times that we live in.

There are many things which we would expect to be truly basic human rights – things that no one should have to fight to secure for their maintenance and thriving in life. The United Nations Universal Declaration of Human Rights[37] enumerated thirty articles, many of which are rights, though not always in specific – for instance (this online translation still uses the masculine pronouns, clearly meaning any gender):

---

[36] GA 23, 2 pages from end of Ch. 2 (p. 81)
[37] https://www.un.org/en/about-us/universal-declaration-of-human-rights

Article 3. Right to life: Everyone has the right to life, liberty and security of person.

Article 4. Freedom from slavery: No one shall be held in slavery or servitude; slavery and the slave trade shall be prohibited in all their forms.

Article 5. Freedom from torture: No one shall be subjected to torture or to cruel, inhuman or degrading treatment or punishment.

Article 25. Right to adequate standard of living: Everyone has the right to a standard of living adequate for the health and well-being of himself and of his family, including food, clothing, housing and medical care and necessary social services, and the right to security in the event of unemployment, sickness, disability, widowhood, old age or other lack of livelihood in circumstances beyond his control. Motherhood and childhood are entitled to special care and assistance. All children shall enjoy the same social protection.[38]

In the US, our social organization does not assure these rights to all. Social services, for example the Supplemental Nutrition Assistance Program (SNAP)[39] – oddly administered by the The U.S. Department of Agriculture's (USDA) Food and. Nutrition Service (FNS)[40] – is tied to work requirements and results, not in increased employment, but rather in decreased enrollment:

By comparing older and younger adults previously getting SNAP benefits, we found that work requirements did not increase employment or earnings 18 months after their reinstatement …

But we did find that work requirements dramatically reduced the number of people enrolled in SNAP. Among the adults subject to work requirements once they were restored in 2013, over half lost their benefits because of the policy.

We also found that work requirements disproportionately led people who had faced great economic hardships, such as those without housing or earned income, to lose benefits.[41]

As to Article 25, the right to adequate standard of living, only Iran ever

---

[38] https://www.ohchr.org/en/what-are-human-rights
[39] https://www.fns.usda.gov/snap/supplemental-nutrition-assistance-program
[40] https://www.usda.gov/sites/default/files/documents/snap_fact_sheet.pdf
[41] https://theconversation.com/snap-work-requirements-dont-actually-get-more-people-working-but-they-do-drastically-limit-the-availability-of-food-aid-204257

fully instituted a Universal Basic Income (UBI) from 2010 to 2016. Four countries, Brazil, United States, United Kingdom (ending in 2025), Kenya have pilot programs to varying degrees. Sixteen countries are discussion the concept and not yet implemented as of 2022.[42]

As to education, the US Constitution does not lay down education as a right. Education is understood to be the province of the states under the Tenth Amendment. And notably missing from the UN Declaration is anything concerning access to clean water, air and soil.

In a truly functioning social organism, the rights domain would act to ensure all of the elements that are necessary to ensure an existence worthy of the human being – of *each* human being. And within the scope of human rights, there are several areas in particular to which Steiner brought important insights; and he explained how these could be applied. These will be taken up next.

QUALITY OF LIFE

Within the three-membered social organism, it is the domain of rights which has the responsibility of ensuring that people are secure in having a decent quality of life throughout life – as Rudolf Steiner characterized it, "a decent human existence."[43] This provision gives recognition and substance to the dignity that is inherent in each and every human being. It is clear in the context of his writing and lectures, that this decent quality of life is beyond mere subsistence. It very much includes the ability of each individual to pursue their self-development/improvement, too, in accord with their own needs and free choosing.

How is this to come about? There are several aspects to this.

We usually think that our quality of life is a matter of finding and holding a job, earning a wage or salary, and with that paying as best we can for our maintenance and desired activities in life. For most of us, it is ingrained in us to engage in selling our labor at a set hourly rate or salary. In this way, much depends upon what an employer decides to expend for our labor. But Steiner explained that the provision of a decent human existence for each "is only possible if [it] is carried out by the political

---

[42] https://worldpopulationreview.com/country-rankings/countries-with-universal-basic-income

[43] GA 23, about 2/3 into Ch. 2 (p. 72)

state independently of economic management."[44] Can we fathom what this means?

To help us begin to approach this, Steiner worked to disentangle human labor from the phenomenon of wages. And here we can come to realize how very much the dignity of the human being is denied by this practice of giving wages in direct exchange for human labor as if labor were a commodity. He stated how the relationship between employer, worker and commodity must be arranged, to reflect the reality of the economic process:

> Within the capitalistic economic form, this labour has been incorporated into the social organism in such a way that it is bought like a commodity from the worker by his employer. An exchange takes place between money (representing commodities) and labour. But such an exchange cannot, in reality, take place. It only appears to do so. In reality, the employer receives commodities from the worker, which can only come into existence by the worker devoting his labour-power to their creation. The worker receives one part of the equivalent value of these commodities and the employer the other. The production of commodities results from the cooperation of the employer and the employed. Only the product of their joint action passes into economic circulation.[45]

We can see that in the current economic system, the human being *makes use of* the human being. What we can begin to understand is, that together with the fundamental right to meet every other human being on an equal footing, face-to-face, each must also be liberated from the commodification of their labor.

Much of this is quite challenging to our current way of thinking about standard of living, wage, and labor, a thinking in which we even go so far as to call human beings 'human resources' and we often see ourselves as a replaceable 'cog in the machine' as illustrated by this May 2023 article:

> A significant majority (85 percent) of employees feel like they are just a cog in the machinery of their organisation and 43 percent have no idea how their performance contributes to business success, according to a new survey of employee experience and expectations.
>
> To feel like a valued part of their organisation, employees want

---

[44] GA 23, about 2/3 into Ch. 2 (pp. 72-73)
[45] GA 23, 3/5 into Ch. 2 (pp. 71-72)

an experience where their voices are heard (56 percent), they have clearly defined goals (49 percent), and they receive support in growing their careers (52 percent).[46]

Our dignity is not recognized even with the 'good intention' of minimum wage laws. For instance, the Fair Labor Standards Act (FLSA) of 1938 enacted a minimum wage to regulate commerce.[47] This is an example of the government attempting to address the problem of a standard of living by setting an hourly labor wage – rather than having the standard of living drive the valuation of the product. At the present time, the Federal minimum wage is $7.25 per hour, last increased in 2009.[48] States also determine their own minimum wage – for example in New York City, the minimum wage is $15.00/hr. and in upstate NY it is $13.20/hr.[49] Compare these minimum wages with the cost of living in New York City – if you include the basic living expenses plus rent plus transportation, a single person renting a single bedroom apartment would be paying (conservatively) over $4,000 per month.[50,51] A full-time minimum wage worker (160 hours a month at $15.00/hr) would make $2,400 before taxes. Clearly, the New York City minimum wage cannot cover the cost of living, so how can the minimum wage provide for even the minimal quality of life?

Technology has created a significant labor force that is only indirectly coupled to the use of natural resources to create products, such as in software engineering and the various industries that it has created – gaming, entertainment, and animation in particular when everything is done through Computer Generated (CGI), record management, digital transactions including blockchain and cryptocurrency. Other industry examples include marketing and advertising (significantly now through social media), and online services and education. As these products are only directly coupled with human labor (not with nature), the question in the rights domain regarding product valuation must rely entirely on the determination of the standard of living.

One might ask, why should a software developer in NYC make $250,000 a year while a line cook is making $30,000 a year? We can only

[46] https://workplaceinsight.net/majority-of-employees-see-themselves-as-cogs-in-corporate-machinery/
[47] https://www.law.cornell.edu/wex/minimum_wage
[48] https://en.wikipedia.org/wiki/Minimum_wage_in_the_United_States
[49] https://www.ny.gov/new-york-states-minimum-wage/new-york-states-minimum-wage
[50] https://www.corporatesuites.com/how-much-is-the-cost-of-living-in-new-york-city
[51] https://www.apartmentlist.com/renter-life/cost-of-living-in-new-york

decouple wage from "this is what you are worth as a human being" and "this is what your labor is worth" if we approach the value of a human being from the perspective of quality of life. To complicate matters, the quality of life currently is also very regional specific. Wichita Falls Texas is ranked (2016-2017) as the city with the lowest cost of living[52]. As a software developer working remotely for a Wall Street firm, is it right that I be paid $150,000 a year (or more) living in Wichita Falls? As technology provides the ability for remote work for some people, the domain of rights has more complicated issues to consider now in the 21st century than in 1919. This regional effect is being considered by companies like Google,[53] cutting pay anywhere between 5% to 25%. And of course, the local government gets involved: "In New York, Mayor Eric Adams sent a memo telling city workers to get back to the office to re-energize the city's economy. 'I'm trying to fill up office buildings,' he said."[54] These are all examples of a dysfunctional rights-economic domain interaction.

As described above, we can only decouple wages from labor if we approach the value of a human being from the perspective of quality of life, gained through our increasing sensibility for what a decent human existence means. We must be realistic that the undertaking to bring into real practice the three-membered organization of social life in one fell swoop would be traumatic (to say the least) to the existing economic and social domains (businesses and people.) However, as discussed later, it is possible to approach the three-membered dynamic individually and locally.

Quality of life also includes factors such as conditions of life for human beings in many settings, most notably in the workplace. The Occupational Safety and Health Administration (OSHA) does not have regulatory standards on break rooms but it does on requirements for bathroom facilities.[55] The FLSA section 7 was amended in 2010 to provide break times for nursing mothers.[56] The Family and Medical Leave Act[57] (FMLA) enacted in 1993 provides certain employees with up to 12 weeks of unpaid, job-protected leave while maintaining group health benefits[58] for medical reasons and for the birth and care for a newborn child. These are examples of issues

---

[52] https://www.businessinsider.com/us-cities-with-the-lowest-cost-of-living-2016-7
[53] https://www.vox.com/recode/22691275/googles-remote-work-home-pay-cut-location-real-estate
[54] https://www.kktv.com/2022/06/09/companies-want-remote-employees-return-office/
[55] https://www.cbia.com/news/hr-safety/employee-break-room/
[56] https://www.dol.gov/agencies/whd/nursing-mothers/law
[57] https://www.dol.gov/agencies/whd/fmla
[58] https://www.dol.gov/general/topic/benefits-leave/fmla

that fall under the purview of the rights domain and pertain to the quality of life at work (the economic domain.)

Finally, security (police, national guard, the military) are under the jurisprudence of the rights sphere. This also includes a business's security guards as well as personal guards.

QUALITY OF NATURE

The rights discussed in the section on Quality of Life point to the basic need of the human being to have their innate dignity and validity affirmed and to be guaranteed an existence worth living. And through becoming fully aware of this as the basic work of the rights domain, we can through our feeling-to-feeling for each other also find that this feeling consideration should not be confined to the realm of the human kingdom. It therefore must encompass our fellow kingdoms, the animals and plants and even the mineral kingdom, the earth, water, air, and the planet itself.

The domain of rights has among its concerns what we now call 'environmental impact' – how natural resources are used, for instance, logged, mined, farmed, fished, and impacted by waste disposal, pollution, and so forth, as well as how they are restored. Environmental impact is "the effect of human activity on the environment in the form of creating environmental imbalance.;"[59] Changes are made in "the natural or built environment ... that can have adverse effects on the air, land, water, fish, and wildlife or the inhabitants of the ecosystem." The resulting "[p]ollution, contamination, or destruction ... "can have short-term or long-term ramifications....."[60] The work of the rights domain of course also includes legislation toward managing other environmental issues that are not directly generated by human activity, for example, forest fire management.[61]

Furthermore, the quality of nature affects the *equality* of people: "Most adverse environmental impacts also have a direct link to public health and quality of life issues."[62] For example, we see US government legislation such as the Clean Water Act, whose "objective is to restore and maintain

---

[59] https://www.mapfre.com/en/insights/sustainability/environmental-impact/
[60] https://www.sciencedirect.com/topics/economics-econometrics-and-finance/environmental-impact
[61] https://www.nifc.gov/
[62] Ibid.

the chemical, physical, and biological integrity of the nation's waters."[63] The difference in the quality of the water that is available for drinking and washing, for fishing and sports clearly creates *inequality* among the people: some do not have this access, while others do.

Another aspect of the work of the rights domain, then, is the question of the *use* of these four kingdoms in the pursuit of economic goals. And especially of concern here is the use of land and other resources.

LAND, NATURE AND THE 'RIGHT OF DISPOSITION'

Steiner wrote and spoke extensively about land and its right place in the functioning of the social organism. Because of societal changes and technological advancements, what Steiner took up as issues concerning land would nowadays include the following:

- Water use rights: mining, nuclear plant cooling, fishing, river and ocean fish farms, etc.
- Air space rights: controlled airspace,[64] sovereign country air space rules,[65] etc.
- Radio frequency rights: allocation of frequency bands[66]
- Near space rights: the use of orbital space, frequency allocation and interference, and managing orbital debris.[67]
- Outer space rights: The Outer Space Treaty "prohibiting nuclear weapons in space; limiting the use of the Moon and all other celestial bodies to peaceful purposes; establishing that space shall be freely explored and used by all nations; and precluding any country from claiming sovereignty over outer space or any celestial body."[68]

With land – and therefore all of the aspects of nature which are available for human use (as suggested in the list above) – the role of the rights domain is to oversee the assignment of the 'right of disposition' (Verfügung) over these as means of production, in order that what is unfolded benefits the

---

[63] https://en.wikipedia.org/wiki/Clean_Water_Act
[64] https://www.faa.gov/Air_traffic/Publications/atpubs/aim_html/chap3_section_2.html
[65] https://en.wikipedia.org/wiki/Air_sovereignty
[66] https://en.wikipedia.org/wiki/Frequency_allocation
[67] https://www.itu.int/en/ITU-R/space/Presentations/Orbit_Spectrum%20International%20Regulatory%20Framework_Henri.pdf
[68] https://en.wikipedia.org/wiki/Outer_Space_Treaty

entire community or social organism. These days, of course, the necessary considerations will not be limited to the local community; impacts can in some cases be very consequential for a large number of people spanning multiple communities:

> The Chinese Three Gorges Dam included the flooding of 13 cities, 140 towns and 1,350 villages as well as numerous sites of cultural, historic and religious heritage. As a result, 1.3 million inhabitants were relocated, many from rural areas to cities (DTK 2002; International Rivers 2008a). It has been reported that many subsistence farmers and fishermen were relocated to cities, or they received tiny slots of barren land as compensation. In total, China's domestic dams are reported to have displaced 23 million people as well as significantly affected water availability and environmental quality (International Rivers, 2012b).[69]

We have a variety of laws in the US that have to do with land use. In New York State, there are zoning laws which:

> … [organize] how land may be used. It establishes an orderly pattern of development across neighborhoods and the city by identifying what may be built on a piece of property. New York City's Zoning Resolution divides land into districts where similar rules are in effect. Zoning regulations are assigned to these districts based on relevant land use issues. These issues include building shape, affordable housing, walkability and climate change resiliency. They do not include factors such as property ownership or financial considerations.[70]

Of note is the statement that zoning laws do not consider the issues of ownership and financial considerations that would otherwise fall into the economic domain. Most zoning regulations are designed to ensure the quality of life of the citizens particularly in relation to pollutants (noise, chemical and so forth), roadway traffic, and safety.

State and federal parks are another example of land use rights that are not associated with the production of commodities in the economic life. President Ulysses S. Grant signed the Yellowstone National Park Protection Act into law which became the world's first national park.[71] Similarly, land conservancies, or land trusts, are community-based,

---

[69] https://www.e-ir.info/2014/01/30/china-dams-the-world-the-environmental-and-social-impacts-of-chinese-dams/

[70] https://www1.nyc.gov/site/planning/zoning/about-zoning.page

[71] https://www.nps.gov/yell/learn/historyculture/yellowstoneestablishment.htm

nonprofit organizations dedicated to the permanent protection and stewardship of natural resources. In New York, "Columbia County's scenic landscapes, diverse wildlife habitats, and fragile natural resources are a trust to be conserved for future generations through sound stewardship practices."[72] Here again we see "land rights" associated with the cultural domain.

In our modern technology age, the use of other resources mentioned above has led to a variety of international agreements that work on coordinating people's activities in the social domain and where economic issues could be seen as secondary concerns.

THE EFFECTIVENESS OF THE RIGHTS DOMAIN AND ITS SUPPORT THROUGH TAXATION

The rights domain largely produces services, of which the functions of legislation are primary. Internal to the domain, many services are exchanged. To itself and to the public, it provides legal papers and forms, legal assistance. As already discussed, the function of adjudication of infractions by judges and juries is attended to in the cultural domain. Like in the cultural domain, in the rights domain the people who are drawn to work in the domain of rights of course also have a right to quality of life, just as those in the area of education.

The rights domain does not produce a *consumable* commodity – there is no economic exchange that occurs except for services the rights domain specifically provides – legal papers and forms, legal assistance, and so forth. These services are not commodities – they are not sold and purchased in an economic exchange. However, the legislation of the rights domain is vital to a functional, balanced, three-membered organization. The people who are drawn to work in the domain of rights of course also have a right to quality of life, which as Steiner wrote would be supported through taxation: "What this political state itself requires for its maintenance will be raised through tax law. This will develop through a harmonization of the requirements of the rights-consciousness with those of economic life."[73] What this "harmonization" looks like is a question and can probably only be conceived of more clearly after disentangling the inappropriate influences that our current economic and political systems have over each other.

---

[72] https://clctrust.org/about/our-mission/
[73] GA 23, about 3 pages from end of Ch. 2 (p. 80)

In the domain of economics and specifically production, it is often clearly quantifiable how many workers are required to produce a commodity and to administer its production and distribution. In the cultural domain, it is often similarly quantifiable as to how many teachers and administrators a school needs, or how many actors a play requires. With the rights domain, the number of people required for legislation, administration and security/enforcement is not so easily quantifiable.

How can one answer the question of how much in taxes should be collected to maintain these functions without first addressing what necessity there actually is for the number of people working in the rights domain at the federal, state, and local level? Is the rights domain effective? Consider:

> Across the U.S., nearly 24 million people – a little over 15% of the workforce – are involved in military, public, and national service at the local, state and federal levels. Of this number, approximately 16 million are employed in state and local governments.[74]

And:

> In 2021, around 18.28 million people were working for state and local governments in the United States. This is much higher than the number of federal government (civilian) employees, which stood at about 2.85 million people in that year.[75]

Also, local, state and federal legislative needs, and therefore the people involved in that legislation, varies based on locale, production and environmental concerns. These legislators also require supporting staff (administration) for their work. Finally there is the question of security – police, national guard and so forth.

Sufficient effectiveness in the rights domain is reflected in the vitality, productivity and services of the two other domains. Millennium Challenge Corporation (MCC) writes the following (see the reference for the sources they site in this statement):

> Countries with more effective governments tend to achieve higher levels of economic growth by obtaining better credit ratings and attracting more investment, offering higher quality public services

---

[74] https://www.brookings.edu/policy2020/votervital/public-service-and-the-federal-government/

[75] https://www.statista.com/statistics/204535/number-of-governmental-employees-in-the-us/

and encouraging higher levels of human capital accumulation, putting foreign aid resources to better use, accelerating technological innovation, and increasing the productivity of government spending. Efficiency in the delivery of public services also has a direct impact on poverty. On average, countries with more effective governments have better educational systems and more efficient health care. There is evidence that countries with independent, meritocratic bureaucracies do a better job of vaccinating children, protecting the most vulnerable members of society, reducing child mortality, and curbing environmental degradation. Countries with a meritocratic civil service also tend to have lower levels of corruption.[76]

The MCC has a number of factors they use to measure a country's government effectiveness to determine eligibility for its assistance programs. And while the above quote is very much entangled with the infrastructures of our existing political-economic way of life as well as existing views on education and health care, it is none-the-less a launching point for further discussion on what 'efficient' and 'effective' actually mean and how they can be quantified so that the rights domain has the resources it needs to legislate quality of life and ensure human dignity. And remember that quality of life is connected with environmental concerns as well, as the quality of the environment affects us locally and globally.

RIGHTS WITHIN THE DOMAINS

Within each of the domains there exists a 'rights domain,' as it must in order to legislate and administrate the rights and rules as they *pertain to the specific activities within the domain.* A simple example is the legal aspect of a home-owners association (within the cultural domain) through which the home-owners legislate (rights domain within the association) bylaws to which they agree to adhere. Similarly, in the economic domain, contracts between two corporations is an example. In the rights domain itself, how legislation is passed is also a form of 'legislation' under the purview of 'the rights within the rights domain' though it might be argued that this is actually under the purview of the cultural domain – for example, would it be the cultural domain that determines whether legislation passes by simple (50%) majority, 2/3rds majority, or 100% consensus, and what

---

[76] https://www.mcc.gov/who-we-select/indicator/government-effectiveness-indicator

legislation requires what majority? If this is still confusing, would not the cultural domain determine that a declaration of war requires 100% consensus but the legislation concerning the building of a dam requires only 2/3rds majority? It is sometimes difficult to discern which domain (and therefore who) is responsible for legislation and this difficulty is increased because of our mostly unconscious indoctrination into how legislation currently works: it can be hard to think 'outside of the box.'

SUMMARY

In summary, equality embodies the concepts that in human relationships we treat each other equally, as human beings. Equality also values personal opinion even if contradictory to our own opinion – in fact we should take interest in contradictory opinions as they provide a counterpoint to our own opinions which renders our opinions more complete and beware of our pride in our own thoughts. These two aspects of equality enhance our freedom in society – our choices and our voice with regard to all aspects of the society.

Healthy social impulses exist within the human being and seek to inform and enliven the social organism. But the human being and these impulses have been pushed to the fringes of that social organism and its potentially health-giving organization. Why? This is because over the last centuries the economic relationships and activities of human beings have undergone a radical transformation and through this, the drive of economic advances – industrial and now technological as well – have vastly outpaced the advances in the cultural and rights domains (as mentioned earlier here). And the economic domain has vastly breached its rightful bounds. Some rethinking is therefore in order, toward understanding and correcting this.

Chapter 5

CHARACTERISTICS *of the* ECONOMIC DOMAIN

The domain of economics redefines economic activity such that economic activity furthers the social organism. Contrast this with our current economic systems (capitalism) where the primary goal is the profitability of individuals and corporations, often disregarding human dignity in achieving that goal, and often producing products and services that are harmful to society and nature and are not wanted except through advertising that manipulates us into wanting the product or service.

WHAT IS A COMMODITY?

In the simplest terms, the economic domain is responsible for the production, distribution, and consumption of commodities, regulated by the rights domain to ensure safety, human dignity and quality of life, and the proper use of natural resources with regard to the well-being of the environment. The modern definition of a commodity[1] is:

1. An economic good such as a product.
2. Something useful or valued.
3. A good or service widely available.
4. One that is subject to ready exchange or exploitation in the market.

Among a long list of terms which Merriam-Webster suggests as synonyms for 'commodity' are also the terms, 'being,' 'individual' and 'individuality.' This is in direct contradiction to the three-membered organization in which neither the person nor their labor is viewed as a commodity. Steiner wrote:

> ... [T]he modern capitalistic economic order, within its own sphere of activity, recognizes only commodities and their respective values.

---

[1] https://www.merriam-webster.com/dictionary/commodity

Within this capitalistic organism something has become a commodity which the proletarian feels [*empfindet*] *may not* be a commodity.

The modern proletarian abhors instinctively, unconsciously [in den unterbewussten *Empfindungen*], the fact that he must sell his labour power to his employer in the same way that commodities are sold in the market-place, and that the law of supply and demand plays its role in determining the value of his labour power just as it does in determining the value of commodities. This abhorrence of the commodity nature of labour power has a profound meaning in the social movement.[2]

This practice of seeing the worker and their labor as a replaceable commodity is, if anything, even more prevalent in today's business practices than in Steiner's time.

As soon as someone produces something and it enters the realm of exchanges or intended exchanges between people, it becomes a commodity in the economic domain. Commodity includes not just the usual goods that come to mind with this word, but also a work of art, a performance, a lesson plan or lecture, etc. that is 'consumed' by others. As Steiner wrote (Kate's translation, which includes translation options to widen the understanding of the noun, 'Leistung,' and the verb, 'leisten,' both of which Steiner used quite often in regard to the results of human activity):

Within the economic domain one has to do with commodity values only. For this domain, the achievements/performance/results [Leistungen] that arise from the cultural and state organization also take the character of commodities. What a teacher achieves/carries out/performs [leistet] for his students is a commodity for the economic cycle. The teacher is no more paid for his individual capabilities/talents than the worker is for his labour. For both, it is only *possible* for them to be paid for what proceeds from them that can be goods, commodities, in the economic cycle. How free initiative, how the law should work so that the goods come about, is just as much outside the economic cycle as the effect of natural forces on the grain yield in a good year or a lean year.[3]

It then follows that the factor that determines whether the business of the producer is viable is whether– without manipulation – a commodity

---

[2] GA 23, 4 pages from end of Ch. 1 (pp. 49-50)
[3] GA 23, Smith translation for reference in relation to Kate's translation, about 4/5 into Ch. 3 (pp. 117-18), ("The economic sector is only….")

or service is wanted and valued or not by society and therefore 'consumed.' This point was well-made by Steiner, in this case in relation to fruits of the spiritual-cultural life:

> What someone practices in the field of spiritual life is his own affair. What he is able to contribute to the social organism however, will be recompensed by those who have need of his spiritual contribution. Whoever is not able to support himself within the spiritual organization from such compensation will have to transfer his activities to the political or economic sphere of activity.[4]

This is challenging to those struggling in our current society where "According to the Bureau of Labor Statistics, the average 2019 wage for high school teachers is $61,660, and lower for elementary teachers, only $59,420. The average salary of an NBA player in the 2018-2019 year, according to The Balance Careers, is $7,422,823."[5] This is not to denigrate professional athletes but rather to point out the *inequality* generated by the coupling of labor and wages in our social organism. And in addition, how do we balance the production of commodities and provision of services, particularly in the arts, that are valued only *abstractly?* Usually, the money in the donation basket utterly fails in providing for the concrete needs of the artist, such that the artist will be provided with a quality of life to sustain and continue their work. As Steiner wrote, when the fruits of activity within the cultural domain enter the domain of exchanges between individuals in the form of goods and services, the economic domain must take hold of them and hold sway; and the right to a decent human existence must also be ensured from the rights domain.

CORE CONCEPTS IN THE ECONOMIC DOMAIN

We have many ingrained concepts regarding economic activities that are challenged by what Steiner described concerning these activities. The primary difficulty in understanding the economic domain is that one cannot just take one idea, such as land ownership, and understand it without understanding the entire architecture and very fluid dynamics of the economic domain. One cannot apply just one concept within the existing

---

[4] GA 23, 4 pages from the end of Ch. 2 (pp. 79-80)
[5] https://thehorizonsun.com/features/2021/02/02/why-are-teachers-still-getting-paid-less-than-sports-players

structure of our current economic system and expect that implementing this one new idea will actually work. Each aspect of the economic domain must be considered in relationship with the other aspects – in other words, holistically.

The roles of land, labor and wage within the economic domain are discussed next. This is by no means comprehensive – topics such as true price, profit, capital, interest, inheritance, the aging of money, the transfer of capital, and international relationships require a separate comprehensive discussion that is beyond the scope of this book and is discussed in detail in the author's book "The Economic Domain in Light of the Work of Rudolf Steiner" (working title, to be published in 2024.)

A summary which will probably raise more questions than answer them follows. This summary and the quotes cited in the following paragraph come from Steiner's fourteen lectures given in Dornach, 24th July - 6th August, 1922, as published in the book <u>World Economy</u> (Rudolf Steiner Press, 1990, 3rd edition.) Here is the summary:

The economic system is the process in which commodities are exchanged between producer and consumer, usually with a distributor in the middle to move the commodity from its point of production to where the consumer can purchase it. Capitalism came about through the introduction of the division of labor which improves production efficiency and capacity and lowers the price of the commodity. People, both producers and consumers, place value on a commodity, and it is partly the tension in the 'value difference' that determines price. Price is also of course determined by the 'cost' of the raw materials and maintenance/upgrades of machinery, as well as labor costs. Because labor is treated as a commodity rather than a 'counter-value', commodities currently have a 'false price', and a 'true price' can only be attained when the 'counter-value' that the worker receives ensures that the worker's needs and those of the worker's dependents are met until the next commodity is produced (there is much further detail on that topic alone that is not discussed here.) Profit is used to re-invest in the production and ensure continued production. Surplus capital (what's left of profit after it applied to the 'cost' of production) is not distributed in dividends or used in the acquisition of competitive companies as it is now, but is instead transferred to the cultural domain and applied to education and research. Surplus capital is also not used to purchase land, as this creates economic congestion (another complicated topic.) The purpose of transferring surplus capital into the cultural domain is so that it can be used to foster new ideas and technologies that are then 'returned' to the economic domain to improve production processes (efficiency, safety, and so forth.) Fundamental to how all of this works together and dynamically is the point that, if a commodity is highly valued, workers can be added to the production, and if a commodity is little valued, workers can be transferred to places of other production. An important factor in this is of course the freedom the worker has to be educated in other work, and here we see how surplus capital, applied to the cultural domain, allows this to happen. All of this is 'wrapped' in the understanding that there are two forms of labor: labor applied to nature, and thinking applied to labor. For example, producing a sweater can be seen as labor applied to nature (the sheep's wool being from nature) whereas an improvement on how the sheep are sheared (efficiency, quality, and the safety of the workers and the sheep) is thinking applied to labor, or a Steiner calls it, "Spirit applied to Labor." Also, there are people with expertise in the markets that determine price – associations of producers, distributors (or traders) and consumers, hence the term "associative economics." This entire process is very fluid and unlike the scientific process, cannot be dissected into its individual components – any specific component, such as price, can only be understood within the framework of the entire system. Lastly, money itself has value to us beyond the value of the currency itself. Money "is nothing but the externally expressed value which is gained in the economic process through the division of Labour and transmitted from one man to another. .... Let us therefore suppose that I sell something and receive money for it. I must gain by giving my commodity away and getting money for it. I must desire the money more than I do the commodity. The buyer on the other hand must desire the commodity more than he desires the money." Money, if treated like any other commodity, can age – it can have less and less 'purchase power' and before it becomes useless, it is at its end of life to be gifted and used one final time. And the author's favorite quote regarding money: "Money is the Spirit realised."

To help 'hydrate' the possible dryness of the discussions, each subject below includes a diagram to vivify the interaction of the three domains in relation to this specific aspect of the economic domain.

Land

When someone acquires a piece of land through purchase, this must be regarded as an exchange of the land for commodities, which the purchase money is taken as a representative. The land itself, however, does not function as a commodity in economic life. It stands within the social organism through the *right* of a person to use it. This right is something essentially different from the relationship in which the producer of a commodity finds himself to the commodity. The essential basis of this latter relationship is that it does not overlap with/encroach upon the completely different type of person-to-person relationship which results through the fact that someone is entitled to the exclusive use of a piece of land. The owner brings other people, who for their livelihood are employed by the owner on the land, or who must live on it, in dependence upon the owner. Through the mutual exchange of real commodities which one produces or consumes, a dependency that works in that same kind of way between human beings does not set in.[6]

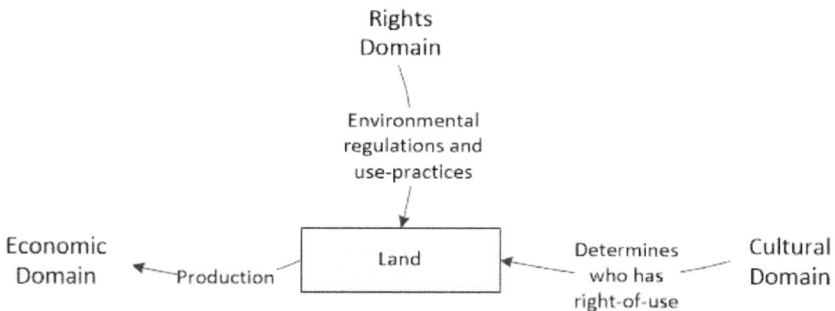

```
                          Rights
                          Domain
                              \
                        Environmental
                        regulations and
                         use-practices
                               |
Economic                  ┌──────────┐         Determines    Cultural
Domain        ◄―Production─┤   Land   ├◄――――     who has      Domain
                          └──────────┘          right-of-use
```

- Land is not a commodity – it cannot be purchased or sold.
- A producer is given "use-rights" to land as determined by the cultural domain.
- Land has no intrinsic value. Instead, what is "valued" is what is produced on or by the land.
- Because one cannot "sink money into the purchase of land" as a proxy for current and future commodities, money maintains its mobility, or one could say, its liquidity.)

---

[6] GA 23, about 1/2 into Ch. 2 (pp. 66-67), KRH translation (italics are in the original German)

Also refer to the quote cited in the Preface regarding the relationship of the rights domain to private property[7].

Labor

There is an understanding that people will be productive through their labor; however, that labor must be meaningful to the individual and society. Furthermore (again): "Whoever is not able to support himself within the spiritual organization from such compensation will have to transfer his activities to the political [rights domain] or economic sphere of activity."[8] This might be startling to some people – the idea that 1) we should work (produce something) and that 2) if the results of what we produce do not sustain our needs then we need to find different work.

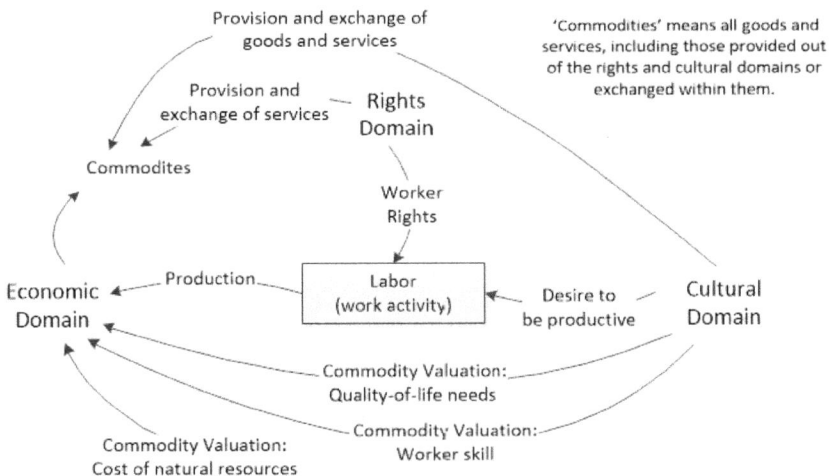

- Labor is not a commodity nor is the person performing the labor a commodity.
- The price of the commodity is determined by the cost of the raw materials and distribution, *and* the labor and skill that are required in its production *and in respect* to the laborer's right for a decent quality of life (the inclusion of this third aspect is mandated by the rights domain).

---

[7] GA 23, about 2/5 into Ch. 3 (pp. 101-102), "The rights-state will not have to prevent....";
KRH translation
[8] GA 23, 4 pages from the end of Ch. 2 (pp. 79-80)

- The entrepreneur (business owner) receives one part of the proceeds from the purchase (for 'consumption') of that commodity or service and the laborer receives the other part.

The Service Sector

Over the last 100 years we have seen a transition from labor associated with the physical production of products to 'service' production. The website Indeed[9] defines service industries to include customer service, management, data, information, education, maintenance and repair, sanitation and health care, to name a few. In 2019, 1.36% of the workforce was involved in agriculture, forestry and fishing, while 19.91% was involved in industry (including construction), and the remaining 78.74% of the workforce was working in the services sector.[10]

This shift is dramatic:

> Whereas in the early part of the 20th century, the United States became the dominant world economy, thanks to its massive manufacturing industry; by the early part of the 21st century, its worldwide economic dominance was based on its massive service sector.
>
> In the U.S., between 1919 and 2019, the service sector grew from accounting for less than 50% of the country's gross domestic product (GDP) to generating roughly 85% of the country's GDP.
>
> The explosion of the service sector has been made possible by the exponential increase in knowledge that has occurred over the past 50 to 70 years, the rapid growth of technology, and the development of instantaneous, worldwide communication through internet connections and cell phones.
>
> Increased automation, which reduces the number of people required for manufacturing processes, is also a key element in the shift from a manufacturing-based economy to a service-based economy.
>
> The massive expansion of government services in developed nations is another significant contributing factor to the increasing predominance of the service sector.[11]

---

[9] https://www.indeed.com/career-advice/finding-a-job/service-industry
[10] https://www.statista.com/statistics/270072/distribution-of-the-workforce-across-economic-sectors-in-the-united-states/
[11] https://corporatefinanceinstitute.com/resources/knowledge/economics/service-sector/

The shift from physical commodity production to service production complicates the valuation of the service 'product,' as this service 'product' is by and large no longer a tangible item but rather an intangible one, particularly with regard to customer services, data, and information. This in turn complicates the determination of what the worker shall receive as 'the other part' of the proceeds from the purchase of the service.

Intangible Commodities

The ability to digitally record a song or even a piece of art and easily and cheaply reproduce it complicates the concept of 'the laborer receives the other part' of the commodity's purchase. The same is true of a software product which is either downloaded from the Internet or is implemented as a 'web application,' such as Google Docs or Gmail. A piece of software or a music album can be reproduced a million times. In the music industry, a record goes 'gold' when 500,000 records are sold, platinum when one million records are sold.[12] Royalties are a means of providing the musician a 'share' of the sales. Conversely, software developers rarely receive royalties (or even equity in the business) for the sale of their software. These issues of mass production of service industry 'products' are new considerations with regards to labor in the 21st century and contribute to the class disparity. Microsoft's revenue in 2022 was $198 billion.[13] Microsoft employed 221,000 people in 2022.[14] Do the math: that's almost $900,000 per employee on that revenue. Is every person's salary at Microsoft nearly 1 million dollars a year? Certainly not. And keep in mind that the revenue of $198 billion is almost entirely derived from cookie-cutter *service production.*

Wage/Salary

It is important to be clear about the definition of 'wage' and 'salary' in the English language. A 'wage' is "a payment usually of money for labor or services usually according to contract and on an hourly, daily, or piecework basis."[15] A salary is a "fixed compensation paid regularly for services."[16]

---

12 https://ew.com/article/1991/03/01/real-meaning-gold-and-platinum-records
13 https://www.statista.com/statistics/267805/microsofts-global-revenue-since-2002/
14 https://www.macrotrends.net/stocks/charts/MSFT/microsoft/number-of-employees
15 https://www.merriam-webster.com/dictionary/wage
16 https://www.merriam-webster.com/dictionary/salary

However note that the term 'wage' is sometimes used to encompass both forms of compensations, an hourly/piecemeal rate or a fixed rate.

Historically, the concept of salary has been around for thousands of years. "Roman soldiers were paid in salt, a highly valued commodity at the time. In fact, the word 'salary' comes from the Latin word 'salarium,' which means 'salt money.'"[17] and hence we have the expression that 'one is worth their salt.' Being paid a salary rather than a 'per widget' wage became predominant for the 'professional class', i.e. managers, as a result of the Industrial Revolution:

> As we moved into the Industrial Revolution of the late 19th century, modern business corporations became a fixture of the professional landscape. With the emergence of this professional class, calculating their output was no longer as easy as recording hours or counting the number of widgets produced. The local currency remained the compensation of choice, but many workers began receiving a fixed salary at regular intervals for the first time in history.[18]

A company determines whether to pay a wage or a salary based on a variety of criteria:

> The greatest benefit of paying employees a salary is attracting more senior workers, who tend to expect a stable paycheck and benefits. Having mostly or exclusively salaried workers also stabilizes your payroll, so costs will remain the same regardless of how much or how little business you do.
>
> The biggest benefit to hourly wages is cost savings for employers. Employee compensation fluctuates with the amount of work they do, so you can adjust your costs based on revenue. Hourly employees can also be employed part-time, which may mean they don't expect benefits, such as health insurance and retirement plans. Norms exist in many industries to dictate whether a role is salaried or hourly.
>
> For example, hourly wages are common in the service industry, where a worker's on-site presence is a necessary contribution, the amount of work available fluctuates in line with the amount of revenue coming in and many workers are seeking less than full-time positions.

---

[17] https://www.paycom.com/resources/blog/from-salt-to-stipends-the-history-of-the-salary/
[18] Ibid.

By contrast, in many roles classified as knowledge work, the employee's contribution isn't about time but about outcomes or deliverables. The outcomes are often scalable, so revenue doesn't correlate with hours worked, and workers may be more likely to seek full-time roles with steady paychecks and benefits.[19]

The last paragraph identifies a key aspect of 'knowledge work' which Steiner calls 'Spirit applied to Labor' (see the summary of economics above.) For example, an improvement to a production process can be applied 'to scale', meaning all the factories producing the commodity. If that improvement took 10 hours of 'knowledge work' but affects the annual production of a million widgets, the significant increase in the company's revenue generated from that production improvement does not correlate to the 10 hours that it took to come up with an idea that improved the production of that widget.

Even more importantly, the worker that came up with the idea usually does not directly benefit from this increased revenue. Yes, the worker may receive a bonus or a pay raise at their annual performance review. However, the practice of recognizing individual achievement is being replaced with different models for recognizing achievements. One model is to give bonuses to the worker's 'team' regardless of whether the 'team' of workers were involved in the idea. Another even more common model is that the revenue increases are partially shared by all the workers in a company. These new models are intended to promote the idea 'we are all a team working together.' While there is a dehumanizing effect of not being individually recognized, at the same time individual recognition can have negative effects.

> ...even though individual recognition can help promote positive reactions within the same team, it might actually incite more negative reactions in other teams. So if company management is going to implement such a recognition system, it's best to roll it out to all teams at once.[20]

In our current economic culture, understanding the difference between wage and salary is useful when negotiating compensation based on the individual's needs. In the economic domain discussed here, the salary

---

[19] https://www.forbes.com/advisor/business/hourly-wage-vs-salary/
[20] https://hbr.org/2016/03/teamwork-works-best-when-top-performers-are-rewarded

model comes closest to the concept that 'the worker receives one part of purchase proceeds.' Steiner wrote (his italics):

> ...what is advocated here is not piece-wages, but the abolishment of the wage system in favor of a contractual sharing system in respect of the common achievements of management and labour – in conjunction, of course, with the *overall structure of the social organism*. To hold that the workers' share of the proceeds should consist of piece-wages is to fail to see that a contractual sharing system – in no sense a wage system – expresses the value of what has been produced in a way which changes the workers' social position in relation to the other members of society. This position is completely different from the one which arose through one-sided, economically conditioned class supremacy. The need for the elimination of the class struggle is therewith satisfied.[21]

Note that in Steiner's time, a salary was given to management and typically not the factory worker:

> From 1870 to 1930, the Second Industrial Revolution gave rise to the modern business corporation powered by railroads, electricity and the telegraph and telephone. This era saw the widespread emergence of a class of salaried executives and administrators who served the new, large-scale enterprises being created.
>
> New managerial jobs lent themselves to salaried employment, in part because the effort and output of "office work" were hard to measure hourly or piecewise, and in part because they did not necessarily draw remuneration from share ownership...
>
> In the 20th century, the rise of the service economy made salaried employment even more common in developed countries, where the relative share of industrial production jobs declined, and the share of executive, administrative, computer, marketing, and creative jobs—all of which tended to be salaried—increased.[22]

In the life of the three-membered organization, the labor of the human being is not subjected to being bought and paid for with money, either as a wage or salary or as a 'widget production within a time interval' wage. This does not mean that ultimately a person does not receive money, but this comes as a proper recompense or compensation for what had been

---

[21] GA 23, 4 pages from end of Ch. 3 (p. 123)
[22] https://en.wikipedia.org/wiki/Salary

produced by that individual, and it will be such as to support a decent quality of life..

In this book, the phrase 'wage/salary' is used when discussing our current society's concept of labor, and the term 'compensation' is used when discussing labor in relation to the three-membered organization.

The following diagram broadly illustrates the relationship between the three domains regarding compensation.

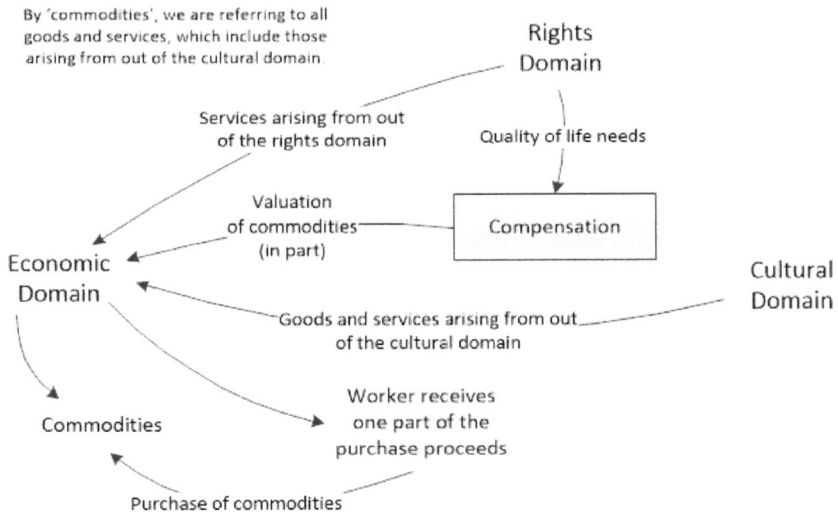

By 'commodities', we are referring to all goods and services, which include those arising from out of the cultural domain.

Rights Domain

Services arising from out of the rights domain

Quality of life needs

Valuation of commodities (in part)

Compensation

Economic Domain

Cultural Domain

Goods and services arising from out of the cultural domain

Commodities

Worker receives one part of the purchase proceeds

Purchase of commodities

- Labor is not compensated for by the number of widgets produced.
- The recompense of a person's productive participation in the economic cycle is determined solely by what ensures the worker's quality of life, including the ability to go through life developing themselves as they choose.

TAXES AND MONEY

In the United States (and elsewhere) we have a complicated tax code. In simplistic terms, we are taxed on both income and expenditures. Our income is taxed by the federal government and, with a few exceptions,[23]

---

[23] The states with no personal income tax are Wyoming, Washington, Texas, Tennessee, South Dakota, Nevada, Florida, Alaska. New Hampshire limits its tax to interest and dividend income, not income from wages. Source: https://turbotax.intuit.com/tax-tips/fun-facts/states-with-the-highest-and-lowest-taxes/L6HPAVqSF

by the state we live in. Local taxes may also be applied to our income. In the United Kingdom, the standard Value Added Tax (VAT) is 20% for most goods and services.[24] European Union (EU) law requires a VAT of no less than 15% for most goods and services.[25]

With regard to spending money, each state in the US also has a sales tax, again with a few exceptions.[26] Most notably, there are several taxes added to the cost of gasoline. As of July 2022, these taxes were 18.40 cents (a federal excise tax and a Leaking Underground Storage Tank fee) and an average state tax of 31.67 cents for, but not limited to, excise taxes, environmental taxes, special taxes, and inspection fees.[27] Taxes on diesel fuel are higher, 24.40 cents and 33.45 cents respectively.

We therefore have a mixed model of taxes on our income, and that income is again taxed when we 'spend money.' Steiner proposes that taxes be applied only when money is spent for something. This is because money is an abstraction, a symbol for commodities, until it is actually spent on the purchase of a commodity (Steiner's italics):

> We earn money; we trade with it. By money we detach ourselves from the sound productive process itself. Money is made into an abstraction, so to speak, in the economic process, just as thoughts are in the process of thought. But just as it is impossible to call up by enchantment real ideas and feelings from abstract thought, so it is likewise impossible to bring forth by enchantment something real from money, *if that money is not merely a symbol for commodities which are produced. if it is not merely a kind of book-keeping, a currency system of book-keeping, in which every piece of money must represent a commodity.*[28]

The money sitting in our bank account, received as recompense for our work, is merely a symbol for the commodities we *could* purchase. Conversely (Steiner's italics):

> *Money only becomes a reality when it is spent for something.* It then takes its place in the circuit of economic life, whether I spend it on

---

[24] https://www.gov.uk/vat-rates
[25] https://taxation-customs.ec.europa.eu/what-vat_en
[26] Four states — Delaware, Montana, New Hampshire and Oregon — have no statewide sales tax, or local sales taxes, either. Alaska has no statewide sales tax, but it allows cities and towns to levy sales taxes. Source: https://www.aarp.org/money/taxes/info-2020/state-sales-tax-rates.html
[27] https://www.eia.gov/tools/faqs/faq.php?id=10&t=10
[28] GA 332a, Lecture 2, several paragraphs from end of lecture (pp. 51-52)

amusement, or for bodily or mental necessities, or whether I bank it to be used in the economic process. Banking my money is a way of spending it. This must, of course, be kept in mind. But money becomes a reality in the economic process at the moment it passes out of my possession into the process of economic life. If people would reflect, they would see that it is of no use for a man to have a large income. If he hoard it, it may be his; but it is of no use in the economic process. *The only thing that benefits a person is the ability to spend a great deal.* In public life to-day, in a life fruitful of results, the ability to spend a great deal is just the sign of a large income. Hence, if a system of taxation is to be created which constitutes a real service of the economic process to the good of the general community, instead of a parasitical growth upon it, capital must be taxed at the moment it is transferred to the economic process. And, strange to relate, income tax comes to be transformed into a tax on expenditure…the moment my capital passes into the economic process, and becomes productive, it shall be taxed.

Precisely by this example of taxation, we see how very necessary is a change in our method of thinking, and how the belief that a tax on income is first in importance is an accompaniment of that financial system which has appeared in modern civilization since the Renaissance and Reformation. When the economic system is once placed upon its own basis, the only matter to be considered is that capital actually involved in the production of commodities shall supply the means for the manufacture of the products necessary to the community. It will then be a case of a tax on expenditure, but never one on income.[29]

In our society, a reason for "a man to have a large income" is for a person's retirement. (One may define a 'large income' as some percentage in excess of what is required for a person's quality of life.)

Retirement experts have offered various rules of thumb about how much you need to save: somewhere near $1 million, 80% to 90% of your annual pre-retirement income, 12 times your pre-retirement salary.[30]

---

[29] GA 332a, Lecture 2, several paragraphs from end of lecture (pp. 52-53)
[30] https://www.merrilledge.com/article/how-much-do-you-really-need-to-save-for-retirement

Unfortunately:

> On average, Americans have around $141,542 saved up for retire-
> ment, according to the "How America Saves 2022" report compiled
> by Vanguard, an investment firm that represents more than 30 mil-
> lion investors. However, most people likely have much less: The
> median 401(k) balance is just $35,345.[31]

Much of this disparity between what Americans are advised to save
vs. what they are actually saving is the result of having to pay college
debt, mortgage debt, and credit card debt. "Debt in any form can be overwhelming, but especially so when it interferes with your ability to build
up your savings."[32]

In the three-membered social organism, in addition to the radical change
of our current system of taxation to one based solely on expenditure, the
concern of retirement savings goes away because the rights domain ensures
the quality of life of people past the age of being able to work.

THE ENTANGLEMENT OF LABOR AND WAGE/SALARY

In 1847, Freidrich Engels wrote:

> Labor is a commodity, like any other, and its price is therefore deter-
> mined by exactly the same laws that apply to other commodities. In
> a regime of big industry or of free competition—as we shall see, the
> two come to the same thing—the price of a commodity is, on the
> average, always equal to its cost of production. Hence, the price of
> labor is also equal to the cost of production of labor. But, the costs
> of production of labor consist of precisely the quantity of means of
> subsistence necessary to enable the worker to continue working,
> and to prevent the working class from dying out. The worker will
> therefore get no more for his labor than is necessary for this purpose;
> the price of labor, or the wage, will, in other words, be the lowest,
> the minimum, required for the maintenance of life.[33]

---

[31] https://www.cnbc.com/2022/07/30/vanguard-how-much-americans-have-saved-for-re-
tirement-by-age.html
[32] https://www.equifax.com/personal/education/debt-management/debt-repayment-vs-sav-
ing-money/
[33] Frederick Engels. "The Principles of Communism" https://www.marxists.org/archive/
marx/works/1847/11/prin-com.htm

The concept "the minimum, required for the maintenance of life" clearly omits any concern for human dignity, the quality of that life, and self-development.

Marx saw this treatment of 'labor as a commodity' to be a function of capitalism:

> Under capitalism, according to Marx, labour-power becomes a commodity – it is sold and bought on the market. A worker tries to sell his or her labour-power to an employer, in exchange for a wage or salary. If successful (the only alternative being unemployment), this exchange involves submitting to the authority of the capitalist for a specific period of time.[34]

In modern parlance, the "market" is the 'job market', also called the 'labor market.' While it is disguised as "the market in which employers search for employees and employees search for jobs"[35] we discover an interesting relationship between labor and wage/salary:

> When employers have a larger pool of applicants to choose from, they can be pickier or force down wages. Conversely, as the unemployment rate drops, employers are forced to compete more heavily for available workers. The competition for workers has the effect of increasing wages. Wages determined by the job market provide valuable information for economic analysts and those who set public policy based on the state of the overall economy.[36]

While selecting the most appropriate worker for a job, the idea of competition in our society is not exclusive to just skill – it is the combination of skill and the asking (or offered) wage/salary. Anyone who has ever worked with an employment agency has noticed that after meeting the skill requirements (at least on one's resume) the very first question is "how much are you wanting in an hourly wage or annual salary?" It is in complete disregard of human dignity and quality of life when competition combines labor skill and labor wage/salary, and where that wage/salary is affected by the availability of skilled labor. Labor is not a commodity to be bought (by employers) and sold (by headhunters) on a fluctuating 'labor market' as is promoted by websites like Indeed, Monster, and LinkedIn.

---

[34] https://en.wikipedia.org/wiki/Labour_power, Citation note 11: https://www.marxists.org/archive/marx/works/1847/11/prin-com.htm
[35] https://www.investopedia.com/terms/j/job-market.asp
[36] Ibid.

Granted, this is a simplistic view – the worker (in any system) receives a share of the proceeds from the purchase of a commodity, but while this has to take into consideration the manufacturing costs, *it really must not in like manner consider the labor.* The cost of the commodity has to instead take into consideration the quality of life of the workers. This frees workers from competing with each other based on wage/salary and instead allows workers to compete based on their skill. However, compensation for skill does come into play – the worker's share is still based on quality of life needs but extra share that is above and beyond the requirements for a quality of life can be based on skill.

A current example of the complexity of this situation is in the threat of the freight railroad strike as written in the CNN article on Sept 9 2022. The dispute is not over pay, "but rather the rules controlling worker scheduling. Many of the engineers and conductors who make up the two-person crews on each train have to be 'on call' to report to work seven days a week, preventing them from making their own plans, depriving them of time with their families and creating a high turnover rate."[37] The article continues with these considerations: "how the 'on call' requirement will affect the quality of their members' lives, denying them any free time with their families even when off of work." Here the engineers and conductors of the two person crew are attempting to address their quality of life needs.

DECOUPLING PRICE, LABOR AND WAGE/SALARY: A THOUGHT EXPERIMENT

Steiner defined the 'true price' (richtiger Preis) of a commodity to be forthcoming "... when a man receives, as counter-value for the product he has made, sufficient to enable him to satisfy the whole of his needs, including of course the needs of his dependents, until he will again have completed a like product."[38] The point that Steiner made: "until he will again have completed a like product" is not one to dismiss. As Steiner pointed out:

> Hence in this formula it is essential to say: "If someone makes a pair
> of boots, the time he took to make them is not the determining

---

[37] https://www.cnn.com/2022/09/09/economy/freight-railroad-strike/index.html
[38] GA 340, Lecture VI, paragraph 2

factor in the economic sense. The determining factor is the time he will take to make the next pair of boots."[39]

For this thought experiment, to build a picture of what this economic movement is, let's start with the premise that the commodity price, labor, and what a person receives as counter-value (the term 'share' is also used) for their labor are completely independent. The decoupling of commodity price, labor and 'share' is a useful thought experiment as it loosens our deeply-rooted concepts of how these three are entwined.

Currently, a product's price is determined by a multitude of factors.[40] The most adjustable costs in a product's price are:

1. The number of laborers and administrators.
2. The hourly rate and salaries of the laborers and administrators.

With regard to the number of laborers and administrators as well as other costs, we see the following occurring in the current economic domain and applies to not just the production of a commodity like a car or an airplane but also to food (farming) production:

1. Laborers are replaced by robotics which also reduces administration costs.
2. Administrators are replaced with automation 'tools' – usually software.
3. Labor is transferred to countries where labor is 'cheaper.'
4. Production is transferred to countries with fewer quality of life and environmental regulations.

The hourly wage and/or salary of the laborers and administrators, as determined in today's economic models, do not consider the quality of life needs of the worker but rather the effect of their wage/salary on the

---

[39] GA 340, Lecture VI, paragraph 3

[40] To list a few:

The cost of the raw materials.

The cost of distribution.

The labor required to produce that product.

The hourly rate/salary of the laborers and administrators.

Competitors.

The perceived value of the commodity by the consumer.

Licensing, taxation, fees, royalties, required services, certificates, maintenance, repair, customer support, advertising, and other costs.

The term 'administrators' refers to everyone not directly involved in the commodity's production, including but not limited to the secretaries, accountants, lawyers, and the CEO.

product's price, which in turn affects shareholder value resulting from profit driven motives.

Rather than profit-driven motives, Steiner places the quality of life needs first (though not to exclude the cost of the production in terms of material issues – raw materials, maintenance, etc.) For this thought experiment, disconnect the worker's quality of life needs, so we can ask:

1. What are the costs of producing the commodity independent of the 'share' the worker receives for having the whole of their needs and the needs of their dependents met?

The answer to this question provides a baseline for the price of the product. We can then ask:

2. What share of the sale of the commodity does the worker receive?
   a. Ask this question completely independent of the amount of labor (time) or difficulty of labor (effort and skill) required to make 'the next product.'
   b. Ask this question completely independent of the share the worker must receive for their quality of life.

This leads to the interesting question:

3. Why should a part-time worker receive less of a share than a full-time worker?

This question may at first seem absurd. It is asked because it is a question that must be consciously considered – how does the time a worker spends on the production of a commodity affect the worker's 'share?' What if the worker can only work part-time, or works slower, due to a disability? Is their contribution less because of their disability? How will 'less of the share' affect the disabled worker's sense of human dignity?

Another question:

4. How does the share the worker receives reflect the worker's skill level?

Again, this question may seem obvious – more skilled workers receive a greater 'share.' But why? How is this determined? Classically, a worker's salary in a white collar job was based on educational achievement – a high school graduate would earn less than a person with a doctorate degree. This situation is much less the case nowadays.

Another question:

5. How does the share the worker receives reflect the physical effort required in the production process?

Unfortunately our society tends to not consider physical effort. "Farmers earn an average hourly wage of $11.21."[41] (This hourly wage varies a bit depending on the source.)

We can then think about the reintegration of the worker's 'share' and the issue of quality of life with deeper questions:

6. What would the commodity price be when factoring in the worker's share such that it meets the quality of life needs of the workers?
7. How is 'share' determined?
   a. By the individual worker's needs?
   b. By the 'position' of the worker?
   c. By the skill of the worker?
   d. Should there be a conscious conversation regarding the individual worker's needs as opposed to wage/salary being based on 'market-force' labor competition?
8. How is 'share' adjusted?
   a. When a child or other dependent joins the worker's family?
   b. When the worker wants to undertake further education?
   c. If the worker makes a contribution to the production of a commodity that reduces production costs or improves quality?
   d. As consumer need increases or decreases, affecting the income of the producer?
   e. As 'acts of God' – weather, for example – affects production, distribution, inventory, etc.?

We can also think about the worker's 'share' when that share only partially meets their quality of life needs.

9. Under what conditions would you price the commodity such that the worker's share *does not* meet the quality of life needs of the workers?

---

[41] https://www.careerexplorer.com/careers/farmer/salary/

10. Under what conditions would a worker accept a share that does not meet their quality of life needs?

To the last question, there are some valid reasons – the worker may have other resources that when combined provide for their quality of life. The worker may simply want to volunteer their time, again having other resources that provide for their quality of life. The share the worker receives may be deferred under, say, a royalty agreement when the commodity goes to market.

The purpose of these questions is to encourage conscious thinking with regard to the interrelationship of a product's price, the labor (time, effort, skill) that goes into producing the product, and the share the worker receives. By considering price, labor, and share as independent concepts, one's thinking can be loosened to consider novel ideas for:

- How the economic domain can inform the domain of rights with regard to the actual interdependencies of price, labor and worker share. Because we are each always involved in all three domains, we are capable of 'switching over' between them whichever domain we find ourselves in and of communicating what we perceive as living in that domain, in order that the other two domains may play their roles appropriately.
- The legislation the rights domain passes to address questions of part time and full time labor, disabilities, and education.
- How the cultural domain informs both the rights domain and the economic domain with regard to the 'quality of life needs' with regard *to each individual's requirements.*

Novel ideas are very much needed. At the moment, anyone who has gone through an interview for a high-tech job is asked "what salary range are you looking for?" and told: "this is the salary range for this job." Where is there a conscious, formal discussion of the individual's quality-of-life needs? When a child or other dependent joins the worker's family, there is no increase in 'share' as a result. Instead we can take a Child Tax Credit in the American Rescue Plan[42]. The name itself is indicative of the crisis.

As the life insurance company Prudential writes on their website (posted Aug 6, 2019):

Every individual has a personal hierarchy of needs they must meet to

---

[42] https://www.whitehouse.gov/child-tax-credit/

achieve financial wellness. In today's diverse workplace, understanding an employers' unique mix of employees can inform their most critical needs for financial wellness. For instance, by asking employees to complete a self-assessment questionnaire, employers can determine whether employees carry student loan debt, serve as a caregiver to aging parents, or are burdened by financial stress.

> Using a data-driven approach, employers can customize a hierarchy of needs for their specific workforce, prioritize the aspects of financial wellness programs best suited for their employees, and address the most needed areas.[43]

While this statement recognizes the unique quality of life needs (termed 'wellness') of each individual, these needs are not met through an appropriate 'share' of the profits received in the sale of a commodity, but through 'programs' such as incoming planning and budgeting, debt management, short term and long term savings, and discretionary assets which is the responsibility of the individual to 'tighten their belt' for planning and budgeting. 'Tightening one's belt' is often a sad euphemism for 'reducing one's quality of life' – yes, there are discretionary expenses (a cost that a business or household can survive without, if necessary) that can be removed, but frequently budgeting involves cutting costs in groceries (affecting nutrition) and education (affecting one's self-development.)

DEBT AND ITS EFFECT ON WAGE/SALARY AND PRODUCT PRICE

The programs mentioned at the end of the previous section exist because our society makes it all too easy to go into debt, especially tuition debt. It takes 21 years on average to pay off student loan debts[44] and 30 years to pay off a mortgage. This leads to one of the most important questions that all three domains need to consider: how do we eliminate going into debt in order to have a decent quality of life?

The irony here is that in our current society:

- Going into debt is a right.

---

[43] https://www.prudential.com/corporate-insights/Understanding-employees-financial-needs

[44] https://www.ramseysolutions.com/debt/how-long-does-it-take-to-pay-off-student-loans

- We have bankruptcy protection laws (rights) to stop debt collection.
- Higher education can only (usually) be obtained by going into debt.
- Entrepreneurs must often go into debt to raise the capital they need to start a business.
- "Most of the interest you owe is front-loaded, meaning that the vast amount of the cash you pay [at first when paying off a debt] is for interest and relatively little is toward repaying the balance."[45]

And the clincher, the 'paying off' of worker and entrepreneurial debt is ultimately reflected in the price of the commodity because this debt has to be 'priced in' to the wage/salary the worker/entrepreneur receives in order to have the means to pay off the debt while sustaining the necessary quality of life. The authors could not find any discussion of this relationship in mainstream literature but a simple thought experiment should make this clear. To employ a worker with a specific level of education, say, a doctorate degree, that worker requires a wage/salary that provides the means for the worker to pay off their student loans. How does the employer ensure the means to pay that wage/salary? It can only come from the pricing of the commodity and therefore affects the cost the consumer pays for that commodity. The same thought experiment can be applied equally to housing debt. In fact, this is one of the relationships that create class disparity – only those workers paid a high wage/salary can live in areas of high housing costs and generally higher cost of living. This also drives (no pun intended) the need for commuting. For example, a company in New York City, in order for the employer to keep commodity costs down so as to be competitive, cannot pay a 'livable wage' for its employees to live in that city and therefore employees must commute an hour or more twice a day from an area with a cost of living where their wage/salary is sufficient. Weekly commute time in New York City adds almost 7 hours of time to the worker's '40 hour' work week.[46]

Regarding the issue of unsecured debt (see the section 'Unsecured and Secured Debt below), some startling statistics:

---

[45] https://www.washingtonpost.com/news/where-we-live/wp/2016/10/19/how-to-pay-off-your-mortgage-sooner

[46] https://comptroller.nyc.gov/wp-content/uploads/documents/Longest_Work_Weeks_March_2015.pdf, chart on pg 2.

- As of 2022, Americans have $887 billion dollars of credit card debt.[47]
- Student loan borrowers in the United States owe a collective nearly $1.75 trillion in federal and private student loan debt as of August 2022, according to the Federal Reserve Bank of St. Louis.[48]
- 54% of student loan borrowers say their mental health issues like anxiety and depression are directly related to their debt.[49]

Contrast our individual credit card and tuition debt in 2022 of over $2 trillion with that of the US federal debt (adjusted for inflation) in Steiner's time, specifically 1920, of $333 billion.[50] It is staggering to think that the American credit card and tuition debt in 2022 is *six times* more than the US federal debt was in 1920.

How can this individual debt not be reflected in the worker's wage/salary and commodity price? It has to be, so that this debt can continue to be serviced.[51]

Even in 1920, personal debt was on the rise, as Paul Thompson wrote regarding 'The Roaring Twenties':

> In the 1920s, with increasing wages and credit now available to many households, the United States became the world's first mass market. Consumer debt skyrocketed to the accompaniment of jeremiads that the nation was abandoning the old virtues. But it turned out that Americans were usually careful in their use of credit and repaid loans on time. Consumer debt was as much a taskmaster as the meanest Victorian boss, requiring steady work, budgeting, and its own kind of thriftiness.[52]

---

[47] https://www.lendingtree.com/credit-cards/credit-card-debt-statistics/
[48] Federal Reserve Bank of St. Louis, Student Loans Owned and Securitized, accessed Aug 10, 2022.
[49] https://www.cnbc.com/2022/09/21/americans-mental-health-continue-to-struggle-amid-student-loan-debt.html
[50] https://www.gobankingrates.com/net-worth/debt/us-national-debt-since-1900/
[51] 'Debt service' refers to the money required to pay the principal and interest on an outstanding debt for a particular period of time.
[52] https://www.cutoday.info/THE-tude/The-Roaring-Twenties-Consumer-Debt-Skyrockets

UNSECURED AND SECURED DEBT

Credit card and tuition debt is considered 'unsecured debt' – debt owed by individuals or households that is not secured by an item of value. Secured debt is associated with physical collateral such as a house, land, a vehicle or farm equipment.

> Unsecured debt like credit cards, personal loans and medical debt are not backed by collateral or any other guarantor, just a promise to pay from the consumer.
>
> While student loans fall under the unsecured category, they are not treated the same way when it comes to nonpayment. Failure to pay any debt will result in some type of collection effort by the creditor. The type of debt will determine the type of collection effort.
>
> Because there is usually collateral attached to a secured loan, the remedy for failing to pay is generally repossession or foreclosure. If another guarantor was used for the secured loan, that person will be pursued next for payment.
>
> Since there is no collateral or other guarantor attached to an unsecured student loan, these remedies do not exist. This means failure to pay an unsecured debt, like a student loan, will require legal action that can ultimately result in a lawsuit and the possibility of having a judgment rendered against the consumer, including garnishment of wages.
>
> … Consumers struggling with student loan debt may not find relief through bankruptcy.[53]

Specifically regarding tuition debt being 'unsecured', the definition of unsecured – "not secured by an item of value"[54] – can be construed as education not having value to our present economic system because it is not associated with a physical item that can be foreclosed or repossessed. The only recourse for the lender is to take action within the economic system – to garnish wages.

It should be self-evident, at least with regard to education, that we need a different model in which the economic system does not hold sway over the individual's right to an education.

---

[53] https://www.usnews.com/education/blogs/student-loan-ranger/articles/2018-12-26/how-student-loan-debt-is-different-from-other-types-of-debt
[54] https://www.apha.org/Policies-and-Advocacy/Public-Health-Policy-Statements/Policy-Database/2022/01/07/The-Impacts-of-Individual-and-Household-Debt-on-Health-and-Well-Being

STAKEHOLDERS

In modern parlance, those people who entrust to another person the means to realize an endeavor are called 'stakeholders':

> A stakeholder is a party that has an interest in a company and can either affect or be affected by the business. The primary stakeholders in a typical corporation are its investors, employees, customers, and suppliers.
>
> However, with the increasing attention on corporate social responsibility, the concept has been extended to include communities, governments, and trade associations.[55]

Notice how the concept of a stakeholder has been expanded to include communities and associations as a result of social responsibility. (Please note that the use of the term 'stakeholder' should not be confused with the concept of stakeholder capitalism which is discussed later – here we simply mean 'those that have an interest in the use of the capital provided to an entrepreneurial effort.')

The previous section on 'Unsecured and Secured Debt' brings us to a few questions with regard to stakeholders when realizing the three-membered organization:

1. If an endeavor fails, should the stakeholders be able to 'recover' those means, particularly with regard to consumable means?
2. If so, how are each of the domains involved in managing this 'recovery?'
3. In particular, how does the rights domain legislate the actions that stakeholders can take?
4. How does the cultural domain adjudicate those laws, particularly with regard that the adjudication must take into consideration the individual circumstances?
5. In our current society, 'consumable means' usually refers to money. What does 'means' look like in a three-membered organization?

These are complex questions that require conscious attention of both the stakeholders and the people involved in the endeavor with regards to the 'means' that they receive from the community.

---

[55] https://www.investopedia.com/terms/s/stakeholder.asp

CREDIT AND DEBT

The question of debt, and the other side of the coin, 'credit', must involve the human relationship. As Steiner wrote:

> Work done in confidence of the achievements of others is the social basis of credit.... In our age, life makes it necessary for people to work with the means that are entrusted to them by others, or by a community, in confidence of their power to achieve a result. Under capitalism, however, the credit system involves a complete loss of any real and satisfying human relationship to the conditions of one's life and work. Credit is given when there is a prospect of an increase of capital that seems to justify it.[56]

In modern parlance, 'trust' has been replaced with 'risk assessment' and 'risk mitigation', as the company LexisNexis states on their financial services web page:

> Sustainable business growth is a delicate balance between revenue opportunity and risk mitigation. Your business thrives on a foundation of trusted relationships that are nurtured and expanded at every point of the consumer continuum. How well can your business effectively prioritize growth opportunities, protect against risky relationships and prevent losses?
>
> LexisNexis® Risk Solutions delivers end-to-end financial services technologies and tools to keep valuable commerce in efficient motion by effectively mitigating risk to protect critical revenue streams. Our solutions combine the advantages of innovative analytics and big data technology, expansive physical and digital identity intelligence.[57]

This applies to whether a person qualifies for a loan and at what interest rate, what the cost of insurance is that the person must pay, and so forth.[58] The risk assessment services provided by companies such as LexisNexis are motivated entirely by protecting "critical revenue streams." There is no consideration of "any real and satisfying human relationship to the conditions of one's life and work." The application of technology by the people

---

[56] GA 24, about 3/7 into Article 4, "The Threefold Order and Social Trust: Capital and Credit" (book, pp. 45-46)

[57] https://risk.lexisnexis.com/financial-services

[58] Author's note by Marc Clifton – having worked in the insurance industry, I was stunned to learn that the number of traffic tickets one has on record is used in the determination of one's credit rating.

in these companies is directly responsible for reducing the human being to a 'credit score.' Nor do the lending institutions consider whether credit is given for an endeavor that actually improves society. Steiner put it very succinctly: "In the long run, credit cannot work in a healthy way unless the giver of credit feels himself responsible for all that is brought about thereby."[59]

With regards to the relationship between producer and consumer and the giving and taking of credit, Steiner wrote:

> The economic life in a threefold social order is built up by the coop-eration of associations arising out of the needs of producers and the interests of consumers. These associations will have to decide on the giving and taking of credit. In their mutual dealings the impulses and perspectives that enter economic life from the cultural and legal spheres will play a decisive part. These associations will not be bound to a purely capitalist point of view. One association will deal directly with another; thus the one-sided interests of one branch of production will be regulated and balanced by those of the other.[60]

This structure of human relationships that Steiner was referring to as "associations" is a replacement of the existing market system of supply and demand:

> The 'market' relationship must be superseded by associations that regulate the exchange and production of goods through an intel-ligent consideration of human needs. Such associations can replace mere supply and demand by contracts and negotiations between groups of producers and consumers, and between different groups of producers.[61]

And:

> It is important to see that what has been proposed here can be put into practice without delay. One need only begin by forming such associations. Surely no one who has a healthy sense of reality can deny this is immediately possible. Associations based on the idea of the threefold social order can be formed just as readily as companies and consortia were formed along the old lines. Moreover, all kinds

---

[59] GA 24, 2 pages from end of Article 4, "The Threefold Order and Social Trust: Capital and Credit" (book p. 50)

[60] GA 24, 5 pages from end of Article 4 (p. 47)

[61] GA 24, 4 pages into Article 4 (pp. 41–42)

of dealings and transactions are possible between the new associations and the old forms of business. There is no question of the old having to be destroyed and replaced artificially by the new. The new simply takes its place beside the old; the new will then have to justify itself and prove its inherent power, while the old will gradually crumble away.[62]

Questions:

1. What kind of contracts and negotiations can replace supply and demand?
2. How would the giving and taking of credit, based on cooperation and the needs of producers and the interests of consumers, be realized?
3. How would these associations work with old forms of business?

These questions should not be asked in the abstract but rather in the context of a real-life, concrete, scenario in which a group of people would like to work in a three-membered manner.[63]

INFLUENCES BETWEEN THE THREE DOMAINS

There are situations in which the autonomy of a domain is sacrosanct and there are situations when one domain influences another domain. Because it is people – not corporations represented by lobbyists, nor Artificial Intelligence systems nor Blockchain 'agreements' – that participate in all three domains, it is people that ensure the appropriate autonomy and influence of and between domains.

Influences of the Rights Domain on the Economic Domain

- The rights domain does *not* influence the economic domain through devices such as tariffs, quota limits, subsidies, price fixing or other means of manipulating the freedom of the economic domain.

---

[62] GA 24, 5 pages from the end of Article 4 (pp. 47–48)
[63] Suggested reading: *Vision in Action: Working with Soul & Spirit in Small Organizations,* Christopher Schaefer and Tÿno Voors, Lindisfarne Books; 2nd Rev ed. edition (July 1, 1996)

- The rights domain *does* assert itself on the economic domain to ensure various "quality of life" concerns are met:
  - Environmental concerns, as in land use administration – proper farming practices, proper mining practices, reclamation, pollution, etc.
  - Production: labor safety and human dignity
  - Laborer compensation is just.
- Commodity safety.

Most importantly, the rights domain is concerned with the inter-relationships of people. With regards to the economic domain, this relates to the dignity of people working for the entrepreneur and the relationship between worker and manager. It also relates to the safety and health of the worker.

Influences of the Cultural Domain on the Economic Domain

- If the cultural domain doesn't want or need the commodity, it should not be produced.
- If the cultural domain reacts negatively to the quality of a commodity, the economic domain either corrects the issue or, because that commodity is not being consumed, the economic domain ceases production of the commodity.

These broad statements need to take into consideration niche markets and the production of a commodity in the economic domain must take into account the number of people actually wanting the product, which is termed 'market demand'--the demand for a given product and who wants to purchase it. It also raises an interesting question that a three-membered organization might want to consider in the producer-trader-consumer associations: should the economic domain support 'the needs of the many, or the few, or the one?' (Apologies for borrowing this phrase from Star Trek.) This question is not a mere abstraction. Consider that each child is a unique individual. What unique education needs does the child have that require a specialized commodity to be produced by the economic domain? The same question can be asked with regards to a disabled person. The deeper question here is, how is the economic domain involved with the unique needs of the individual in their activities (education, research, science, etc.) in the cultural domain? As usual, the answer is something that can be explored further in the evolution of the three-membered organization.

Influences of the Economic Domain on the Rights Domain

Conversely:

- The economic domain does *not* influence the rights domain through devices such as lobbying and campaign contributions.
- Concerns of the economic domain with regards to natural resources and human dignity are brought into the rights domain.

As was described earlier, the internal role of rights and administration in the economic domain inform the rights domain. A topic for further discussion is to come up with examples that demonstrate this.

Influences of the Economic Domain on the Cultural Domain

Also:

- The economic domain does not manipulate consumers through advertising into believing they need the commodity.
- The cultural domain is improved through production of commodities, both in terms of human dignity and the usefulness of the commodity.

With regard to advertising, Stephen E. Usher, Ph.D, wrote:

> Since then [1919] the enormous forces of commercial psychology and advertising have conspired to manipulate needs and transform them into desires. For a good discussion of this very significant and sinister transformation of civilization see the film, *Century of the Self*, by Adam Curtis which describes, in particular, the work of Freud's nephew, Bernays, who was the father of public relations and manipulative advertising. The basic point is there are real needs that can be made visible when the impact of powerful subliminal manipulation is weeded out of the soul.
>
> In Steiner's picture of the economic domain, associations of the

economic life collect price data and use a combination of market forces and other policy tools to keep prices true.[64]

And the influence of Bernays Freud:

> Intrigued by [Sigmund] Freud's notion that irrational forces drive human behavior, Bernays sought to harness those forces to sell products for his clients. In his 1928 book, 'Propaganda,' Bernays hypothesized that by understanding the group mind, it would be possible to manipulate people's behavior without their even realizing it. To test this hypothesis, Bernays launched one of his most famous public relations campaigns: convincing women to smoke.[65]

Questions:

1. Is the manipulation of people's behavior through advertising an ethical activity of the economic domain?
2. What are legitimate advertising practices?
3. If an entrepreneur develops a new commodity, how does the entrepreneur 'advertise' this product to the consumer in an ethical manner?

One should be careful not to confuse 'marketing' with 'advertising.'

> In basic terms, marketing is the process of identifying customer needs and determining how best to meet those needs. In contrast, advertising is the exercise of promoting a company and its products or services through paid channels.[66]

4. Is marketing (as a process of research) something that should be performed in the cultural domain as a means to *inform* the economic domain?

REPLACING HUMAN LABOR WITH MACHINE LABOR

When Steiner wrote GA 23 in 1919, factory automation, first by simple machines and now by sophisticated robotics, was not a consideration. As

---

[64] https://www.rudolfsteinerweb.com/Threefold_Social_Order.php/Rudolf_Steiner_and_Art.php
[65] https://www.apa.org/monitor/2009/12/consumer
[66] https://www.ama.org/pages/marketing-vs-advertising

an example, we have most likely noticed how toll booth workers have been replaced by E-ZPass and other automated toll collection systems.

> Machines have made jobs obsolete for centuries. The spinning jenny replaced weavers, buttons displaced elevator operators, and the Internet drove travel agencies out of business…. Robots could replace as many as 2 million more workers in manufacturing alone by 2025, according to a recent paper by economists at MIT and Boston University….Many Black and Latino Americans are cashiers, food-service employees and customer-service representatives, which are among the 15 jobs most threatened by automation, according to McKinsey. Even before the pandemic, the global consulting company estimated that automation could displace 132,000 Black workers in the U.S. by 2030.[67]

It is argued that the very technology that replaces jobs also creates new jobs, for example:

> In the late 15th century, the scribes' guild of Paris successfully lobbied to delay the introduction of the printing press into their city for 20 years. There was widespread worry that mechanised printing would put entire rooms full of monks out of work. It eventually became clear that this would happen very gradually, and the printing press itself gave rise to thousands of new job functions not foreseen by preemptive fearmongers.[68]

However, this is usually not a one-to-one relationship 'job replacement' – mechanization often replaces many more workers than the new jobs it creates. Furthermore, using the printing press example, a monk trained to be a scribe requires new training to build and maintain a printing press.

Concerning the use of machine labor, Steiner wrote:

> But if people will only open their eyes to facts, nothing can be more evident than the immense importance of the part directly played by technical science in economic affairs. One example, a really typical one, may be given here. By multiplying machines, technical science has, to put it in a few words, succeeded in providing commodities for public consumption and to the existence of this machinery is

entirely due the fact that from four hundred to five hundred millions of tons of coal were brought to the surface per annum for industrial purposes before the War. Now if one calculates the amount of economic energy and power required by those machines, which are entirely the result of human thought and can only be worked by human thought, the following interesting result is arrived at. If we reckon an eight-hour day, we get the startling result that by these machines, i.e. through the human thought incorporated in the machines, through the inventive gift of the mind, as much energy and working force are used as could be produced by seven to eight hundred millions of men!

Hence, if you picture to yourself that the earth has a working population of about 1500 million men, it has gained, by the inventive genius of human beings in the recent periods of modern civilization, seven hundred to eight hundred millions more.

… It is of the utmost significance that facts like these, which might easily be multiplied, should be grasped. For they show that technical science cannot be treated with indifference and lightly put aside; but that it cooperates actively and ceaselessly in industrial life and is inseparable from it. Modern economic life is altogether unthinkable without the basis of modern technical science and without special knowledge and expert skill.

To overlook these things is to set out with preconceived ideas, inspired by human passions, and to close our eyes to realities.[69]

One cannot ignore the fact that "[m]odern economic life is altogether unthinkable without the basis of modern technical science and without special knowledge and expert skill."

Some questions:

1. What are the responsibilities of the economic domain, working with the rights domain, to ensure that the workers affected by job loss due to automation are capable of finding other work?
2. Is this strictly the responsibility of the worker?
3. Should the rights domain be involved in legislation that ensures that workers receive new education, while maintaining their quality of life, so they can work at other jobs?
4. How should the worker's dignity be considered when the worker is replaced by a robot?

---

[69] GA 332a, Lecture 2, a bit before the middle of lecture (pp. 38-39)

5. Is the economic domain as a whole, or the 'company' specifically, taxed to support the new education the worker needs?

Concerning education, Steiner suggested:

> The right to education could be arranged in that the economic organization's administration, in accordance with the general economic situation, calculates the amount of educational income possible, while the rights-state, in consultation with the [cultural] organization, determines the rights of the individual in this respect.[70]

When a worker cannot continue in a given line of work, the worker would undertake preparation through the schooling (trade or professional, at their choice as circumstances like consumer needs might suggest) provided by the cultural domain. And in as much as the worker is not yet productive in this new line of work that the worker aspires to (hopefully rightly, with aptitude and interest!), the worker's decent human existence would be assured, just as it would be for all who are unable to be productive, such as the disabled and elderly, and the young.[71] They would apply themselves fully to their task of becoming newly productive.

As should be evident by these questions, finding answers is challenging and involves the participation and coordination of all three domains.

THE DIVISION OF LABOR

We usually do not produce a commodity on our own – the production of the commodity (or service) is divided among many workers. While a factory assembly line is a good example, when one considers what is required in order to produce the parts that an assembly line puts together to build, say a car, one begins to form a picture of the vast number of people that can be involved in the production of a completed commodity in modern day. As Steiner pointed out:

> Whoever works in a social organism which is based on the division of labour never really earns his income by himself; he earns it through the work of all the participants in the social organism. ... [I]t is not even possible to work for oneself in an economic organism based on the division of labour. One can only work for others, and

---

[70] GA 23, about 3/4 into Ch. 3 (p. 115)
[71] GA 23, a bit over 3/4 into Ch. 3 (p. 116)

let others work for oneself. One can no more work for oneself than one can devour oneself.[72]

Division of labor is not restricted to the people working on the assembly line. It also includes the people, such as the managers and administrators, whose labor is also required in the production of a commodity. For example, a factory will cease to function without people ensuring that the materials needed for production are available and that there is a balanced flow between the factory's use of materials and the delivery of those materials to the factory.

At present, this leads to 'class' formation – the perception that the managers, their manager, the senior officers, the president, are more and more important as one goes up the hierarchy. Their skill is considered higher and their education is in reality often higher. This perception is reflected in their wage, which in turn results in external class division because the more one is 'paid' the higher one's standing is in social class.

But as Steiner wrote, this incredible sharing of labor in the production of commodities gives us the means for quite a different outcome than this! And we need to investigate why we are not responding to this in a healthy way:

> The division of labour exerts pressure on the social organism which has the effect of causing the individual in it to live according to the conditions prevalent in the overall organism; economically, it precludes egoism. Should egoism be present nevertheless in the form of class privilege and the like, an untenable situation arises which leads to severe disturbances in the social organism. We are living under such conditions today.[73]

And today, those conditions create considerable contrasts in social class. "In Ford's 2021 proxy statement filed Friday, the automaker said [Chief Executive James] Farley's total compensation was $22.81 million."[74] Compare this to: "[The] average Ford Motor Company Line Assembler yearly pay in the United States is approximately $42,691, which is 20% above the national average."[75]

Questions:

---

[72] GA 23, about 5 or 6 pages from end of Ch. 3 (pp. 120-21)
[73] GA 23, about 5 pages from end of Ch. 3 (p. 121)
[74] https://www.marketwatch.com/story/ford-ceo-james-farley-sees-2021-compensation-nearly-double-to-228-million-2022-04-01
[75] https://www.indeed.com/cmp/Ford-Motor-Company/salaries/Line-Assembler

1. Would this almost 500 times difference in earnings be something that the rights domain would address, working together with the economic domain? And if so, how?
2. In the three-membered organization, how does the economic domain work with the social domain to prevent the creation of social classes?
3. Are we capable, as human beings today, to preclude egoism in our economic affairs?
4. How did the perception evolve, that those in 'higher' positions in the structure of an entrepreneurial effort receive more 'share' of the income?
5. Why does society 'value' the labor of a CEO in the boardroom above that of the labor of the worker on the factory floor?

These questions are not intended to imply that the CEO's wage should instead be distributed amongst all the workers, nor that the price of the commodity should be reduced. These questions are intended to offer contemplations related to the division of labor and creation of social classes resulting from wage differences.

To inject a counterpoint with regards to CEO's, consider:

> Today's CEO, at least for major American firms, must have many more skills than simply being able to 'run the company.' CEOs must have a good sense of financial markets and maybe even how the company should trade in them. They also need better public relations skills than their predecessors, as the costs of even a minor slipup can be significant. Then there's the fact that large American companies are much more globalized than ever before, with supply chains spread across a larger number of countries. To lead in that system requires knowledge that is fairly mind-boggling.
>
> ...major CEOs still have to do the job they have always done—which includes motivating employees, serving as an internal role model, helping to define and extend a corporate culture, understanding the internal accounting, and presenting budgets and business plans to the board. Good CEOs are some of the world's most potent creators and have some of the very deepest skills of understanding.[76]

Again, the questions posed above are not intended to devalue the

---

[76] https://time.com/5566816/ceo-pay-income-inequality/

contributions of management and administrators. The deeper questions might be:

6. Is the 'replaceability' of a worker, based on the skills needed for a job, the factor in determining the 'share' of the commodity's sale that they receive?

7 And if so, is this 'replaceability' actually in line with the issues of human dignity and quality of life?

The only way to answer these questions is to look at the 'share' that a person receives from their labor in an egoless manner, with the required shift in thinking that 'I do not work for myself, I work for others and they work for me.'

Chapter 6

The PRIMARY TYPES *of* CAPITALISM

There are at least ten forms of capitalism, some more predominant than others and each with a particular motivation regarding control over social behavior and profit. The meaning of 'capitalism' is based on what Adam Smith called the 'Mercantile System'[1] in his book *The Wealth of Nations* published in 1776. Adam Smith is considered the 'forefather' of capitalist thinking, summarized as:

> [Adam Smith's] assumption was that humans were self serving by nature but that as long as every individual were to seek the fulfillment of her/his own self interest, the material needs of the whole society would be met. Therefore, there was no need for the government or any outside force to interfere or try to regulate the market. Privately held property and making profit would be the norm and help provide incentive.[2]

It is striking that this view considers people to be self-serving, which contradicts Steiner's insight regarding work: "One can only work for others, and let others work for oneself."[3] It is also clear that Smith's concept is idealistic. The idea that neither "the government [n]or any outside force" would need to interfere with the 'market' is clearly not what has occurred since the Industrial Revolution and the advent of large corporations.

While the International Monetary Fund claims:

> Capitalism is often thought of as an economic system in which private actors own and control property in accord with their interests, and demand and supply freely set prices in markets in a way that can serve the best interests of society.

The essential feature of capitalism is the motive to make a profit.[4]

---

[1] https://www.vistage.com/research-center/business-leadership/business-innovation/the-importance-of-entrepreneurial-capitalism-in-todays-society/
[2] http://hrlibrary.umn.edu/edumat/sustecon/others/capitalist.htm
[3] GA 23, about 5 or 6 pages from end of Ch. 3 (pp. 120-21)
[4] *What is Capitalism?*, https://www.imf.org/external/pubs/ft/fandd/2015/06/basics.htm

We see that capitalism is not necessarily about profit nor is it oriented to "serve the best interests of society." An understanding of the different forms of capitalism in relation to the three-membered organization serves to deepen our appreciation of the importance of having *autonomous* domains, equally weighted, where one domain does not have control over the other two. *All* of the existing forms of capitalism, and a couple proposed new forms, *always* position either a small group of people or a particular domain as the dominant 'force' dictating the function of the other domains.

OLIGARCHIC CAPITALISM

> Under oligarchic capitalism, a small group of elite capitalists (the oligarchs) have taken over not only the economic system but also the political system.
>
> The oligarchs may be corrupt and will, in any case, use their power to prevent competition in the economy and in politics. This is because they have amassed the power to control who else can try to have access to capital.
>
> Oligarchs use their existing wealth to buy off competitors or corrupt politicians.
>
> The United States has often been argued to be sliding towards oligarchy. As large corporations such as Amazon or Walmart have ever more power over the economy and politics, they may be heralding a shift towards an oligarchic system.[5]

Under oligarchic capitalism, the oligarchs, typically the CEO's of large corporations, use their financial clout to manipulate the economic and political/rights domains for their own purposes without regard for the interests of society in so far as what interests the oligarchs is continued profit and power. With regards to the three-membered organization, the oligarchs are essentially an outside influence on all three domains.

---

[5] *The 6 Types Of Capitalism (With Examples),* https://helpfulprofessor.com/types-of-capitalism/

STATE-GUIDED CAPITALISM

...under state-guided capitalism the economy is mostly controlled by the state (the government).

State control may be either for the benefit of the country when a democratic government has decided that it needs to intervene in the economy to improve it, or it may be just another form of oligarchic control but with bureaucrats (state officials) instead.

Governments usually guide the economy through a mixture of regulations and direct economic activities.[6]

Here the rights (political) domain has complete control over the economic domain. The purpose of this is often to ensure that a particular ideology is maintained to control its society.

CORPORATE CAPITALISM

Corporate capitalism refers to an economic system where big companies (corporations) have a controlling position on the market. It is usually achieved through neoliberal policies [i.e., policies that promote private, market-based interests at the expense of public, usually state-supported institutions].[7]

...[T]hose with an advantage on the market due to their size will try to use their position to further their advantage ever further. We often refer to this as 'anti-competitive behavior.'

Corporate capitalism is therefore also not a truly free market system.

However, corporations can also be bad for the economy and society if they are able to rig the market for their benefit. They may be able to establish a monopoly on the market, which means that a company faces no competition and can raise its prices or drop its standards voluntarily.

Another issue arises if they are able to affect politics [the rights domain] in a way that frees them from social responsibilities, such as paying decent wages or not damaging the environment. Sometimes

---

[6] Ibid.
[7] https://helpfulprofessor.com/neoliberalism-examples

we call collusion between corporations and governments 'crony capitalism.'[8]

Corporate capitalism differs somewhat from oligarchic capitalism in the sense that the corporation itself manipulates the economic domain to have market influence over other corporations. Once this dominance is established, the corporation can control the rights domain with regards to human dignity and quality of life, as well as abusing environmental rights. In the corporate capitalism model, the rights and cultural domains are under the control of the corporations.

CRONY CAPITALISM

Crony capitalism:

> ...is an economic system in which businesses thrive not as a result of free enterprise, but rather as a return on money amassed through collusion between a business class and the political class. This is often achieved by the manipulation of relationships with state power by business interests rather than unfettered competition in obtaining permits, government grants, tax breaks, or other forms of state intervention over resources where business interests exercise undue influence over the state's deployment of public goods, for example, mining concessions for primary commodities or contracts for public works. Money is then made not merely by making a profit in the market, but through profiteering by rent seeking using this monopoly or oligopoly. [Oligopoly is a state of limited competition, in which a market is shared by a small number of producers or sellers.] Entrepreneurship and innovative practices which seek to reward risk are stifled since the value-added is little by crony businesses, as hardly anything of significant value is created by them, with transactions taking the form of trading. Crony capitalism spills over into the government, the politics, and the media, when this nexus distorts the economy and affects society to an extent it corrupts public-serving economic, political, and social ideals.[9]

Crony capitalism has a particularly nefarious quality to it because of

---

[8] *The 6 Types Of Capitalism (With Examples),* https://helpfulprofessor.com/types-of-capitalism/
[9] https://en.wikipedia.org/wiki/Crony_capitalism

the collusion between the economic and rights domains for pure profit motives at the expense and corruption of the cultural domain.

ENTREPRENEURIAL CAPITALISM

Entrepreneurial capitalism is based on the work of free market entrepreneurs. These will typically be small-scale businesses, perhaps composed of just one owner and a few employees.

Entrepreneurial capitalism could be argued to be the purest form of capitalism. It was a capitalist system developed before industrialization brought factories and other forms of large-scale capital that allowed the formation of corporations.

It is also the closest to how economic theory describes ideal markets.

However, entrepreneurial capitalism can be hard to maintain, as inevitably some entrepreneurs will be more successful than others and will expand by buying the competition. This then leads to a process of ever bigger businesses, until corporate capitalism is reached.

Trying keep the capitalist economy purely entrepreneurial will on the other hand require massive intervention from the state, thereby leading towards state-guided capitalism.

It therefore might be that entrepreneurial capitalism is unlikely to exist for very long outside of economics textbooks.[10]

The point that the staff writer of HelpfulProfessor.com makes regarding the requirement of intervention from the state to maintain entrepreneurial capitalism is demonstrated by how small entrepreneurial businesses (for example, Microsoft and Apple, which both started in the garage of their respective founders) have become mega-corporations which require rights-domain regulations regarding business practices and monopolies:

The Microsoft antitrust case came to be one of the high-profile cases a few decades ago. In the 1990s. U.S. federal regulators sued Microsoft, which was at that time the world's leading software company. The Federal Trade Commission launched an investigation as a response to the rising market share of the company in the personal computer market.

---

[10] *The 6 Types Of Capitalism (With Examples),* https://helpfulprofessor.com/types-of-capitalism/

The investigation aimed to determine whether Microsoft was trying to monopolize the personal computer market. The federal agency soon ended its investigation, only to be brought up again by the U.S. Department of Justice in 1998.[11]

Similarly, Google, which "began as a research project of Larry Page, who enrolled in Stanford's computer science graduate program in 1995"[12] was (and continues to be) the subject of antitrust lawsuits:

> A top court largely rejected Google's appeal of a record European Union antitrust fine imposed for throttling competition and reducing consumer choice through the dominance of its mobile Android operating system. It marks another win for EU regulators taking a global lead in controlling the power of big tech companies.
>
> The European Court of Justice's General Court mostly confirmed a 2018 decision by the EU's executive Commission to slap Google with a fine of more than 4 billion euros ($3.99 billion).[13]

Antitrust issues are not limited to technology companies. Regarding the grocery store Kroger purchasing Albertsons (another grocery store) so as to be more competitive with Walmart, which is the lead grocery retailer with 25% market share in 2021[14], Reuters wrote on Oct. 18, 2022, "U.S. senators who scrutinize antitrust issues expressed 'serious concerns' about grocery company Kroger Co's plan to buy rival Albertsons Cos Inc (ACI.N), and said they would hold a hearing next month on the $25 billion deal."[15]

The question of entrepreneurial capitalism with regards to the economic domain in three-membered organization is relevant – how do all three domains participate in managing the growth of a small entrepreneurial endeavor into a large company? Ideally, the situation should never evolve to the point where antitrust lawsuits are required, but how is this accomplished?

With regards to the three-membered organization, in entrepreneurial

---

[11] https://corporatefinanceinstitute.com/resources/knowledge/strategy/microsoft-anti-trust-case/
[12] https://www.theverge.com/2018/9/5/17823490/google-20th-birthday-anniversary-history-milestones
[13] https://apnews.com/article/technology-european-union-commission-e1d46538091a0608-500117a156bcac1
[14] https://www.reuters.com/article/albertsons-m-a-kroger-idTRNIKBN2R911X, see chart
[15] https://www.reuters.com/markets/deals/us-lawmakers-set-hearing-big-grocery-merger-amid-fears-price-hikes-2022-10-18/

capitalism the cultural and economic domains are the predominant forces, with the rights domain having no influence over their activities, at least until the company requires the intervention of the rights domain to ensure that new entrepreneurial efforts can be competitive in the market.

LAISSEZ-FAIRE CAPITALISM

> Laissez-faire (French for "let do") capitalism is based on letting people do as much as they want, with minimal interference from the state. It is the complete absence of state intervention in the market.
>
> The justification for this system is that it is the purest form of a free market. This, however, assumes that free markets emerge naturally without government intervention.
>
> As the above section noted, however, it is in fact the case that over time there will be continuous consolidation of individual companies within the market. This then leads to the unfree markets of corporate capitalism.
>
> There is therefore a paradox in laissez-faire capitalism in that the opposition to government intervention in the hopes of maintaining the competitive free market will eventually create the need for government intervention in order to preserve competitiveness within the market.[16]

Laissez-faire capitalism is similar to entrepreneurial capitalism except that the government (rights domain) does not interfere with "letting people do as much as they want." As the staff editor of HelpfulProfessor.com points out, this ultimately is an untenable situation for the same reason that entrepreneurial capitalism ultimately requires government intervention – companies will grow to the point of monopolizing the market and thus eliminating people's ability to engage in competitive entrepreneurial efforts.

As with entrepreneurial capitalism, in laissez-faire capitalism the cultural and economic domains attempt to function without the influences of the rights domain.

---

[16] *The 6 Types Of Capitalism (With Examples),* https://helpfulprofessor.com/types-of-capitalism/

WELFARE STATE CAPITALISM

> The government plays a major role in welfare state capitalism. Unlike in state-guided capitalism, welfare state capitalism is based on using the state to redistribute some of the resources of the economy.
>
> These resources usually include money, with people receiving unemployment benefits or support for raising children. It may, however, also include direct provision of services, such as healthcare and education.
>
> In a welfare state capitalism system, the competitive private market continues to operate, but taxation is used to provide for people who have not succeeded within the market.
>
> The welfare state capitalist model is therefore different from the laissez-faire model in having a bigger role for the state in taxing and redistributing profits generated by the market.[17]

In welfare state capitalism, the rights domain mandates taxes on the economic domain for services and commodities that people are deemed to need. While this seems reasonable on the surface, it creates an imbalance in the actual valuation of commodities such as health care and education because it disconnects 'quality of life,' a concern of the rights domain, from the cost of the commodity. For example, the resulting cost of higher education is such that students are required to take out loans that take years to repay.

Tuition

The Biden administration's response is a loan forgiveness program for "a full or partial discharge of loans up to $20,000"[18] – a kind of welfare state provision. Note that the average tuition for a private college in the academic year of 2021-2022 was $38,000;[19] thus a four year degree from a private college would put a student, assuming 100% loans on their tuition, at over $152,000. Biden's loan forgiveness program covers only 13% of that debt.

The real issue, the cost of education, is ignored. Also, given that the student is going to school in order to obtain potential future employment

---

[17] Ibid.

[18] https://studentaid.gov/manage-loans/forgiveness-cancellation/debt-relief-info

[19] https://www.collegedata.com/resources/pay-your-way/whats-the-price-tag-for-a-college-education

with an income that will allow the student to repay their debt, the issue of the 'quality of life' that the student will then require is put aside and projected onto the future.

Historically:

> A series of social and legislative changes in the 60's ended an era of tuition-free state universities in the US and started the current student loan crisis.
>
> Up until the 1960's, and since Lincoln's land grants in the 1860's, state universities used to be tuition-free (college wasn't "free," it was "tuition-free" at state schools and otherwise inexpensive).[20]

The move to charge for tuition, which spurred the need to go into debt to obtain an education, is recognized as having started in 1966 with Ronald Reagan, then governor of California, as a political move:

> When people involved in the fight to cancel student debt demand free college education they are not calling for a new, radical idea. Countless numbers of lawmakers, for example, got their educations [sic] at free colleges that they now say are out of reach to the nation's students.
>
> One of the best examples was the City University of New York whose many four year colleges and community colleges were tuition free until the late 1960's. They even had an open admissions policy resulting in not just the admission of minority students but the opening of their doors to countless white working-class students.
>
> And, of course, countries in Europe and elsewhere offer free college education to this day, enabling working-class students to gain an education that allows them entrance into professions out of reach to U.S. students today.
>
> ...In California, Ronald Reagan ... was elected governor of California in 1966 and proposed that the University of California system should charge tuition to attend college. In his words, this was to "get rid of undesirables [...] those who are there to carry signs and not to study might think twice to carry picket signs." His was a campaign to maintain white supremacy by making public colleges and universities cost money. Reagan succeeds and by the 1990s, every "formerly public" school began being paid for by tuition costs, which in turn turned into student debt. This was a slap in

---

[20] http://factmyth.com/factoids/state-universities-began-charging-tuition-in-the-60s

the face to those who were protesting white supremacy, capitalism and imperialism because it put these folks in debt.

...To sum it up, from 1964 to 2019 tuition costs soared by 3,819% thanks to Ronald Reagan.[21]

And as wikipedia.org states:

> During the late 1960s, as the nation's economic growth slowed, the question of who should pay for higher education came under fresh political scrutiny. Decades-old no-tuition policies at some campuses fell by the wayside as politicians promoted new austerity policies. In California, Governor Ronald Reagan promoted cuts to higher education as a way to win favor with business interests and conservative voters. He justified tuition as necessary given voters' aversion to any increase in taxes. In New York, federal and state politicians forced austerity on New York city to satisfy bond holders. New York reformers claimed that The City University of New York's longstanding no-tuition policy was no longer financially feasible. In the context of a stagnant economy and a growing conservative movement embracing government austerity, no-tuition policies fell out of favor in many areas of the country during this period.[22]

The social impact of tuition debt is considerable:

> Besides economic effects of rapidly-increasing debt burdens placed on students, there are social ramifications to higher student debt. Several studies demonstrate that students from lower income families are more likely to drop out of college to avoid debt. Middle class families are at risk because the increasing cost of college tuition may limit their acquisition of the education that allows them to succeed in their communities.
>
> Recent reports also indicate an increase in suicides directly attributable to the stress related to distressed and defaulted student loans. The adverse mental health impacts on the student population because of economic-induced stress are becoming a social concern.[23]

---

[21] https://www.peoplesworld.org/article/free-college-was-once-the-norm-all-over-america/
[22] https://en.wikipedia.org/wiki/College_tuition_in_the_United_States
[23] Ibid.

Healthcare

The issue of healthcare is even more complicated. The cost of healthcare is dissociated from the actual cost of the services provided (either under or over) by the insurance company that 'covers' the cost of the healthcare service, excluding deductibles and copays. The basis of profit for the insurance company is that collectively, the majority of people are healthy, so that the insurance premiums the healthy people pay more than covers the cost of the services the sick people receive. Hence we have 'group insurance' policies, and the insurance premiums can be viewed as a taxation on all the people. Because there are so many players making a profit (see figures in the footnotes) – the insurance companies,[24] the medical equipment manufacturers,[25] the drug companies,[26] the hospitals (health systems)[27] – the cost of a medical service/procedure reflects all of these for-profit associations but fails to reflect what the actual cost would be if there were not all of these for-profit associations.

The complexities discussed here regarding educational and healthcare costs, and many more that welfare state capitalism is concerned with, need to be examined thoroughly in light of the three domains as to which is doing what, why and how.

SHAREHOLDER CAPITALISM

> In Shareholder Capitalism the owners of the business are the primary stakeholders whose principal goal is to increase business profits.

---

[24] "The health insurance industry continued its tremendous growth trend, but it experienced a significant (41%) decrease in net earnings to $19 billion and a decrease in the profit margin to 2.1% in 2021 compared to net earnings of $31 billion and a profit margin of 3.8% in 2020." https://content.naic.org/sites/default/files/2021-Annual-Health-Insurance-Industry-Analysis-Report.pdf

[25] Due to the COVID-19 pandemic, "Seven of the top 15 medical device companies by revenue posted losses in fiscal year 2020, but eight managed gains..." https://www.beckersasc.com/supply-chain/top-15-medtech-companies-by-revenue-2021.html

[26] "New figures from the Peoples Vaccine Alliance reveal that the companies behind two of the most successful COVID-19 vaccines —Pfizer, BioNTech and Moderna— are making combined profits of $65,000 every minute." https://reliefweb.int/report/world/pfizer-biontech-and-moderna-making-1000-profit-every-second-while-world-s-poorest

[27] "While many hospitals face financial hardships and rising expenses from the COVID-19 pandemic, several large health systems ended 2021 with profits above $1 billion." https://www.beckershospitalreview.com/finance/7-health-systems-reported-profits-over-1b-in-2021.html

> Short-term profit maximization is the key driving force and all other
> considerations are of lesser importance.[28]

A shareholder is a person, company, or organization that holds stock(s) in a given company. Here we see the economic domain holding sway over the rights and cultural domain to maximize short term profits. Any consideration for long term effects on the environment and human beings is "of lesser importance." Not stated is the implicit influence of the stakeholders over the rights domain to ensure that legislation is passed to maximize short-term profits. Hence we have lobbyists (which are of course not limited to shareholder capitalism):

> Lobbyists are professional advocates that work to influence political decisions on behalf of individuals and organizations. This advocacy could lead to the proposal of new legislation, or the amendment of existing laws and regulations....In 2014, the top industries that employed lobbyists were pharmaceuticals/health products and business associations. These groups combined for nearly $300 million in spending on lobbying. The total amount spent in the United States on lobbying in 2014 was $1.62 billion.[29]

Shareholder capitalism has come under criticism:

> ...two distinguished Harvard Business School professors – Joseph L. Bower and Lynn S. Paine – recently declared in Harvard Business Review[30] that maximizing shareholder value is 'the error at the heart of corporate leadership.' It is 'flawed in its assumptions, confused as a matter of law, and damaging in practice.' Bower has long held this view: back in 1970, he told NPR that maximizing shareholder value was 'pernicious nonsense.'
>
> Jack Welch, who in his tenure as CEO of GE from 1981 to 2001 was seen as the uber-hero of maximizing shareholder value, has been even harsher. In 2009, he famously declared that shareholder value is 'the dumbest idea in the world.'[31]

Unfortunately, even with this criticism, "Shareholder value thinking,

---

[28] https://www.advanceesg.org/what-is-stakeholder-capitalism/
[29] https://lobbyit.com/what-is-a-lobbyist/
[30] https://hbr.org/2017/05/the-ceo-view-defending-a-good-company-from-bad-investors
[31] https://www.forbes.com/sites/stevedenning/2017/07/17/making-sense-of-shareholder-value-the-worlds-dumbest-idea/

say Bower and Paine, 'is now pervasive in the financial community and much of the business world.'"[32]

STAKEHOLDER CAPITALISM

In 2021, Louis Marmon wrote the following regarding stakeholder capitalism. Please note that Marmon includes a definition written by Paul Tubor Jones.

> Stakeholder Capitalism envisions that all stakeholders, the owners, customers, employees, suppliers, essentially anyone who is impacted by business decisions, matter equally. The key characteristic is the emphasis on improving society and increasing the well-being of everyone rather than to generate a financial return. This form of capitalism focuses on long-term value creation and ESG parameters. In this system, individuals, private businesses and public corporations can still innovate and compete freely while also being protected and guided to ensure that the general direction of economic development is for the greater good.
>
> "Stakeholder capitalism is a vow to do business in service of all stakeholders, rather than just profits and returns. Shareholders are of course important, but it's vital that companies also consider workers, communities, the environment, and more when defining success – especially because doing so has demonstrated benefits not just to society, but also the bottom line. This approach is neither status quo nor abandoning capitalism altogether. It's simply recalibrating the system to take a deeper view of business, and ensure an economy that works for all." – Paul Tudor Jones, founder of Tudor Investment Corporation and The Robin Hood Foundation, Co-Founder and Chairman of JUST Capital[33]

The concept of stakeholder capitalism goes back to 1932;[34] and since 1971 has been championed by Klaus Schwab, the chairman of the World Economic Forum. In particular, the Davos Manifesto has evolved since its first publication in 1971 to state the following in 2020 (selected excerpts):

---

[32] Ibid.

[33] https://www.advanceesg.org/what-is-stakeholder-capitalism/

[34] "[Stakeholder capitalism] was launched by the 1932 management classic, *The Modern Corporation, and Private Property* by Adolf A. Berle and Gardiner C. Means." https://www.forbes.com/sites/stevedenning/2020/01/05/why-stakeholder-capitalism-will-fail/

[Item] A. …The best way to understand and harmonize the divergent interests of all stakeholders is through a shared commitment to policies and decisions that strengthen the long-term prosperity of a company.

i. A company serves its customers by providing a value proposition that best meets their needs. … It has zero tolerance for corruption. … It makes customers fully aware of the functionality of its products and services, including adverse implications or negative externalities.…

ii. A company treats its people with dignity and respect.…

iii. … [A company] integrates respect for human rights into the entire supply chain.

iv. … [A company] acts as a steward of the environmental and material universe for future generations.[35]

Much of the 2020 Davos Manifesto uses the same phrases we have been using in this book: 'dignity,' 'respect,' 'human rights,' and 'environment.' Underlying this "recalibration" that Paul Tudor Jones spoke of in the above quote is Schwab's statement in 2019:

Stakeholder capitalism, a model I first proposed a half century ago, positions private corporations as trustees of society, and is clearly the best response to today's social and environmental challenges.[36]

This statement, "trustees of society" has evolved from the 1977 Davos Manifesto which stated: "The management has to serve society. It must assume the role of a trustee of the material universe for future generations."[37]

Schwab's perspective is entirely from that of the economic domain. It is the economic domain that is entrusted with all aspects of society – customers, suppliers, collaborators, government, the environment. In particular is the idealistic concept that a company "has zero tolerance for corruption." But as "trustees of society," how do *private* corporations (or corporations in general) ensure that they are not corrupt, without the oversight of an independent rights domain?

---

[35] https://www.weforum.org/agenda/2019/12/davos-manifesto-2020-the-universal-purpose-of-a-company-in-the-fourth-industrial-revolution/
[36] https://www.theglobeandmail.com/business/commentary/article-what-kind-of-capitalism-do-we-want/
[37] https://www3.weforum.org/docs/WEF_First40Years_Book_2010.pdf, p. 16 of the PDF

Steve Denning, Senior Contributor to Forbes, has additional criticisms, published on 1/5/2020:

> When many big firms attempted to implement [stakeholder capitalism] over decades, the perpetual need throughout the organization to keep balancing conflicting claims among stakeholders led to mass confusion and what came to be known as garbage can organizations.[38]
>
> Cynics have concluded[39] that stakeholder capitalism is nothing more an elaborate public relations stunt espoused by big business to get through the current PR crisis. Business, they say, will go on doing what it has done since time immemorial: making money for itself.
>
> The attraction of stakeholder capitalism as a public stance is that it doesn't commit big business to do anything in particular. Firms can go on privately shoveling money to their shareholders and executives, while maintaining a public front of exquisite social sensitivity and exemplary altruism.[40]

And with regards to Schwab's statement "to understand and harmonize the divergent interests of all stakeholders," Denning writes:

> What the original founders of stakeholder capitalism overlooked was that big firms are comprise[d of] coalitions of participants and groupings whose personal goals, attitudes and values often conflict. Goals and policies are constrained by past behavior, decisions, policies, values, attitudes, rivalries, and differing objectives of individuals and different divisions and subsets of the organization, as well as differing interpretations as to how long and how strongly any new goals and strategies may be retained. External forces like the stock market, the shareholders, regulators, politicians, and the press also bear down on the firm. Actual decisions are compromises among these different and often conflicting elements.
>
> 'Stakeholder capitalism' with its call to balance the claims of different stakeholders on a case-by-case base was an invitation to allow innumerable decisions in this morass of differing viewpoints, values,

---

[38] https://en.wikipedia.org/wiki/Garbage_can_model
[39] http://www.bos-cbscsr.dk/2019/09/25/business-purpose-big-trouble-but-wait-here-is-one-surprising-point-of-agreement/
[40] https://www.forbes.com/sites/stevedenning/2020/01/05/why-stakeholder-capitalism-will-fail/

attitudes and ambitions, to be made by different people at different levels o[f] the organization.[41]

Here we see how stakeholder capitalism not only has failed in the past but will continue to fail if it becomes the predominant capitalistic model in the future, for the very reason that placing the economic domain, and specifically "private corporations as trustees of society" results in a complete lack of cooperation with a rights and cultural domain.

CUSTOMER CAPITALISM

In a Forbes article on 1/10/2020, Denning addresses his critique of stakeholder capitalism (as discussed in the previous section) with the solution: customer capitalism.

> The good news is that there is a better idea: customer capitalism. As Peter Drucker declared in his book, *The Practice Of Management*, in 1954, and reiterated in the years that followed, 'There is only one valid purpose of a corporation, to create a customer.'
> "... To be sure, Drucker noted that successful corporations need to take care of many other things besides customers, including safety, integrity, legality, profitability, sustainability, great workplaces, respect for the community, the environment, and so on. But the purpose, the overriding goal, and the very raison d'etre of the firm, to which the firm must single-mindedly direct its efforts if it is to survive, is to create customers.[42]

Customer capitalism reverses the relationship between consumers and producers. Instead of the consumer having a need that an entrepreneur perceives and seeks to meet, being supported by the cultural domain through being granted the right of disposition of capital and means of productions, the idea of customer capitalism is that the corporation's purpose is to "create a customer."

How do corporations 'create customers'? Denning writes:

> Peter Drucker's customer capitalism is a moral posture. It is the opposite of the institutionalized selfishness of shareholder capitalism,

---

[41] Ibid.
[42] https://www.forbes.com/sites/stevedenning/2020/01/10/the-triumph-of-customer-capitalism/

in which the purpose of a firm is to make money for itself and its shareholders. In customer capitalism, work, firms, management are in their essence about human beings creating more value for other human beings.[43]

One should pause here on the idea of "human beings creating more value for other human beings" as a "moral posture." While this sounds like a principle of the three-membered organism, the concept of "value" in customer capitalism is an emotional, subjective experience:

> The shift in the center of the corporate universe from firm to customer is a radical idea. As my colleague, Hunter Hastings of Economics For Entrepreneurs points out:
> "Value is in the mind of the customer. It's an experienced bene-fit, a feeling, an emotion. That's why it's called subjective. ... Firms can create customers, and they do so by facilitating the customer's value experience. Meeting the needs of customers lies entirely in the customer domain."[44]

WHAT IS VALUE?

Customer capitalism spurs the question, what actually is 'value?' and is an important question to consider with regard to capitalism in general.

The Harvard Business Review (HBR) article, "The Elements of Value,"[45] includes a diagram of "The Elements of the Value Pyramid" (the article states that the source of this diagram is copyright 2015 Bain & Company Inc. and is therefore not included in this book; so please refer to HBR reference). The pyramid consists of four tiers, from top-to-bottom:

- Social Impact
- Life Changing
- Emotional
- Functional

Even though some of the "30 'elements of value'" discussed in the HBR article are personal subjective experiences, such as "Rewards me" and "Fun/entertainment," the value of the experience is still being

[43] Ibid.
[44] Ibid.
[45] https://hbr.org/2016/09/the-elements-of-value

objectively quantified. The experience of most of the 'value-items' are in the 'Functional' category, such as "Saves time" and "Organizes" are likewise objectively quantifiable.

With regards to customer capitalism, the first problem is its focus on facilitating "the customer's value experience" as a means of creating customers. This can lead to scenarios in which the economic domain's attempt to facilitate the subjective, egocentric value experience of one group of customers is detrimental to another group or society and/or the environment. This is an issue that the rights domain, informed by the cultural domain, would have to take up.

The second problem involves the idea that value is subjective.

> The subjective theory of value is an economic theory which proposes the idea that the value of any good is not determined by the utility value of the object, nor by the cumulative value of components or labour needed to produce or manufacture it, but instead is determined by the individuals or entities who are buying or selling the object in question.[46]

A subjective value experience has no relationship with the "moral posture" of Drucker's customer capitalism, in which "human beings [create] more value for other human beings" in reality, in actuality. It is entirely disconnected from the objective valuation of a commodity.

As Steiner wrote regarding the real value of commodities:

> Let us begin with the old system of natural economy, though it is not so much in evidence in our day. The only factor in the economic process is the commodity produced by the individual. This he can exchange for something produced by another; ... For if I wish to barter one commodity for another, I must have something that I can exchange for it and that the other accepts as of equal value. This means that people are forced to produce if they want anything. They are forced to exchange something which has a real, an obviously real, value. In place of this exchange of commodities which have a real value in human life, we have introduced finance, and money has become the medium with which one buys and sells, as one buys and sells with real objects in the natural economic system.

The fact that money has become the medium of exchange for commodities does not reduce the value of a commodity to a subjective

---

[46] https://en.wikipedia.org/wiki/Subjective_theory_of_value

experience – the commodity continues to have "a real value in human life." And we keep in mind that money is merely standing-in for commodities and services to be claimed from others in return for what one has produced for others. As Steiner wrote:

> Money, in a healthy social organism, can be nothing other than a draft on commodities produced by others, which the holder may claim from the overall social organism because he has himself produced and delivered commodities [and services] to this sector.[47]

Should we be questioning whether, in today's society, many commodities are being produced that have no real value in human life? And should we be questioning the natural resources, energy and labor that goes into the production of those commodities?

We can also ask, should not the customer consider the value of a commodity objectively, at least for the most part? One may choose the color of a vehicle that is being purchased based on personal taste, but there are (mostly) objective, quantifiable reasons for purchasing a specific make and model. Clearly there are many commodities that we do not objectively need but are still of subjective value to us. However, an economic model based on companies whose *sole* purpose is to create customers that subjectively value the commodity is concerning, as this is a reversal of the trends in consumer consciousness. For example:

> When Brooklyn resident Melissa Hinnen goes grocery shopping, the most important dollar amount she's looking for isn't the price of her lettuce. It's the wages of the person who stocked it on the shelf, the driver who delivered it to the store, and the farmworker who grew it.
>
> "When workers don't make enough money to buy food or medicine, it just doesn't work, and it's so unfair," she says. 'It's not a system I want to contribute to."
>
> Hinnen, who is 49, started researching the business practices of several large retail stores that focus on convenience about 15 years ago. She made a list of companies that, in her assessment, don't support living wages for their workers or suppliers. To this day, she refuses to spend her money with any of them.[48]

---

[47] GA 23 Ch. 3 p. 117
[48] https://meansandmatters.bankofthewest.com/article/sustainable-living/taking-action/the-evolution-of-the-conscious-consumer/

The article referenced in the above quote is worth reading in full. It demonstrates the objective valuation of a commodity based on human dignity, quality of life, the environment, supporting companies owned by diverse ethnic groups, and so forth. This is not only the antithesis of customer capitalism but is in fact an example of the individuals practicing a three-membered organization – the individual is engaged in conscious thinking[49] in all three domains. We bring all three domains with us, and we are beginning to bring our rights consciousness to bear on what products we choose to purchase, because the rights domain is not doing this. As Steiner wrote:

> We may say that actually for centuries the most important impulses of humanity have been tending unconsciously in the direction of this threefold membering; only they have never gained sufficient force to carry it through. The failure to develop this force is the cause of the present state of things, and of the misery in our surroundings. The time is ripe to say that the work must now be taken in hand for which preparation has been made for centuries, the work of bringing order into the social organism. The first thing we see is that the really free spiritual and intellectual life has broken away from the political and economic bodies.[50]

We see in Hinnen's choices and the choices described by others in the aforementioned article (their capitalizations), "The EVOLUTION of the Conscious CONSUMER," the very thing Steiner wrote of, that "the really free spiritual and intellectual life has broken away from the political and economic bodies."

TOWARD TRUE SOCIAL RENEWAL

The three-membered organization that Steiner outlines in GA 23 is neither capitalism nor socialism. Certainly corporations must be profitable, but this profit is the result of consumers wanting or needing the commodity. The commodity's price is not propped up or regulated through government intervention, nor does the corporation engage in psychological manipulation to convince the consumer that they need the commodity. Each domain interacts autonomously and yet with an interdependence

---

[49] See the section, "Free and Ethical Action," which concerns ethical individualism
[50] GA 332a, Lecture 5, several paragraphs into lecture (p. 110)

that is inherently harmonized as a result of that autonomy, particularly with regards to the rights domain. In each of the capitalistic models presented above, the rights domain is either:

- subservient to the economic domain,
- or has no role to play in the cultural–economic relationship,
- or manipulates the economic and cultural domains,
- or all of the above to varying degrees.

The other shift that takes place in the three-membered organization is that profit is not the primary motive of a corporation. Profit is instead the result of meeting the needs of human beings and the environment, and doing so in a manner that ensures their dignity. While some of the capitalistic models described above appear to take on that paradigm shift, they do so in a way that does not honor the autonomy of each domain. The models described above preserve an unbalanced, unharmonious relationship between the three domains. The social organism cannot accomplish true renewal under these conditions.

Chapter 7

INDIVIDUAL *and*
GROUP REALIZATION *of the*
THREE-MEMBERED
ORGANIZATION

The three-membered organization is the foundation of every initiative whether it is an individual or group initiative. This may not be obvious at first – however when one considers these three questions:

1. What is the initiative contributing to society?
2. What are the initiative's economic needs?
3. What aspects of the initiative concern the individual or group's rights and also in respect to the larger society?

One can almost always recognize that the initiative is entwined in all three members as well as the administrative needs of each of the three members that require the attention of the individual or group.

Inner capacities need to be developed when an initiative works out of the principles of the three-membered organization. In 1919, Steiner wrote:

> People are asking today — and rightly so — what is the first step to be taken in order to satisfy the demands which are arising in the social movement. Even the first step will not be taken in a worthwhile manner if it is not known what relation this step should have to the foundations of the healthy social organism.[1]

This question still needs to be asked, and it must be asked in concrete terms, not abstract terms. As Steiner said: "What really matters most of all is to learn the truth that human beings must not conduct themselves in one way or another in the various parts of the world according to abstract notions...."[2]

---

[1] GA 23, 2 pages into Ch. 3 (p. 84)
[2] GA 186, Lecture I, "East and West From a Spiritual Point of View," November 29, 1918, about 1/6 into the lecture (p. 7)

An understanding and interest in both the human being and each other is also required:

> If we desire to achieve a social understanding, as I have said in various connections, the most important thing of all is that we shall acquire an understanding of the human being, interest in human beings, a differentiated interest in persons, that we should desire to know human beings.[3]

This interest must include tolerance:

> We can save ourselves only by having inner tolerance, by being able to enter into the opinions of others even when we think them wrong. If we can bring a deep understanding for the opinions of other souls even when considering them mistaken, if we can take what the other thinks and feels in the same way as we take what we think and feel ourself, if we adopt this faculty of inner tolerance, we may overcome these prejudices due to the human cycle in which we were born.[4]

And as has been described, the capacity for "an understanding of the human being" requires the continual development of our *Empfindung* regarding human dignity and human rights.

BEGIN SMALL AND WITH CONVICTION

As Steiner wrote:

> One need not do away with state schools and state economic institutions overnight; but from out of perhaps small beginnings one will see the possibility grow up that a gradual dismantling of the state education and economics will take place. Above all, however, it would be necessary that those individuals who are able to permeate themselves with conviction concerning the correctness of the social ideas presented here, or of similar ones, attend to their dissemination. If such ideas are understood, then confidence is created in the possibility of a healthy transformation of the present conditions into ones which do not exhibit harm. But this confidence is the only thing from which really healthy development can emerge. Indeed,

---

[3] GA 186, Lecture I, about 3/5 in the lecture (p. 24)
[4] GA 189, The Social Question as a Question of Consciousness, Lecture II

whoever would win such confidence must be able to survey how new arrangements/adaptations can be practically tied into the existing ones. And the essence of the ideas that are being developed here appears to be exactly this, that they do not wish to bring about a better future by destroying the present yet further than has already come to pass; but that the realization of such ideas builds on what already exists and in building further, brings about the dismantling of that which is unhealthy.[5]

What Steiner wrote in the above quote are the essential elements for how to engage in social renewal:

- Begin small.
- Permeate ourselves with conviction regarding the correctness of the three-membered organization.
- By understanding the ideas of social renewal, confidence is created.
- Given that confidence, look at how "new arrangements/adaptations" can co-exist with existing ones.
- Do not destroy the present – build on what exists.

Furthermore, there is also the possibility of similar ideas – as Steiner wrote: "or of similar ones". For example, with today's concerns of global warming, pollution, deforestation and species extinction (to name a few), it may be valid to consider the environment as its own domain having an independent administration and interpenetrating the economic, rights, and cultural domains. Certainly one could argue that the environment is impacted not just by economic processes but by people's activities in general. The administration of the environment (research, study, remediation, etc.) as a separate domain can then also be decoupled from the current situation where environmental 'administration' is usually funded by the local, state, or federal government.

BEGIN WITH OURSELVES

We can begin with ourselves. Just as the human body consists of the nerve-sense system, the rhythmic system, and the metabolic-limb system – the aspects of thinking, feeling, and willing respectively – so we can

---

[5] GA 23, Smith translation, a bit over 1/2 into Ch. 3 (p. 108)

explore the three domains of the social order: cultural/spiritual, rights and economic.

Cultural/Spiritual Domain	Rights Domain	Economic Domain
Thinking	Feeling	Willing
Nervous System / Senses	Rhythmic System	Limb / Metabolic System
Egypto-Caldean Epoch	Greek-Roman Epoch	our fifth post-Atlantean Epoch
Comes from the past	In the present	Leading us to the future

The relationship of each domain to the human body is an analogy rather than something imposed on the domains and Steiner himself made different analogies in different places in GA 23 and his lectures, such as when he wrote of the flow of commodities (and money/capital) through the economy domain this would naturally suggest the circulation of blood (rhythmic system); and he wrote that "This member [the economy] is comparable to the head system of the human organism which conditions individual aptitudes...."[6] As a result, there is some confusion in the literature regarding the correspondence of the human body systems and of thinking, feeling and willing to the cultural domains.

The spiritual-cultural domain is associated with the head, the nervous system and senses and thinking:

> ...the human being demanded that the part of his being that was connected with his head should appear to him in the mirror of external social reality. So we observe that, from the ... Egypto-Chaldean epoch, the endeavor was made to achieve a theocratic social arrangement in which everything pertaining to theocratic social institutions was in some way permeated by religion.[7]

While theocratic means 'relating to or denoting a system of government

---

[6] GA 23, about 1/3 into Ch. 2 (p. 62)
[7] GA 186, Lecture III, Dec. 1, 1918, "Mechanistic, Eugenic and Hygienic Aspects of our Future," about 1/7 into the lecture (p.75ff). This is where Steiner discussed the 3rd, 4th and 5th post-Atlantean epochs and what the human being required/requires to be reflected in external social life rather than being brought about instinctively.)

in which priests rule in the name of God or a god,' the salient point here is not a system of governance but that this governance was determined by the priests and therefore the religious aspect of the spiritual/cultural domain. It is through our thinking that we understand what we experience through our senses. Through thinking we lay hold of the spiritual content – the concepts – which belong to these experiences. (See *The Philosophy of Spiritual Activity*.).

Following what Steiner said in that lecture, with the rights domain being an external reflection of the rhythmic system – breathing, heart beat – we would associate it with feeling. This may seem contradictory in our society where rights is something we might attribute to thinking. However, rights are very much related to our *Empfindung* regarding human rights, dignity and quality of life, that leads to the laws governing all three domains.

And with the economic domain being an external reflection of the metabolic-limb system we would associate it with willing :

> For instance, you do not understand Greek culture if you do not know that the situation was such that the merely metabolic life, which is expressed externally in the economic structure, still remained instinctive, inner and without the need of external reflection.[8]

This instinctiveness of the economic domain began to mature into consciousness around the 15th century.

Core Questions in Light of These Correspondences

We can first ask ourselves (bearing in mind that 'feeling' in each case means *Empfindung*):

1. What is my thinking regarding culture, education, science, art and the human being?
2. What is my feeling of rights and laws in the rights domain?
3. What is my willing (my work as a producer or an entrepreneur) in the economic domain?

These questions can also be asked in relation to the other domain:

---

[8] GA 186, about 1/8 into Lecture III (p. 78)

1. What is my thinking regarding the cultural domain in relation to the economic and rights domains?
2. What is my feeling of the rights domain and its laws in relationship to the economic and cultural domains?
3. What is my willing (my work as a producer or an entrepreneur) in the economic domain and its relationship to the rights and cultural domains?

And lastly with respect to human dignity and rights:

1. What is my thinking regarding the cultural domain in terms of human dignity and human rights?
2. What is my feeling/sensing of rights and their laws in terms of human dignity and human rights?
3. What is my willing (my work as a producer or an entrepreneur) in the economic domain in relation to human dignity and human rights?

These questions are intended to first place our individual thinking/feeling/willing into the appropriate domain, then to look at thinking/feeling/willing in the relationship of each domain to the other two domains, and finally to look at thinking/feeling/willing in relationship to our fellow human beings. Each set of questions will most likely yield different answers and ideally move us from the abstract to the concrete.

OURSELVES AND OTHERS

The next set of questions is intended to bring concrete awareness of the three-membered organization in relation to ourselves and others (again bearing in mind that 'feeling' in each case means *Empfindung*):

1. Thinking-cultural domain: How do I act *for myself* with regards to my self-development and quality of life?
2. Feeling-rights domain: How do I act *for myself* with regards to my own sense of ethics?
3. Willing-economic domain: How do I act *for myself* with regards to the work that I do and its benefit to society?

The same questions can be asked in relation to other people:

1. Thinking-cultural domain: How do I act *towards others* with regards to my self-development and quality of life?
2. Feeling-rights domain: How do I act *towards others* with regards to my own sense of ethics?
3. Willing-economic domain: How do I act *towards others* with regards to the work that I do and its benefit to society?

Thinking, feeling, and willing are not restricted to their respective domains of cultural/spiritual, rights, and economics. While each of these domains requires all three, it is an important foundation from which to start from with regards to our relationship to these domains and each other.

As a Consumer

As a consumer, some basic questions help to deepen our relationship to the product we are 'purchasing':

1. How aware am I of the producers, distributors/traders, wholesalers, and retailers involved in the production of a commodity?
2. How aware am I of the capital, particularly natural resources, used to manufacture the product?
3. How aware am I of the worker's quality of life in each the production and distribution of the product?
4. How can I apply my personal valuation of the product with regards to the purchase of the product?
5. Are other forms of exchange possible besides the use of money?

The first two questions may remind one of Steiner's 'control of thought' exercise and can certainly be applied in Steiner's first of his six basic exercises. Tom van Gelder gives as an example the question "How are the raw materials mined?"[9]

The question of personal valuation is not limited to monetary exchange. One can express the personal value of a product by recommending the product to friends, blogging about it, writing reviews on the producer's website, and so forth.

The question of other non-monetary forms of exchange, particularly in direct producer-consumer relationships, is often very open to

---

[9] https://tomvangelder.antrovista.com/pdf/basic.pdf

a service-for-a-service exchange. Time banks are an example of this non-monetary service exchange:

> 'Once upon a time' we lived for decades or generations in neighborhoods and villages. Everyone knew one another; knew their gifts and their needs. It was natural to share and to give help.
>
> For most of us that is a distant memory, as technology and the economy have split us apart. The TimeBank uses technology to help change that. Members use a 'Pay it Forward' approach to connect and share their time, exchanging favors and services.[10]

An example of the interplay of rights, culture, and economic domains, as a consumer might include a recognition of the following factors:

> *As I believe in supporting producers directly and in consuming food free of pesticides, and having an income that exceeds my basic needs, I purchase food as much as possible from local farmer's markets and often pay more than the asking price because I value the producer's work beyond what the producer is asking in terms of 'capital exchange', i.e., money. Furthermore, the environmental impact of purchasing goods from a local producer is much less than from a "remote" producer. I also have a direct relationship with the producer.*

As an individual, this is only possible because of the direct producer-consumer relationship.

Another example, and notice the rewording:

> *As I believe in supporting stores that provide food free of pesticides from a variety of producers, and having an income that exceeds my basic needs, I purchase food as much as possible from such stores to support the store and its employees even though I recognize that the food is most likely not local, that the price of the food must include the overhead of the store and employee wage, and that the employee's wage probably is not meeting the quality of life requirements of the employee. Furthermore the environmental impact of purchasing goods from a "remote" producer is greater than from a local producer. I do not have a direct relationship with the producer.*

Here, as an individual, I recognize the real-life necessity of an intermediary – this is no longer a direct producer-consumer relationship but rather a producer-retailer-consumer relationship. It is less ideal but necessary.

The interplay of my personal thinking/feeling/willing and its

---

[10] https://www.hudsonareatimebank.org/

relationship to other people shifts as this producer–consumer relationship becomes more abstract. For example, when purchasing something from a chain store, also known as a retail chain, "a retail outlet in which several locations share a brand, central management and standardized business practices"[11] there is often a considerable network of distributors/traders and wholesalers between the producer, retailer, and consumer.

As an Entrepreneur

An entrepreneur could ask the following questions:

1. Is the commodity being produced valued by society?
2. Does the consumption of the commodity being produced sustain my quality of life?
3. If I engage workers in the production of the commodity, does the consumption of the commodity being produced sustain their quality of life? What kind of agreements do I have with the workers regarding their quality of life?
4. If the production requires access to capital (land, machinery, etc), do I and does the community feel that I am qualified to have access to that capital?
5. How do I work with the current external domains of the current society with regards to taxes, land use, wage, and issues such as sole-proprietorship, non-profit, limited liability corporation, and so forth?

Depending on the commodity, the term 'society' encompasses the appropriate region for the commodity such as local or regional communities, including global communities. Thus, the community has a responsibility in valuing the entrepreneur's production sufficient to sustain that production. Donations most likely do not provide an artist with the required quality of life to sustain the production of their 'art.' Even if the community highly values the work of the entrepreneur, the production of the commodity is not sustainable for the entrepreneur if their quality of life cannot be met, perhaps not even in terms of basic needs. In such situations the entrepreneur would be required to meet their quality of life needs

---

[11] https://en.wikipedia.org/wiki/Chain_store

through being a producer (worker) and possibly relegate their entrepreneur "work" to their free time more in the category of a hobby.

The availability of capital (usually expressed in terms of money in our existing social systems) to promote entrepreneurship has expanded considerably from the days of finding a patron to fund creative and scientific endeavors.

> Kings, nobles and the extremely wealthy would often pay artists a living wage while they created a majestic work of the patron's choosing. While artists today are often held in high regard for innovating new ideas and creating masterpieces, they were once treated as skilled laborers who were simply following creative orders from someone with an extravagant vision and a lot more prestige.[12]

While there are various organizations that provide grants such as the National Endowment for the Humanities[13] which has "[s]ince its creation in 1965, ... awarded more than $5.6 billion for humanities projects through more than 64,000 grants," modern technology has enabled entrepreneurs the ability to acquire funding directly from individuals in society through websites such as GoFundMe[14] and Patreon.[15] Social media platforms such Facebook, Twitter and Instagram are frequently used to reach broader communities regarding an entrepreneur's commodity.

Copyright laws work to control ownership, use, and distribution of creative and expressive works.

> A patent is the granting of a property right by a sovereign authority to an inventor. This grant provides the inventor exclusive rights to the patented process, design, or invention for a designated period in exchange for a comprehensive disclosure of the invention.[16]

Copyright and patents are means of protecting the entrepreneur's work and engaging in the rights-economic domain to receive compensation for the use of that work – royalties, for example.

Nowadays there are also numerous free resources available to an entrepreneur, from legal counsel and tax help to open source software for the administration of the capital and production.

---

[12] https://www.tubefilter.com/2016/06/16/history-future-funding-art/
[13] https://www.neh.gov/grants
[14] https://www.gofundme.com/
[15] https://www.patreon.com/
[16] https://www.investopedia.com/terms/p/patent.asp

Even if the entrepreneur wishes to unfold the dynamics of a three-membered organization, interfacing with the existing external systems for obtaining the needed capital and sustaining the production of the commodity is often essential. Local communities often do not have adequate capital, and even if they do, one must recognize the reality that this capital has been obtained by means *external* to the three-membered environment. This situation will likely continue as long as the three-membered organization is only being realized at the local level.

As a Producer / Worker

As a producer (as in, a person providing labor for an 'entrepreneur' to create a commodity) the predominant questions are:

1. Is the work sustaining the quality of life that is required for my needs?
2. Is the work adhering to my concepts of human dignity?
3. Am I being seen as a creative human being or am I seen as a replaceable commodity? (Here using the term 'commodity' in our existing social system.)
4. Does the work enrich my life or is it just a job and therefore I seek/find enrichment in my life outside of work?
5. What are my rights as a worker in the existing political-economic domains and are those rights adequate and appropriate in a three-membered model?
6. Am I applying myself diligently to the work or am I applying the minimum effort because the work does not meet my concepts of human dignity, rights, and creativity?
7. Does my employer see me as a replaceable commodity?
8. Do I see myself as a replaceable commodity?

These questions are not intended to create a feeling of judgment on either the part of the worker or the employer – if approached neutrally, these questions are intended to be informative as to how the worker views their relationship to their work and to the employer (the 'entrepreneur.') When approached neutrally, the answers, as well as deeper questions regarding one's sense of purpose, one's relationship to society, and the work one is doing, can be informative. It can inform needed conversation and life changes, whether they are minor or major.

GROUP REALIZATION

When a group takes on an endeavor in a the three-membered manner, the three domains are represented in the microcosm ("a community, place, or situation regarded as encapsulating in miniature the characteristic qualities or features of something much larger"[17]) by the members of the group.

The following questions may be asked:

1. What are the group's capital needs?
2. Does the group have the capital it requires or is one of the tasks to obtain the necessary capital?
3. What is the group's 'product'?
4. How is work distributed amongst the members of the group?
5. Does the group require active involvement of others outside of the group's members? How is this realized?
6. Does the group work through consensus and is this a simple majority consensus or a 100% consensus?
7. What communication tools does the group use to resolve conflicts between the members of the group?
8. How is the administration of the three domains realized?
9. Does the work the group is undertaking serve the interest to improve the local society?
10. Does the local society express a desire for the group to undertake their endeavor?
11. How do the three domains in the group interface with the existing structures of the 'external' society?
12. Does the group require legal recognition in the form of a non-profit organization, limited liability corporation, or other?

First, some preliminary remarks on group endeavors. While we form groups, as Mark Leary, Ph.D, Duke University wrote, to "help each other in need, cooperate to reach goals, share resources, and, last but not least, provide opportunities for social interaction, companionship, and support,"[18] group work is not easy, as Leary points out:

> If a group member treats others badly, nobody will be willing to share with them anymore. At the same time, an exploiter can easily take advantage of others in a group. Hence, people try to cooperate

---

[17] Oxford English Dictionary
[18] https://www.wondriumdaily.com/why-and-how-do-people-form-groups

with those that are less likely to take advantage of them, not any random person that they meet.[19]

One should be aware of the group's bias towards other groups. As Leary further wrote:

> Group members develop positive biases about their own group and negatively discriminate against other groups. A social psychologist called Henri Tajfel tried to conduct a study on factors that create prejudice, and he concluded that merely putting people in groups, even randomly, makes them view their own group better than the others, even if they have never met the others.[20]

Within the three-membered organization of the group's activity, balance in the three domains is essential. "The goal is for this independence [of the three domains] to arise in such a way these three realms mutually balance each other, providing healthy cultural equilibrium."[21]

It is often easiest to work with just the economic domain and its relationship to the cultural domain of the three-membered organization because of the lure to create an artificial financial independence to external society. However, how useful is it really to create a local currency that farmers (as entrepreneurs) would use as a medium of exchange with the consumers, when that local currency cannot pay for the diesel fuel their farm equipment runs on? A useable local currency must be tied to the external currency (the dollar), as BerkShares are:

> Our Currency for the Berkshire Region, BerkShares are a local currency that can be used at participating businesses in the region to keep money in local circulation. BerkShares are fully backed by US Dollars held at our community banks. ... Currently, USD is exchanged for BerkShares at nine branch offices of three local banks and spent at 400 locally owned participating businesses.[22]

Even so: "When one redeems their BerkShares for US Dollars, a 1.5% fee applies."[23] Thus the farmer who has been paid in BerkShares has to exchange their Berkshares for a 1.5% loss to acquire the equivalent USD to purchase their diesel fuel, and this loss would most likely be passed on

---

[19] Ibid.
[20] Ibid.
[21] https://en.wikipedia.org/wiki/Social_threefolding
[22] https://berkshares.org/
[23] Ibid.

to the consumer. (At the time of this writing, I did not find any gasoline/ diesel retailers listed in the directory.)

Balance in a local endeavor can only be achieved by integrating all three domains in that endeavor. Unfortunately most local endeavors (in our current societal structure), such as producing a play, putting on an event, or providing a service or manufacturing a product, do not have sufficient capital (including money) to achieve the 'quality of life' the group and its workers require. *This does not mean that plays, events, services, and products should not be brought into existence.* Rather, it is a recognition of the compromise that the people involved in the endeavor will still need to make to meet their quality of life requirements through interfacing with the existing non-three-membered systems that are external to the group's three-membered organization. Examples include working for 'entrepreneurs', depending upon retirement income, acquiring grants, crowd-funding, and patrons.

Chapter 8

The FUTURE
of the THREE-MEMBERED
ORGANIZATION

A s Steiner wrote:

> ...the social organism is constantly *becoming* and *growing*. It is not
> possible to ask how something that grows should be organized in
> order that this organization, which is thought to be correct, be pre-
> served into the future. One can think in this way about something
> which remains unchanged from its beginnings. But it is not valid
> for the social organism. As a living entity it is constantly changing
> whatever arises within it. To attempt to give it a supposedly best
> form, in which it is expected to remain, is to undermine its vitality.[1]

The three-membered organization is not intended to be a utopian one-
time fix. It needs to be flexible and resilient to the ever developing and
changing activities of each domain and society as a whole. Over the last
100 years since GA 23 was written, we have seen significant developments
in each of the domains and the model as a whole needs to reflect those
developments through the work within each domain and the interrelationship of each domain. This can only be accomplished by human beings
and drives home the primal necessity for each human being to develop
their *Empfindung* concerning human life in its social aspects.

As Steiner wrote regarding the domain of economics:

> The threefold social order recognizes that at the present stage of
> human evolution, the economic sphere must limit itself exclusively
> to economic processes.... [skipping one page] ... It is this mistake
> that makes people say constantly, 'to realize the threefold order,
> human beings must be different than they are now.' No! Through
> the threefold order, people will be educated in such a way that they

---

[1] GA 23, Smith translation, about 1/3 into Ch. 3 (p. 97)

will grow up to be different than they were previously under the economic state.[2]

To restate this: given the current limitations on the economic domain we can however move forward with the three-membered organization, which will result in people being educated such that the economic domain can take its rightful place in its interaction with the other domains of rights and culture. Again we come back to the importance of education; and one of the proposals in this book is that the goal of developing a healthy *Empfindung* should not be focused solely on our children and our children's educational institutions. We, as adults and parents, need to take up this development of a healthy *Empfindung* directly, in ourselves. Particularly as parents, our own development becomes a model for our children.

THE WILL TO WORK

Currently, our will to work is driven by the fact that we each need to purchase commodities to sustain our life and we can only do so if we have the money to buy them; hence we work. When that sustenance is met, the other motive to work is for personal profit. In order for our will to work to orient in a different direction, a restructuring of the way the three domains function presently is required. Studying Steiner's article, "Ability to Work, Will To Work, and the Threefold Social Order" (in GA 24), we can understand that this restructuring has to happen more-or-less simultaneously in all three domains:

1. The *economic domain* can no longer be the impetus for work.
2. A free spiritual-cultural life must be fostered in the *cultural domain* to shift our egoistic profit motive for personal gain to one of working for society as a whole.
3. The *rights domain* must be democratically ordered such that each adult has a voice in the government and is co-equal with every other adult. This kind of 'real relationship' is what will motivate people to work for the community instead of themselves.

Referring to what Steiner wrote in the article, regarding point #1 above:

---

[2] GA 24, article, "Ability to Work," 2nd and 4th pages (p. 81, p. 83)

The demand that in the future one shall not work for oneself but for the community, remains quite empty as long as one has no concrete idea how human souls can be induced to work as willingly "for the community" as they do for themselves. ...

It should be obvious that a new incentive to work must be created the moment there is any thought of eliminating the old incentive of egotistical gain. An economic management that does not include this profit motive among the forces at work within the economy cannot of itself exert any effect whatever upon the human will to work. And precisely because it cannot do so, it meets a social demand that a large part of humanity has begun to raise in the present stage of development. This part of humanity no longer wants to be led to work by economic compulsion. They want to work from motives more befitting human dignity. ...

If the economic system is to be organized in a way that can have no effect on our will to work, then our will to work must be stimulated in some other way.

Regarding point #2 above:

It aims at establishing within an independent, self-sustaining cultural life a realm where one learns in a living way to understand this human society for which one is called upon to work; a realm where one learns to see what each single piece of work means for the combined fabric of the social order, to see it in such a light that one will learn to love it because of its value for the whole. It aims at creating in this free life of spirit the profounder principles that can replace the motive of personal gain. Only in a free spiritual life can a love for the human social order spring up that is comparable to the love an artist has for the creation of his works.

Regarding point #3 above:

The democratically ordered life of the legal sphere will provide the impulses for the will to work. Real relationships will grow up between people united in a social organism where each adult has a voice in government and is co-equal with every other adult: it is relationships such as these that are able to enkindle the will to work "for the community." One must reflect that a truly communal feeling can grow only from such relationships, and that from this feeling, the will to work can grow.[3]

---

[3] GA 24, article, "Ability to Work," near end of article (p. 83)

These are not changes that can be made overnight, nor at the large scale of our current economic, cultural, and governance systems. While they can conceivably be accomplished locally, even the majority of our local systems of governance fail to meet the concept of each adult having a voice and being co-equal with every other adult. Where is the relationship that enkindles the will to work if local organizations have a Board of Directors that *is* the governance, and adults do *not* have a voice in that governance and are not co-equal with every other adult? If a person is to feel truly motivated to work, that person must feel that they have a voice and that they are treated as equals. Our current legal system requires a Board of Directors for non-profit organizations (which are classified as corporations, just doing business not for profit); but there, too, we must not carry forward the attitude that the board members are an authoritative non-democratic body in the decision making, and that they are somehow 'above' the other adults in the organization. Instead, those involved could practice discerning which aspects of their activities and decisions belong to each of the three domains, and seek then to carry the nature of the appropriate domain into their work as a board and with the membership of the organization, i.e., to honor the equality of individuals in matters concerning rights, to honor special expertise that is relevant to economic exchanges, and special contributions out of the spiritual-cultural life of each member. The members of these boards frequently ask "why is it so hard to find people interested in becoming involved?" The answer may be quite simple – people do not experience 'the will to work' when there is an obvious hierarchy of authority and the healthy dynamics of each of the domains do not hold sway.

As Steiner wrote: "The mere awareness that one is working for society will not give any sensible satisfaction; accordingly it cannot provide an incentive to work."[4] Clearly, we are continuing to see what Steiner wrote more than 100 years ago, that people want "to work from motives more befitting human dignity." This must be coupled with an experience of democratic and co-equal participation in enterprise. Only then will the economic domain loosen its grip on us as the motivation to work.

One final requirement, the right to a decent human existence, is particularly difficult to achieve even locally at the present time. We live with the fact that both the local enterprise and the people working for it must exist within society's current economic and rights systems; therefore both

---

[4] GA 24, first paragraph of "Ability to Work" (p. 80)

producer and consumer are still engaging in a system where money is not just a proxy for commodities, money is in fact a commodity in and of itself. What the producer can pay the employee and the local cost-of-living requirements that the employee must 'pay' into the existing economic system is not balanced – there is in fact great disparity between the two, as has been discussed in this book. Again, this limits people's choices. While people might have the will, the 'commodity of money' does not afford them the means to work *where they will*. And if they do, it is often by sacrificing the quality of life they wish to have. Especially for young people, this means relying on financial help from their parents:

> Nearly 30% of millennials (ages 25 to 40) still receive financial support from their parents. This is even higher among Gen Zers (ages 18 to 24) at 67%, though many within this generation are still in college. Across all age groups, 22% of adults still receive financial support from their parents.
>
> While not everyone still receives money help from mom or dad, 56% of Americans say their parents helped them financially at some point during adulthood, such as paying for college (24%), living at home rent-free (22%) and buying a car (16%).[5]

Creating a self-sustaining community that is alive with a healthy functioning of the three domains, that insulates both the producer and consumer from the rest of society's existing systems of rights, commerce and culture, is one of the greatest challenges for bringing the three domains into reality and truly fostering people's will to work for the community rather than personal profit or needs. It would seem that at best, an interim approach involving grants, loans, donations and gifting from people who are willing to direct profits obtained by working 'in the system' towards a three-membered organization of our social life is achievable. We see this being done in indirect ways – just go to any farmer's market and one will see the expensive cars of 'the wealthy' in the parking lot as they shop for the locally grown, organic and niche products being produced by local entrepreneurs. One rarely sees the 20 year old 'beater' vehicle driven by the struggling artist, unless that artist is themselves a performer at the farmer's market! (Author's note: on weekends the parking lot of the Hawthorne Valley Farm Store in Ghent NY is filled with the BMW's and Mercedes of the wealthy visiting the county from New York City.)

---

[5] https://www.magnifymoney.com/news/parental-financial-support-survey/

Unfortunately, these indirect ways are merely a drop in the bucket (if even that) towards sustaining a community as it works with the dynamics of the three domains, hoping to achieve this social renewal.

It should also be brought to consciousness that in our current society, a hierarchical system of authority is the typical template for administrative structures and the organization of work. In a three-membered organization, administrative structures and organization are still necessary but they do not create hierarchies of authority. This is a significant rethinking of how we work together and is directly related to our concept of human dignity with regard to equality. One of the fundamental aspects of scientific thinking that has pervaded our society is the analytical process of understanding the natural world as a hierarchy of systems, and this almost always applies to our thinking in relation to any organization of people. Conversely, a holistic approach, "relating to or concerned with wholes or with complete systems rather than with the analysis of, treatment of, or dissection into parts,"[6] maintains equality.

> "The whole is greater than the sum of its parts" expresses the essence of holism, a term coined by the great South African general and statesman Jan Smuts in 1926. Holism generally opposes the Western tendency toward analysis, the breaking down of wholes into parts sometimes to the point that "you can't see the forest for the trees".[7]

The modern term for this non-hierarchical system of work is 'holacracy':

> Holacracy suggests a more decentralized structure, while hierarchy stands on a centralized one. In [the] holacracy concept, power moves from leaders to processes in an organization as a whole. Further, holacracy also provides a concrete framework for encoding autonomy, agility, and purpose-alignment into the organization's DNA. Somehow holacracy replaces the conventional management hierarchy with a new structure. In holacracy, instead of operating top-down, power is distributed throughout the organization – giving individuals and teams freedom while staying aligned to the organization's purpose.[8]

As holacracy is in the purview of the rights domain, we can see how it supports the impulse for the will to work, as it establishes individual

---

[6] https://www.merriam-webster.com/dictionary/holistic
[7] Ibid.
[8] https://msocialsciences.com/index.php/mjssh/article/view/600

and team freedom, the very 'real relationships between people' that Steiner wrote of, which needs to characterize a democratically-ordered rights domain.

The dynamic nature of holacracy, in which groups of people organize and disband as needed, is a fundamental requirement of the three-membered organization in order for the members of the social organism to be 'co-equal.' This includes:

- Within a particular entrepreneurial endeavor.
- Between entrepreneurial endeavors.
- Between the three domains themselves.

Rather than pigeon-holing a person's role based on the specific skills required for the work (and formalized in their title, such as 'Mid-level software engineer III'[9] or 'Chief Financial Officer'[10]), the will to work is enhanced by the recognition that people have multidisciplinary and cross-disciplinary skills. Both the individual and society benefit when it is recognized that an individual can contribute to different areas of an entrepreneurial endeavor and that people can also contribute in each of the three domains. This flexibility is part of the 'co-equal' concept of the three-membered organization.

THE FOUR DAY WORK WEEK

On June 6, 2022, the United Kingdom began "a six-month experiment to test the efficacy of a four-day work week, which was organized by the nonprofit 4 Day Global."[11] A key point here is the decoupling of labor hours, productivity, and wage: "4 Day Week Global said that this is the biggest pilot program of its kind, where, as long as workers maintain 100% of their productivity, they will also maintain 100% of their salary while working 80% of the traditional work week."[12] Three months into this 'experiment', the results reveal increased employee wellbeing and surprisingly some increase to productivity.

This represents a significant shift to the five day workweek, which:

---

[9] https://www.indeed.com/career-advice/finding-a-job/engineer-level
[10] https://blog.ongig.com/job-titles/c-level-titles/
[11] https://gizmodo.com/four-day-work-week-work-from-home-return-to-office-1849562791
[12] Ibid.

…became part of American labor law partly due to Henry Ford. In 1926, the founder of the Ford Motor Company took his six-day-a-week operation down to five days per week, with no changes in employee compensation. He believed doing so would make his workers more productive—and more inclined to spend money during their downtime. With days off, people would have more time for leisure activities and shopping, spending their earnings, perhaps, on vehicles. This landmark change made Ford one of the first companies in the nation to set the standard of a five-day workweek.[13]

Furthermore, "86% of survey respondents [indicated] that they would be likely or extremely likely to retain the four-day work week." The article concludes:

The four-day work week is a tantalizing concept for the working class, and one that appears to be more and more legitimate as pilot programs such as this one gather illuminating data on the concept. Microsoft flirted with a four-day work week in Japan and saw higher sales figures and levels of happiness in employees. The big hurdle moving forward will be getting buy-in from enough companies and executives to make the four-day work week a permanent fixture in the world's labor market—but results from large projects such as the one from 4 Day Week Global are only getting us closer to that end goal.[14]

While one might argue that Ford's motives were economic, we see this shift occurring in other countries as well:

The United Arab Emirates, for example, became the first nation in the world to adopt the concept of the four-and-a-half-day work-week, which went into effect on Jan. 1, 2022. Belgium is one of the most recent countries to try out the four-day workweek and the U.K. has invited companies to participate in a national trial to determine if a four-day workweek mandate would be viable. There are companies even in the U.S. that have just implemented four-day workweeks, with others planning trials for reduced work hours.[15]

---

[13] https://firmspace.com/theproworker/from-strikes-to-labor-laws-how-the-us-adopted-the-5-day-workweek
[14] https://gizmodo.com/four-day-work-week-work-from-home-return-to-office-1849562791
[15] https://firmspace.com/theproworker/from-strikes-to-labor-laws-how-the-us-adopted-the-5-day-workweek

Here is an opportunity for furthering the issues of human dignity and quality of life by applying the principles of the three-membered organization, particularly the relationship of the economic and cultural domains. A reduced workweek with no reduction in productivity reveals that the accepted norm of a 40 hour work week should be questioned and that labor, productivity, and wage is a dynamic relationship.

IS TECHNOLOGY THE ANSWER?

There is also a growing idea that technology can facilitate the three-membered organization:

> ... [T]here has increasingly been felt a need for a consideration of these technology trends [Narrow AI, Blockchain, and Global Open Source] in balancing the cultural, political, and increasingly powerful economic domains [sic]. In helping facilitate such a threefold balance, the decentralizing effects of open source data science and Narrow AI ... and blockchain technologies can also be noted.... Indeed, it could be possible for humanity to transform closed-source Narrow AI initially ... towards open source ... to extend human freedom, while helping generate sustainable abundance for all through a global threefold open source Narrow AI platform with decentralized open source blockchain foundation ... and social movement. Such an initial movement to 'Open Source the AI' could build the momentum and digital literacy in global civil society to fully address the follow up global transhuman ... and ASI agendas.... Because much or all of the narrow AI/deep learning source code could be made open to the public, humanity as a whole (technical and non-technical alike) could study, discuss and debate issues on its operation and proposed additions – ensuring safety, economic and political freedoms, and charting an initial path towards a positive human future. Such a distributed Narrow AI codebase could then be openly programmed to serve humanity's interests, as opposed to the reverse.[16]

Utilizing these complex technologies with the assumption that they would balance the political, cultural, and economic domains and extend human freedom is a topic that should be approached with the utmost

---

[16] https://demo.firepad.io/#FgaYvF17ff

caution lest we end up with Artificial Intelligence (AI) systems that determine how we interact with each other and between and within the three domains, *accessible only to those within a certain technology 'class' that understand and can work with the technology.* Society has leapt toward so-called technological solutions for decades only to discover not just undesirable consequences but that technology has in fact specifically not solved social issues. Would it not be wiser to first understand the underlying issues, primal thoughts, and truths that we are trying to address? How can an AI understand ethics, morality, human dignity, when we ourselves struggle with those concepts? Is an AI even capable of 'learning' what those concepts mean? Even more salient, how can those concepts be 'encoded' into 'rules' that an AI uses in its decision making algorithms? The very idea that an AI can encompass the 'contracts' between people and the three domains of the social order contradicts and disregards the point that Steiner repeatedly made, that such contracts are dynamic and individual.

As technology plays an ever growing role in people's lives, we must not forget what Steiner wote:

> The producer is of course at the same time the consumer. He whose business it is to produce must have an understanding not only of the process of production, but also of the life of his fellowmen, so that he can devote himself to the work of production in a manner corresponding to their needs.[17]

Steiner repeatedly states that the relationship between production, distribution and consumption is based on human interrelationships:

> Production and distribution of commodities, administration, human intercourse, and so on, are necessary to supply human requirements.
> ... [I]t will be necessary that the entire economic process be reflected in the economic interests of the individual [human being].[18]

Furthermore:

> Men will be there who will make it their task to regulate production in conformity with their observation of the needs of the consumer. So that the market will consist in commodities which the associations, already mentioned, will be able to produce; these

---

[17] GA 332A, Lecture 6, about 1/3 into lecture (pp. 136-37)
[18] GA 332a, Lecture 6, about 1/4 and 3/8 into lecture (p. 136, p. 139)

associations having first studied and observed intelligently the needs of consumption.[19]

Artificial Intelligence cannot replace studying and observing "intelligently the needs of consumption." This is a human endeavor. Using technology as a proxy for real human interaction might seem simpler and more efficient in dealing with the complexities of human interaction in today's world. Instead, it is "By the work of the human spirit alone can that spirit come into the world."[20] that accomplishes human development through "human intercourse."

While technology is obviously an important and necessary *tool* for facilitating communication, bookkeeping and the transactions between producer, distributor/trader, and consumer, it is vital that the technology does not replace human intelligence, but rather that human skills in inter-relationships, observation, and thinking continue developing.

COUNTRY AND LOCAL REALIZATION OF THE THREE-MEMBERED ORGANIZATION

The country of Bhutan (a country in south-central Asia north of Bangladesh) has realized a Buddhist 'middle path'[21] four-membered structure to measure what is called the 'gross national happiness' of the people of Bhutan. This four-membered structure consists of:

1. Preservation and promotion of a free and resilient culture.
2. Sustainable and equitable socio-economic development.
3. Good governance and equality before the law.

and permeating the above three is:

4. Ecological sustainability.

This structure bears a striking resemblance to the three-membered organization, with the addition of ecological sustainability which has become a significant issue in the 21st century, all of which clearly stems from an awareness of the same primal thoughts. Furthermore, this approach

---

[19] GA 332a, Lecture 6 (p. 136, p. 139)
[20] GA 332a, Lecture 6 (p. 136, p. 139)
[21] https://en.wikipedia.org/wiki/Middle_Way

is endorsed by the United Nations General Assembly and is being promoted by Bhutan's Prime Minister internationally:

> The term 'Gross National Happiness' as conceptualized by the 4th
> King of Bhutan, Jigme Singye Wangchuck, in 1972 was declared as,
> 'Gross National Happiness is more important than Gross Domestic
> Product.' The concept implies that sustainable development should
> take a holistic approach towards notions of progress and give equal
> importance to non-economic aspects of wellbeing.
>
>   In 2011, The UN General Assembly passed Resolution
> 'Happiness: towards a holistic approach to development' urging
> member nations to follow the example of Bhutan and measure hap-
> piness and well-being and calling happiness a 'fundamental human
> goal.'
>
>   In 2012, Bhutan's Prime Minister Jigme Thinley and the
> Secretary-General Ban Ki-Moon of the United Nations convened
> the High Level Meeting: Well-being and Happiness: Defining
> a New Economic Paradigm to encourage the spread of Bhutan's
> GNH philosophy. At the High Level meeting, the first World
> Happiness Report was issued. Shortly afterward, the 20th of March
> was declared to be International Day of Happiness by the UN in
> 2012 with resolution 66/28.
>
>   Bhutan's Prime Minister Tshering Tobgay proclaimed a pref-
> erence for focus on more concrete goals instead of promoting GNH
> when he took office, but subsequently has protected the GNH
> of his country and promoted the concept internationally. Other
> Bhutanese officials also promote the spread of GNH at the UN and
> internationally.[22]

Variations of this four-fold structure have been taken up in (same
source as the above citation):

- Victoria, British Columbia, Canada.
- Communities in some cities in the state of São Paulo, Brazil.
- Thailand.
- the Philippines.
- as well as Seattle Washington and Vermont in the United States.

Variations such as 'Beyond GDP'[23] also exist (GDP: Gross Domestic

[22] https://en.wikipedia.org/wiki/Gross_National_Happiness
[23] https://ec.europa.eu/environment/beyond_gdp/index_en.html

Product). All of these works recognize that human dignity and quality of life go beyond economic measures. These are fine steps forward, yet In light of a strong understanding of what impulses hold sway in each of the three domains, care must be taken as to how the four aims are attempted, because it is not the role of the political/rights domain to administer and regulate the economic and cultural domain, nor to determine out of itself what 'sustainable' means. If the political/rights domain takes these roles, this mistake will result in just another form of unitary governance (also in the form of an organization such as the United Nations), unable to unfold livingly the three domains. As Steiner explained at length in Chapter I of GA 23, this was a key mistake in the thinking of the workers in his time who were bringing forth issues that point to the need for a three-membered social organism, but who nevertheless looked to a unitary state to administer the three. Their grasp of the primal thoughts was not clear enough.

THE THREE-MEMBERED ORGANIZATION AND THE ENVIRONMENT

Regarding capitalism and the agriculture, Carl Marx wrote:

> {A]ll progress in capitalistic agriculture is a progress in the art, not only of robbing the labourer, but of robbing the soil; all progress in increasing the fertility of the soil for a given time, is a progress towards ruining the lasting sources of that fertility.[24]

Organic agriculture practices are designed to correct this ruining of "the lasting sources of that fertility," as is biodynamic agriculture. In biodynamic agriculture, initially developed in 1924 by Steiner:

> Each biodynamic farm or garden is an integrated, whole, living organism. This organism is made up of many interdependent elements: fields, forests, plants, animals, soils, compost, people, and the spirit of the place. Biodynamic farmers and gardeners work to nurture and harmonize these elements, managing them in a holistic and dynamic way to support the health and vitality of the whole. Biodynamic practitioners also endeavor to listen to the land, to sense

---

[24] *Capital: Volume 1: A Critique of Political Economy*, Penguin Classics, 1990

what may want to emerge through it, and to develop and evolve their farm as a unique individuality.[25]

Furthermore, here are the results of a recent survey:

> As of 2020, biodynamic techniques were used on 251,842 hectares in 55 countries, led by Germany, Australia and France. Germany accounts for 41.8% of the global total; the remainder average 1,750 ha per country. Biodynamic methods of cultivating grapevines have been taken up by several notable vineyards.[26]

However, today we face environmental challenges that did not exist in 1919. Climate change / global warming.[27] rainwater that is no longer safe to drink anywhere,[28] severe drought around the world,[29] wildfires,[30] insect populations have declined by 40% globally and animal populations have declined globally by 70% over the last 50 years.[31] The list of alarming environmental issues being reported in the mainstream media is extensive and is no longer limited to farming practices.

In the three-membered organization, the economic domain and the production of commodities which frequently impacts the environment would be regulated by the rights domain with regards to natural resources and the impact of production on the environment, as this affects the quality of life for everyone on the planet. However, it is to be remembered that it is not a matter of 'saving' the planet by ridding it of human beings and human freedom, for the Earth is the setting and means by which all four kingdoms are developing further. There is much that needs to be done in the cultural domain with regards to the environmental impact of human activities – everything from commodity consumption, the way we power our world, fuel our cars and recycle our waste. This is because it is from the cultural domain that both awareness and advancements in environmental management originate, informing the economic and rights domains with regards to the use of natural resources, the effects of production, and laws affecting both economic and cultural domains.

---

[25] https://www.biodynamics.com/biodynamic-principles-and-practices
[26] https://en.wikipedia.org/wiki/Biodynamic_agriculture
27 https://www.joboneforhumanity.org/global_warming
[28] https://www.businessinsider.com/rainwater-no-longer-safe-to-drink-anywhere-study-forever-chemicals-2022-8
[29] https://www.vox.com/policy-and-politics/2022/8/21/23315264/droughts-extreme-heat-climate-crisis
[30] https://www.reuters.com/world/europe/wildfires-breaking-out-across-world-2022-07-19/
[31] https://www.earthday.org/fact-sheet-global-species-decline/

This is a completely unexplored area of the three-membered organization. Who can take up the question of how the three-membered organization can concretely address the environmental issues through the interaction of the three domains? Who can provide the necessary education to decrease our personal impact on the environment through the three-membered awareness? These are important questions that can begin to be addressed in new and more effective ways within the three-membered organization of our social life.

THE GIFT ECONOMY

As Wikipedia states:

> A gift economy or gift culture is a system of exchange where valuables are not sold, but rather given without an explicit agreement for immediate or future rewards. Social norms and customs govern giving a gift in a gift culture; although there is some expectation of reciprocity, gifts are not given in an explicit exchange of goods or services for money, or some other commodity or service. This contrasts with a barter economy or a market economy, where goods and services are primarily explicitly exchanged for value received.[32]

A gift economy is essentially the antithesis of the three-membered organization at our current stage of human development. Logical thinking should suffice to demonstrate that a gift economy can only exist as an aspect of the larger economic domain. One can 'gift' another person with a ride to the airport, but one will have had to participate in the larger economic domain as a worker in order to be able to acquire the commodities of the vehicle and the gasoline required for the trip. Currently there is no sustainable scenario in which a gift economy can function as the *exclusive* form of commodity exchange, as the question can always be asked, 'how did I acquire the commodity that I am gifting?' In the future (far future) a true gift economy may be possible.

The reality of today's world is that the transaction of commodities requires the exchange of money, where money is a proxy for commodities. Here we uncover the tension of the economic system, even in the context of producing something that is for the betterment of society.

---

[32] https://en.wikipedia.org/wiki/Gift_economy

That tension is that we work not just for the betterment of society but to receive, from our labor, 'a share in the proceeds' of the commodity we produce, from the purchase by others of that commodity. That 'share' enables us to purchase other commodities to fulfill our quality of life needs. Granted, certain quality of life needs, such as access to clean water and education, might be considered a right rather than something we need to purchase. Conversely, flying to Hawaii for a vacation might fall outside of that 'right' with regards to how one vacations.

Currently, a gift economy is a vital aspect of society because of the inequality between people in their quality of life. Examples include homeless shelters, soup kitchens, and aid to refugees. All three domains of the three-membered organization are required to participate in a gift economy during the transition from the current system of capitalism to a functional three-membered system, and even more importantly, as long as there is conflict and war which destroys people's quality of life, undermines their human dignity, and leaves people in desperate need.

At some point in the future it may be possible to completely decouple the rights domain from the economic domain. At the moment, the rights domain is needed to legislate aspects of the economic domain to ensure a person's quality of life via their share of the purchase proceeds from the sale of commodities. In a true gift economy, this legislation would not need to exist. Because the rights domain would ensure the necessary quality of life, what one produces out of one's personal interest in doing 'work' would be a gift to the community, and the raw materials necessary for that work would be 'gifted' to the workers. It is not clear how quality of life would be ensured in a dominant gift economy. Is there still a rights domain mandating anything? For this future to manifest and therefore a gift economy that can become the dominant method of exchange of commodities, necessitates not just that each human being's quality of life is met but also that conflict, at any level, is eliminated. This would also eliminate all concepts of societal class. One could go as far as to say that a gift economy, as a dominant economy, would require the human evolutionary change that Steiner wrote about, that if one person in the world is suffering, all feel that suffering. As scripture states:

> ... that there may be no division in the body, but that the members

may have the same care for one another. If one member suffers, all suffer together …[33]

If we truly had the ability to sense another person's suffering, we would also know what 'gift' they need to receive to ease that suffering.

IMAGINING THE THREE-MEMBERED ORGANIZATION

As discussed in the Preface, the term 'sphere' conjures up an image of a ball with distinct edges. Hence when talking about the social organism, we might imagine 'something' flowing out of one such sphere and into another and the exchanges between three spheres, for culture, economy and rights. Picturing discrete spheres is convenient (certainly for diagrams) and appeals to culturally-indoctrinated thinking in which separate entities interact with discrete packets of exchange. It appeals as well to today's cultural tendency to emphasize the individual over the group. However, we should strive to remove this imagination of 'spheres' regarding the three-membered organization as it fails to recognize the interpenetration and permeability of the realms of culture, economics, and rights.

Even the term 'domain' fails to express well enough the interpenetration and permeability of the three realms. To be vital, our activity within the economic realm must be permeated by the 'fabric' of rights considerations and of spiritual-cultural inspirations.. Similarly, our activity within the realm of rights must be permeated by what is developing in the spiritual-cultural realm and be permeated by its living relevance within the economic and cultural domains And even in the realm of culture we must permit our activity to be permeated by what belongs to the realms of rights and economics. As a metaphor, consider a painting which expresses color, form, light/dark, and density/dilution. We can observe the painting as a whole and yet we can also differentiate the aspects of color, form, light, and density. Another example: the interpenetration of blood vessels, nerves, and muscles are necessary for a living organism to move about, yet we can also describe the blood vessels, nerves, and muscles discreetly though we lose the context of the whole.

Similarly, the three-membered organization must be imagined as an

---

[33] 1 Corinthians 12:25 – 26, https://biblehub.com/esv/1_corinthians/12.htm

interpenetrated organism – each member permeated by the other members. If we move more towards this imagination, we have a better picture from which we can work to discern how the members function by themselves and in relationship with each other. We will have an imagination that expresses that in order to function, each member is both independent from *and dependent on* the other members.

Applying this same imagination to the human being, to our interactions with each other, helps to reveal these members working in us individually and even what member, culture, economics, or rights, is the primary concern of the individual at any given time. In all seriousness, would it not be an interesting greeting to ask the other person: 'Which of the members of the three-membered organization is your concern today?'

WORKING OUT OF AN INDEPENDENT LIFE OF THOUGHT

As Steiner wrote:

> Not until we are capable of bringing down onto a material level what we think of as being spiritual shall we be able to grasp the actual nerve of the social question.
>
> Thus it is virtually a matter of aiming towards a way of thinking that really develops a knowledge of man that is at one and the same time a social impulse. A way of thinking based on anything else is not adequate. A mentality based on the life of the state or the life of economics creates clerks and officers. But the sort of mentality we need creates human beings. This can only be the sort of thought life that breaks away from the sphere of economics and the life of the state. That is why our "Threefold Social Organism" had to happen. We had to show in a radical way that any kind of dependency of thought life on economics or on the life of the state had to stop, and thought life had to be set up on its own basis. Then thought life will be able to give economics and the life of the state what economics and the state cannot give to the life of thought.
>
> That is the important thing, that is what is vital! Whole human beings will only arise again when we work out of an independent life of thought.[34]

---

[34] GA 191, bottom

It is not for the authors of this book to mandate what "being spiritual" means to the reader – this a personal concern. What is key in the above quote is that our thinking must become independent of the economic and rights domains. In "Another Brick in the Wall" by Pink Floyd, the lyrics:

> We don't need no education
> We don't need no thought control
> No dark sarcasm in the classroom
>
> Teacher, leave them kids alone
>
> Hey, teacher, leave them kids alone
> All in all, it's just another brick in the wall
> All in all, you're just another brick in the wall

were relevant in 1979 when the song was written, as well as prescient with regards to the indoctrination of our thinking influenced not just by education but by the economic and rights domains of our present society as well. As children in earlier society, we experienced our father going off to work and our mother being the 'homemaker.' In present society, we as children experienced both our parents going off to their 40 hour a week jobs. One might argue that school busing indoctrinates us into accepting long commutes to work as adults. As children, we learn about hierarchical systems (in nature, in governance, etc.) rather than relational systems, so is it no wonder we accept a hierarchical work environment? These are just a few of the many examples in which we have grown up with our thinking dependent on existing economic and political influences, and even cultural influences.

In order to work out of 'an independent life of thought,' the questions need to be asked:

1. On what preconceptions is this thought dependent?
2. What is the primal thought that is the source of my thinking?
3. How do I engage 'what I think of as being spiritual,' my Empfindung, to inform new ideas in relation to inculcated thoughts?

It is not easy nor is it necessarily safe to ask these questions. Society considers people to be 'social' when they think the same thing and 'anti-social' when they think independently. Galileo was put under house arrest by the Inquisition for the remainder of his life for his thoughts on heliocentrism. John Wilkes Booth assassinated Abraham Lincoln based on the belief that the Confederacy could be restored.[35] Martin Luther King was assassinated out of hatred and racism.[36] Nelson Mandela, a South African anti-apartheid activist, was imprisoned for 27 years.[37]

This is not to say that an independent life of thought will lead to assassination or imprisonment, but more and more we see examples of how the economic and rights domains have become involved in mandating our behavior when we try to act freely out of our independent thinking. While this brings to mind certain controversial topics, the mandates of the economic domain even impacts issues such as the ability to work remotely.

An independent life of thought leads to independent action, and independent action requires freedom. It is in the interest of all three domains for the freedom of people to act out of their independent thinking. Just as society 'should not' have a religious entity in the cultural domain mandating laws in the rights domain that lead to the persecution of independent thinkers, it is relevant, as quoted at the beginning of this book and worth restating here, that:

> [P]eople cannot be social if they do not see the human quality in one another, but live entirely within themselves. Human beings can only become social if they really meet one another in life, and something passes between them. This is the root of the social problem.[38]

Without 'meeting one another in life,' the path to an independent life of thought will be very challenging because an independent life of thought will continue to be seen as antisocial. Ironically, a true meeting of one another in life, each with an independent life of thought, is also challenging due to our biases (conscious and unconscious) and our egocentric ways of thinking. The fallacy that occurs in meeting one another in life, is that by trying to achieve a unity in thinking, we can fall into imposing our thinking on others.

> Henri Bortoft expressed Goethe's focus on the multitude of phenomena, through the phrase "multiplicity in unity," as opposed to "unity in multiplicity"(Bortoft, 1996). The former is possibility, including all differences and remaining all encompassing as we shift from one phenomenon to the next; the latter tries to generalize what many

---

[35] https://ahec.armywarcollege.edu/exhibits/CivilWarImagery/edwards_Assassination.cfm
[36] https://www.history.com/this-day-in-history/dr-king-is-assassinated
[37] https://en.wikipedia.org/wiki/Nelson_Mandela
[38] GA 191, *Social Understanding Through Spiritual-Scientific Cognition* Lecture II, October 4, 1919, a few paragraphs from the end of lecture

phenomena have in common and thereby excludes differences. It is the latter approach, which Goethe calls a mistake.[39]

Considering that 'phenomena' includes our individual thinking, the "multiplicity in unity" of our thoughts is where the possibilities of a true meeting of one another occurs, not in the "unity in multiplicity." This is the thing to strive towards in our own independent life of thought – to also take in the multiplicity of other's thoughts to find the unity in our individual thinking.

In today's society we often hear the phrase, 'we need to find the middle path'. Regarding this, Steiner wrote:

> The truth cannot be found by a one-sided adoption of this or that standpoint but by applying the modes of knowledge appropriate either for materialism or idealism. The world does not progress by undeviating adherence to a middle course: a middle course is appropriate when the opposing sides are also present and are recognised as forces. If something has to be weighed, the two scalepans are needed as well as the beam. ...Life needs antithesis; life progresses in and through polarity.[40]

The drive to solve a disagreement by either adopting a one-sided standpoint or finding the middle path does not acknowledge the necessity of the polarities. Rather than trying to solve the polarities, those polarities must be worked "in and through." The middle path is only valid when there are strong opposing sides. The middle path is not a passive compromise but rather an active, evolving and creative space that constantly works with the polarities.

The middle path requires concrete, human work. It is not sufficient to repeat abstract phrases about love and altruism. As Steiner said:

> We must not, however, think that the mere repetition of phrases to the effect that the spirit must govern the world will bring about, as by enchantment, the coming of the spirit. No! By the work of the human spirit alone can that spirit come into the world. In this respect also we must be true. We must not allow the falsehood to ring through the world, that the spirit must come. The truth must be proclaimed that the spirit will not appear until there are places in

---

[39] https://designforsustainability.medium.com/the-tip-of-the-iceberg-goethe-s-aphorisms-on-the-theory-of-nature-and-science-ba6e12ebd5f1

[40] GA 141, *Between Death and Rebirth*, Lecture 7, about 4 paragraphs from end of lecture

which not only the materialistic study of outer nature will be carried on, but in which a spiritual conception of life will be striven after.[41]

The ability to create an independent life of thought for ourselves *and* to integrate the independent thoughts of others requires creating the space, *together*, to arrive at "a spiritual conception of life." Following the lecture in which he pointed to this was a question and answer period. In one of his responses he counseled (according to the notes taken, Kate's translation):

> The truth lies in the middle between the opposing assertions/claims, just as the real tree lies in the middle between two photographs that I take from one side or the other. In this regard, one must point out the dangers of one-sided thinking.[42]

It would appear that the key is to keep 'the tree' at the center of the discussion. If we consider and seek the tree itself, it is then clear that no one's perspective can achieve the whole truth of what it is. The truth is what is in 'the middle' between all of the perspectives. We are of course trusting that the photographs don't lie. But there is something more to consider in the case of our beholding. What if the vision of the beholder is poor or the beholder did not observe accurately or gave the tree just a peripheral side glance from their particular vantage point? We are not attempting a compromise as an abstract, artificial 'middle' between opposing views. We learn the characteristics and nature of the tree itself and we are attempting to find out how the seemingly opposing views might be suggesting, filling out and pointing to the same truth, within which we could then be united, in communion with each other. And this is what we need for our work together toward the realization of a healthy three-membered organization of our earthly social life!

ASSOCIATIVE ECONOMICS

Why 'associative economics' rather than 'associative rights' or 'associative culture?' One answer to this question is that in the rights and cultural domains, the human being and associations between human beings are already more or less both the means and the central focus of all concerns

---

[41] GA 332a, Lecture 6, near end of lecture (p. 153)
[42] *Soziale Zukunft*, GA 332a, Question/Answer following Lecture 6, https://archive.org/details/rudolf-steiner-ga-332a (requires downloading as a PDF or other format)

within these domains. The rights domain, even in our current society, passes legislation primarily through direct interaction of people, as is evidenced by Senate and House proceedings and the adjudication of infractions such as speeding tickets in town courts (which should actually be a function of the cultural domain). For the most part in the cultural domain, education, religious teaching, artistic presentations and scientific research involve associations between people – parents and teachers, clergy and lay people, etc. This is not so for the economic domain. Here, producers, distributors/traders and consumers are typically disconnected from each other and entrepreneurs as well are disconnected from those who provide capital. As Steiner said:

> The idea of the Threefold Social Organism starts from realities. It requires, in the first place, that men should be there, who can produce, who have technical knowledge and special skill. On them must depend the business of production. And these experts in technical knowledge and skill must unite and carry on the economic activity founded on the production which springs from individual initiative. This is the true principle of Association. Commodities are first produced and then brought to the consumer on the basis of the union of the producers.[43]

This is the first principle of associative economics: that people with the technical knowledge and skill to produce something are united with the initiatives of other individuals toward the same or similar ends. How difficult is it in our current economic system to find those people with the technical knowledge and skill for an idea, for an initiative that another person has?

A second principle underlying associative economics is that associations of producers and consumers communicate with each other to adjust commodity production based on actual consumer needs. This also includes commodity distribution. As Steiner said:

> The task of the future will be to find, through associations, the kind of production which most accords with the needs of consumption, and the most appropriate channels from the producers to the consumers.[44]

Thirdly, associative economics also includes how capital is lent, how

---

[43] GA 332a, Lecture 2 (p. 40)
[44] GA 23, Chapter 3, about 2/3 into lecture (p. 112)

commodity prices are set and how workers are transferred to meet changing production needs.

Vitally, the essence of associative economics is a malleable, responsive
and multifold approach that brings people into direct relationship with
each other with regard to commerce and to create real human relationships in the place of impersonal markets, financial institutions and prof-
it-motivated business. "With its many and wide-ranging implications for
modern economic life, associative economics places human beings at the
centre of all economic processes."[45]

Associative economics is an ambitious concept and requires that the
primal thoughts which inform each of the three domains be helped to
emerge and that the three-membered organization be brought to realization. And in particular, the independence in the functioning of the rights
and cultural domains *must* be established in order for the economic domain
to function properly. As Steiner said:

> Not until the economic body is supported by the two other depart-
> ments of social life, the independent political and the independent
> cultural body, not until then can the economic system be established
> independently in a sound way on its own foundation.[46]

Once an endeavor or organization of whatever size (local, regional
state or national) accomplishes this three-membered functioning (and this
is no easy task), it becomes possible for it to engage associatively with other
endeavors or organizations regardless of the nature of their internal functioning. These other organizations need not have brought a three-membered social organism to realization as yet:

> Should a social organism form itself according to the three natural
> sectors, the representatives of each sector could enter into interna-
> tional relations with others, even if these others have not yet adopted
> the same forms.[47]

Once the rights and cultural domains are organized and functioning
independently, the reworking of the economic domain can begin. One
such starting point is the existing financial institutions (Steiner's italics):
"A deep gulf has opened between one human being and another. They do not get

---

[45] https://economics.goetheanum.org/research/associative-economics
[46] GA 332a, Lecture 2, about 1/8 from end of lecture (p. 51)
[47] GA 23, Chapter 4, a few paragraphs into Ch. 4 (p. 129)

near to each other under the financial system of economy."[48] The impersonal[49] financial lending systems that exist now would be eliminated by bringing intellectual and manual workers directly together with those human beings who lend capital. Rather than going through the apparatus of a bank or loan agent where the holder of the capital and the person seeking the capital are completely disconnected, the direct association creates a relationship between the two. Again, to emphasize that the principle of associations is to directly bring people together, Steiner said: "This, however, can only be done through the principle of Association, by which men will again unite with each other as men."[50] And as has been previously mentioned, in associative economics the lenders of capital involve themselves with the work of the entrepreneur and the workers who are involved in the entrepreneurial effort, rather than remaining impartial or absent in relation to what unfolds.

One of the effects of having associations of producers and consumers is that, rather than profit – which is only an indicator of degree of demand – being the motive for production under the sway of the chaotic and impersonal market forces of supply and demand, it is associations of producers and consumers that "will determine whether a commodity shall be produced or not."[51] While an entrepreneurial effort is expected to be profitable, the salient point here is that the needs of human beings are what determine production rather than solely profit for the entrepreneur. This shift of focus from individual/corporate profit to one of meeting people's needs eliminates the vast marketing mechanisms and psychological manipulation of advertisements (as discussed earlier), and it eliminates as well the sheer cost of this marketing and this manipulation of the consumer: in 2021 "It was calculated that the total advertising expenditure in North America in 2021 amounted to about 297.5 billion U.S. dollars."[52]

Also, given that commodities will be produced as needed and valued by society, determining the price of a commodity will be done through associations that will bring in people "whose business it will be to find out the relation between the value of a manufactured commodity and its price."[53]

---

[48] GA 332a, Lecture 2, a bit over 1/2 into lecture (p. 43)
[49] Impersonal: for example, we can apply for a line of credit or a credit card simply by clicking a button on a web page – there is zero contact with another human being.
[50] GA 332a, Lecture 2, a bit over 1/2 into lecture (p. 43)
[51] GA 332a, about 3/4 into lecture 2 (p. 48)
[52] https://www.statista.com/statistics/429036/advertising-expenditure-in-north-america/
[53] GA 332a, Lecture 2, about 3/4 into lecture (p. 48)

The value of a commodity corresponds to its value to the community and there is a *relationship* between value and price; but value does not directly determine price. The price of commodities "must fit the value of the commodities and correspond to it,"[54] yet at the same time, "those who quite justifiably must have [the] commodities must be able to pay for them."[55] Among other things, this correspondence prevents price gouging – overcharging in times of crisis. Instead, when people value a commodity or service, this "gives the impulse to demand,"[56] which in turn informs production and price. It is necessary to work at gaining new ways of thinking (and feeling) about these matters.
Furthermore, as Steiner said:

> The price of the product is conditional on the number of persons engaged in its production. But, through these arrangements, the price will really correspond to the value attached to the commodity in question by the community in accordance with its requirements.[57]

However, from the production side of the economic cycle, the number of people engaged in production is determined in turn by how much that commodity is valued/needed (Steiner's italics): "*When a product shows a tendency to become too dear, that is a sign that there are too few workers engaged on it.*"[58] This increased value ("too dear") would have the effect of increasing the commodity's price, which is then brought back within reasonable reach of the consumers who need to be able to purchase it by increasing production to meet the need. Conversely, "If a commodity tends to become too cheap, that is to say, to earn too little profit, arrangements must be made to employ fewer workers on that particular product"[59] – the consumer needs and values it less. Here again we see the relationship between value/need, profit and price. If the need diminishes, the product's value decreases and fewer people purchase the product; this results in lower profits and the number of people producing the product will be reduced. As described earlier, if the product is no longer valued at all, production would cease.

In our current economic thinking, it seems contradictory that adding

---

[54] GA 332a, Lecture 2 (p. 48)
[55] GA 332a, Lecture 2 (p. 48)
[56] GA 332a, Lecture 2 (p. 48)
[57] GA 332a, Lecture 2, about 3/4 into lecture 2 (p. 49)
[58] GA 332a, Lecture 2 (p. 49)
[59] GA 332a, Lecture 2 (p. 49)

workers decreases the price. We would imagine that the price would surely increase because of the additional cost of having to 'pay' the wages or salaries of more workers. We need to keep in mind that in the three-membered organization, the price of a commodity is not coupled to the compensation the worker receives. The price is instead coupled with the relationship of commodity value to the consumer and the costs of production. More workers means that more of the commodity is produced; but the production costs *per commodity* do not increase, only the quantity.

> For sound prices can only be fixed within an independent economic system. Sound prices can only be fixed when they develop in accordance with the true valuation of human activity. Therefore the idea of the Threefold Order of the Social Organism is to detach labor completely from the economic process.[60]

Cooperation between entrepreneurial efforts is key aspect of associative economics:

> Negotiations must then be carried on with other branches of production to transfer workers from one branch to another where the need lies, in order that more of the lacking products may be supplied.[61]

This negotiated transfer of workers eliminates the labor market where people and their labor are treated and marketed just like commodities are. What we call 'layoffs' in our society is replaced by a conscious process of transferring workers to where they are needed. This supports human dignity when the workers' involvement in the production of commodities is as Steiner described:

> In a healthy social organism the proletarian worker should not merely stand at his machine, concerned with nothing but its operation, while the capitalist alone knows the fate of the produced commodities in economic circulation. Through fully active participation the worker should be able to develop a clear idea of his own involvement in society through his work on the production of commodities. Regular discussions, which must be considered to be as much a part of the operation as the work itself, should be arranged by management with a view to developing ideas which circumscribe

---

[60] GA 332a, Lecture 2, a bit under 2/3 into lecture (p. 45)
[61] GA 332a, about 3/4 into lecture 2 (p. 49)

employer and employed alike. A healthy activity of this kind will result in an understanding by the worker that correct management of capital benefits the social organism and therewith the worker himself. By means of such openness, based on free mutual understanding, the entrepreneur will be induced to conduct his business in an irreproachable manner.[62]

In our current economic system, "Feeling anxious and depressed, having trouble sleeping, not being able to enjoy activities that you are used to enjoying are all normal feelings that you may experience after a layoff."[63] Conversely, while changes can be stressful, that stress is mitigated by the knowledge that society and in particular the economic domain is cooperatively engaged in, ensuring that people have both productive work that benefits society and, as discussed previously, the will to work because they are assured a voice in the rights domain and are treated co-equally..

However, much has changed in the last 100 years. Moving workers from one branch of production to another is no longer a straightforward task, if it ever was. Both manufacturing and 'intellectual' work requires training. A machine shop worker cannot simply move from one product and its manufacturing process to another without training on new or different equipment. Training in safety and the product itself are also required. Similarly, a software developer cannot move to another product without learning new programming languages and tools and being trained on the new product's existing code written by other software developers. This applies whether the worker moves to another branch of production within the same company or to another company.

Furthermore, industrial robots are now heavily involved in manufacturing. "The new World Robotics 2020 Industrial Robots report shows a record of 2.7 million industrial robots operating in factories around the world – an increase of 12%."[64] The idea that we can "transfer workers from one branch to another where the need lies" must now consider how robots would need to be retooled for different manufacturing requirements to satisfy new needs. This is a clear challenge for associative economics as the use of robots in manufacturing will only continue to increase.

---

[62] GA 23, Chapter 3, 1/6 into Ch. 3 (pp. 88–89)

[63] https://helpcenter.stanford.edu/resources/work-related-resources/coping-emotional-impact-layoff

[64] https://ifr.org/ifr-press-releases/news/record-2.7-million-robots-work-in-factories-around-the-globe

Is our society even ready for associative economics at any scale? When Steiner said:

> Men will be there who will make it their task to regulate production in conformity with their observation of the needs of the consumer. [This is so] that the market will consist in commodities which the associations, already mentioned, will be able to produce ... having first studied and observed intelligently the needs of consumption.[65]

It is perhaps difficult to imagine how in today's world the people whose task it is to 'regulate production' will not be corrupted, just as we see corruption occurring in all three domains today. Regarding associations "having first studied and observed intelligently the needs of consumption," one can again imagine how at present these associations could easily be manipulated by others to produce biased reports on 'the needs of consumption.' The stark reality appears to be that we are not ready, individually or as a society, for associative economics, at least not at a large scale. The question, 'who watches the watchers?' is pertinent today. At some point in the future that question, through human development, must become obsolete. Only at that point does associative economics become realistic.

Regarding the question of 'studying and observing' the needs of consumers, Steiner wrote (Kate's translation):

> For this [the meeting of consumers' needs] it is necessary that, under the influence of the principle of association, the possibility really will be brought about of producing goods in such a way that they correspond to the observed needs; that is, there must be people organized to study the needs. Statistics can only record/take in one moment; they are never definitive for the future. The needs that exist in each case must be studied, after which the arrangements for producing must be made.[66]

As technology continues to pervade our society, the draw and drive to analyze human interactions through statistics only increases. One can imagine that the study of the needs of consumers will continue to result not in human interaction and conversation, but instead the technological reporting, in real-time, of the purchases of consumers. As an indicator of what consumers need, this misrepresents those needs, since the statistics only reflect which *existing* products consumers are purchasing at

---

[65] GA 332a, Lecture 6, about 1/3 into lecture (p. 137)
[66] GA 332a, Lecture 2, about 1/5 from end of lecture (p. 49)

the moment. Furthermore, such a system would require that all consumer purchases be tracked, and to make this possible would most likely result in legislation to remove cash from the economy so that all purchases would be carried out digitally (debit or credit cards or digital wallets) which banks would track and feed into the statistical engines. Those statistics would then most likely be analyzed by artificial intelligence to make changes in production and distribution. Sweden is already planning to become the first cashless country. "A longstanding innovator when it comes to finance and currency, Sweden is leading the way to cashless adoption, with reports predicting it will be fully digital by March 2023."[67] Sweden's government is directly involved in this transition. We need to ask ourselves if we can perceive anything of the rightful roles and limits of activity of the three domains here at all. Clearly, the rights domain is thoroughly enmeshed with and overtaken by driving forces in the economic domain:

> The fact that consumers are so willing to embrace change when it comes to payments is no accident, and in fact has been ushered in by progressive legislation on the government's part. Throughout the retail and hospitality sectors, it's not uncommon to see 'card only' or 'cash free' signs at point of sale. This is thanks to a law that gives merchants the right to only offer digital payment options, despite cash still being recognised as legal tender.[68]

In a digital economy, the consumer's purchases can be used in a variety ways without the consumer's consent, as the Commonwealth Bank in Australia has implemented regarding tracking consumer's carbon footprint:

> Commonwealth Bank (CBA) has included a new feature on its internet banking that tells customers how many trees they've destroyed with their carbon footprint based on monthly spending. The bank is attempting to encourage more sustainable purchases by highlighting the damage its clients have on the environment. ... The bank calculates a customer's carbon footprint based on the 'transactions made on your CommBank credit or debit cards'.[69]

The obvious next step would be to charge people for exceeding a

[67] https://www.globalprocessing.com/news/blog/swedens-2023-cashless-goals
[68] Ibid.
[69] https://www.dailymail.co.uk/news/article-11313965/Commonwealth-Bank-tracking-carbon-footprint.html

carbon footprint allotment that has been assigned to them. The fundamental principle of associative economics is that associations are composed of people, not of technologies. The lure of an ever more digital economy undermines human associations via increasingly more sophisticated information gathering and analysis. These are concerns that were not on the horizon in the early 1900's and that must be considered with conscious thought with regards to the three-membered organization and associative economics.

The dystopian future described above is in direct conflict with associative economics in which real human interaction determines not just future needs for *existing* commodities, but also the need for entrepreneurial efforts to create commodities and services *that do not yet exist.* These needs can only be determined through human interaction and conversation. No artificial intelligence system will ever be able to do this. People working in the cultural domain whose role is to study the needs of society would create avenues of communication and bridges between these needs and the entrepreneurs and those with the knowledge and skill to produce new commodities and services to fulfill these needs; and the necessary capital would be liberated for this production and the disposition of the capital granted within the economic domain.

It should be noted that associations are not unions. "Unions promote economic equality and build worker power, helping workers to win increases in pay, better benefits, and safer working conditions."[70] In our society, unions exist because the rights domain is laggard in doing its job with regard to work safety, human dignity and quality of life, leaving the existing economic domain to do what it will in determining pay and benefits, meaning that it determines the quality of life of the workers. Furthermore, the pay and benefits that unions promote is made obsolete by the three-membered organization.

While this discussion of associative economics is by no means comprehensive, a web page posted by the Goetheanum (the center of Anthroposophical Society, located in Switzerland) addressed the importance for humanity of proceeding through human association. This must be continually borne in our hearts and minds:

> Pointing to the next step after market economics, [associative economics] describes the landscape that comes into being as and

---

[70] https://www.epi.org/publication/unions-and-well-being/

when humanity, individually and collectively, thinks and acts associatively.[71]

In order to move towards associative economics, we must learn to think and act associatively, meaning that the connection between human beings is key: How am I associated with another person and their ideas in the cultural domain? How am I associated with legislation in the rights domain? How am I associated with the processes of production, distribution, and consumption? We must come to concrete thoughts on what these associations mean to us individually and act associatively in accordance with that thinking.

The beauty of associative economics is that it proceeds naturally from organizations practicing social renewal. The three-membered organization establishes independent rights and cultural domains, which in turn establishes a sound economic domain. A sound economic domain is motivated by meeting the needs of society rather than being driven solely by profit. We will also find that key to this sound functioning are the human-to-human contracts between associations within economic activity. As Steiner said:

> The purely business operations and measures which take place should be based upon contracts entered into by the association. In the economic world everything should rest on contracts, everything should depend upon mutual service rendered. Corporations should carry on business with other corporations; expert knowledge and efficiency in particular branches should have the decisive voice. My opinion as a manufacturer, let us say, as to the importance of my particular branch of industry in political life will have no weight when the economic department is independent. I shall have to be productive in my own branch, to enter into contracts with the associations of other branches of industry and they will render me reciprocal services. If I am able to get a return of services for mine, I shall be in a position to carry on my work. An association of efficiency will be formed by means of contract. These are the facts of the case.[72]

Once established, the ability to interact with other organizations (whether or not they are as yet three-membered organizations) through contracts on "mutual service rendered" would be conducted in a manner

---

[71] https://economics.goetheanum.org/research/associative-economics
[72] GA 332a, Lecture 3, a bit over 1/2 into lecture (p. 67)

that ensures human dignity and quality of life for all the organizations entering into the contract.

And lastly, efficiency and quality would be the norm, not the exception. As Steiner said:

> It will not be possible in future to carry on business by means of money and for money; for economic institutions will have to deal with the respective values of the commodities. That is to say, society will again return to goodness of quality, excellence of workmanship and the capability of the worker.[73]

This is not merely a futuristic dream of how the world community could function in relation to human needs and our mutual fulfillment of them.It is a reality that can be created locally if we would conduct our affairs in the manner prescribed by the three-membered organization.

---

[73] GA 332a, Lecture 2, about 1/6 from end of lecture (p. 50)

CONCLUDING THOUGHTS

There is much more in Steiner's seminal book, GA 23, which our book has not covered, particularly the complexity of the aspects of property, inheritance, access and transfer of commodities, savings, etc., described in Chapter 3 of GA 23. International commerce, associations, and different cultural mores (social norms that are widely observed within a particular society or culture) that are described in Chapter 4 are also not covered here. Also, this book does not cover the complexities of our current society's insurance systems (property, health, risk, life, disability, and others) and how these insurance systems would be applied (and even if they are applicable) in a three-membered structure. Also not discussed are the intricacies of the self-correcting nature of the three-membered organization in the context of current economic concerns such as inflation and recession and the measurement of economic growth with statistics such as the Gross Domestic Product. Again, Steiner discussed this self-correcting nature of the three-membered organization in Chapter 3 of GA 23. The reader is encouraged to read GA 332a, *The Social Future*, as much of that book covers specific details on bringing about the realization of the three domains of the social organism that are not covered here, in this book.

By bringing Steiner's work into the context of today's society and its successes and challenges, this book hopefully provides a glimpse of a foundation for further deepening our understanding of our current social order and the potential for its future social order. Hopefully, by outlining some thoughts on individual and small group endeavors in the context of the three-membered organization, further discussions and actual individual and local group initiatives will be created.

Also, the motivation of this book is not to come up with hard conclusions and 'how to' guidance but rather to inspire individual interest in oneself and discussion amongst ourselves with regards to the three-membered organization in the 21st century. Many positive steps have been taken over the last 100 years, as well as many not so positive steps. There are many whose innate sensibility, *Empfindung*, can easily identify the positive and less positive steps. We often find ourselves in disagreement as to what steps have been positive and what steps have not. It is critical to discuss these differences with open mindedness and interest. It is not for this book to judge nor conclude but rather to ask questions, particularly in the area of realizing endeavors as individuals and small groups. If there is a conclusion to be made, it is that the three-membered organization is a significant guiding work in how to achieve human dignity in its external form, and Steiner's seminal works, including the *The Philosophy of Spiritual Activity* (GA 4) and *Knowledge of Higher Worlds* (GA 10) can teach us how to approach human dignity as an inner sense and sensibility, which in turn informs us with regards realizing a three-membered structure.

Lastly, there are several continually recurring themes in this book. They are:

- The need to cognize the need for human dignity, rights, and quality of life.
- That the environment is also a consideration nowadays with regards to dignity, rights, and the quality of its life, as the quality of the environment directly impacts human quality of life.
- The need for self-development, particularly the development of a conscious *Empfindung* with regards to the future of the social organism.
- That the realization of a three-membered organization can happen now in concrete steps.

Hopefully these themes, as illustrated in the context of historical and current events, allows the reader to approach Steiner's work, GA 23, *Towards Social Renewal*, with a fresh and much needed perspective.

BOOKS, LECTURES,
and ONLINE RESOURCES

THE SEMINAL WORKS OF RUDOLF STEINER

Listed according to the GA number (GA, Gesamtausgabe; or CW, Collected Works).

The Science of Knowing: An Outline of an Epistemology Implicit in Goethe's World View (GA 2, *Grundlinien einer Erkenntnistheorie der Goetheschen Weltanschauung, mit besonderer Rücksicht auf Schiller*, 1886):

> GA 2 translated by William Lindeman under the above title, Mercury Press, 1988

> GA 2 translated by Olin D. Wannamaker under the title, *A Theory of Knowledge Implicit in Goethe's World Conception*, Anthroposophic Press, 1968, 2nd Edition 1978

> The Lindeman and Wannamaker translations plus the German (we recommend that the reader rely on these two older translations of GA 2)

The Philosophy of Spiritual Activity (GA 4, *Die Philosophie der Freiheit*, 1894)

Christianity as Mystical Fact and the Mysteries of Antiquity (GA 8, *Das Christentum als mystische Tatsache und die Mysterien des Altertums*, 1901/1902)

Theosophy: An Introduction to the Supersensible Knowledge of the World and the Destination of Man (GA 9, *Theosophie: Einführung in übersinnliche Welterkenntnis und Menschenbestimmung*, 1904)

Knowledge of Higher Worlds (GA 10, *Wie erlangt man Erkenntnisse der höheren Welten?*) Steiner collected a series of single essays he began to publish in 1904

The Stages of Higher Knowledge (GA 12, *Die Stufen der höheren Erkenntnis*). This volume is a continuation of the series of single essays that Steiner published as GA 10.

Occult Science: An Outline (GA 13, *Die Geheimwissenschaft im Umriss*, 1909

BOOKS AND LECTURES ON THE SOCIAL ORGANISM

Works by Rudolf Steiner

Listed according to the GA number

GA 23: Here are two English versions of Rudolf Steiner's primary book on the three-membered organization of the social organism, *Die Kernpunkte der Sozialen Frage in den Lebensnotwendigkeiten der Gegenwart und Zukunft*, published in 1919. A close translation of the title would be: *The Core Points of the Social Question in the Necessities of Life of the Present and Future*. We strongly recommend the translation by Frank Thomas Smith over that by Frederick C. Heckel. The F. T Smith translation is unabridged.

> *Die Kernpunkte der Sozialen Frage in den Lebensnotwendigkeiten der Gegenwart und Zukunft*, 1919: http://anthroposophie.byu.edu/schriften/023.pdf

> Unabridged translation by Frank Thomas Smith under the titles, *Basic Issues of the Social Question* (as found online, date not stated); *Towards Social Renewal: Basic Issues of the Social Question*, 1977, Rudolf Steiner Press, London; and *Towards a Threefold Society: Basic Issues of the Social Question*, 2019, Rudolf Steiner Publications

> Translation by Frederick C. Heckel under the title, *The Threefold Social Order*, Anthroposophic Press Inc., New York, 1966, 1972

The Renewal of the Social Organism, GA 24, volume of articles written by Steiner in 1919 and 1920, translated by E. Bowen-Wedgwood and Ruth Mariott, revised by Frederick Amrine, Anthroposophic Press, Spring Valley NY, 1985 (and Rudolf Steiner Press, London)

"Anthroposophy and the Social Question," GA 34, essay in three parts by Rudolf Steiner, published in 1905/1906 in This Mercury Press edition of Anthroposophy and the Social Question, first published in 1982, is a translation of three essays by Dr. Rudolf Steiner which first appeared in the journal "Lucifer-Gnosis", October 1905/1906, under the title Geisteswissenschaft and soziale Frage.

The most recent German edition appeared in Vol. 34 of the Rudolf Steiner Gesamtausgabe published by the Rudolf Steiner — Nachlassverwaltung in Dornach, Switzerland, 1960.

"The Social Question and Theosophy," GA 68d (which contains a disparate collection of lectures), lecture given by Rudolf Steiner on October 26, 1905, Berlin, translated by John Root, Sr. (This lecture was replaced by another where it is found within a series of lectures, under the title, "Anthroposophy and the Social Question.")

"The Work of the Angels in Man's Astral Body," in GA 182, lecture given by Rudolf Steiner on October 9, 1918 in Zurich, Switzerland

The Challenge of our Times, GA 186, six lectures given by Rudolf Steiner in November and December 1918, translated by Olin D. Wannamaker, Anthroposophic Press, Spring Valley NY, 1941

Social Understanding Through Spiritual-Scientific Knowledge, GA 191, fifteen lectures given by Rudolf Steiner In October and November, 1919

The Esoteric Aspect of the Social Question, GA 193, three lectures given by Rudolf Steiner in February and March, 1919, translated by Charles Davy, Anthroposophical Press, 1950, Rudolf Steiner Press, London, 1974; also published as The Inner Aspect of the Social Question

The Threefold Order of the Body Social I and II, Study Series,, GA 330 and GA 335/GA 337 respectively, Rudolf Steiner.

The Social Future, GA 332a, six lectures given by Rudolf Steiner in October 1919, with an Introduction by Bernard Behrens in August of 1945, translator not given, Anthroposophic Press; also published by the Anthroposophic Press in 1972 and by Steinerbooks in 2013, translator not known, revised by Henry B. Monges.

World Economy, GA 340, fourteen lectures given by Rudolf Steiner in July and August 1922

WORKS ON THE SOCIAL QUESTION BY OTHERS

Associative Economics: Spiritual Activity for the Common Good
Gary Lamb, Waldorf Publications; 1st edition, August 26, 2016

Steinerian Economics: A Compendium
Edited by Gary Lamb and Sarah Hearn, Adonis Press, March 31, 2016

Vision in Action: Working with Soul & Spirit in Small Organizations,
Christopher Schaefer and Tÿno Voors, Lindisfarne Books; 2nd Rev ed.
   edition, July 1, 1996

HOLDING CONVERSATION, STUDY GROUPS, AND WORKSHOPS

Open Space Technology / Forum
https://openspaceworld.org/wp2/what-is/

Liberating Structures
https://www.liberatingstructures.com/
Summary here: https://marcclifton.wordpress.com/2013/05/20/
   liberating-structures/

Marjorie Spock's essay, *The Art of Goethean Conversation*
http://westdalechildrensschool.weebly.com/uploads/1/7/7/9/17799545/
   article_-the_art_of_goethean_conversation.pdf

Marc Clifton's commentary on *The Art of Goethean Conversation*
https://marcclifton.wordpress.com/2012/12/24/
   marjorie-spocks-the-art-of-goethean-conversation/

GROSS NATIONAL HAPPINESS

Gross National Happiness and Development (Proceedings of the First International Seminar on Operationalization of Gross National Happiness)
   The Center for Bhutan Studies, Edited by Karma Ura & Karma Galay
   https://www.rybinski.eu/uploads/gross_national_hapiness_book.pdf

"Gross National Happiness: Towards Buddhist Economics," Sander G.
   Tideman, 38 page article: https://www.researchgate.net/publica-
   tion/238787860_Gross_National_Happiness_Towards_Buddhist_
   Economics

"Will 'Middle Way Economics' Emerge from the Gross National Happiness
   Approach of Bhutan?," Hans van Willenswaard, chapter of a book, pp.

214-21: https://fid4sa-repository.ub.uni-heidelberg.de/377/1/Middle_Way_Economics_and_GNH.pdf

OTHER SOURCES

Harvard University Implicit Association Test: https://implicit.harvard.edu/implicit/takeatest.html

BIBLIOGRAPHY

For the books and lectures by Rudolf Steiner, the first listing is the first known publication of the book or lecture in German along with the original German title. Following the German publication reference are one or more references to English translations.

GA 4

Steiner, R., *Die Philosophie der Freiheit*. Rudolf Steiner Gesamtausgabe, Vorrede zur Neuausgabe, 1918. First German Edition published 1894

Steiner, R., (1963, 1980) *The Philosophy of Spiritual Activity*. Translated by Rita Stebbing. Rudolf Steiner Publications

GA 23

Steiner, R. *Die Kernpunkte der sozialen Frage in den Lebensnotwendigkeiten der Gegenwart und Zukunft*. Rudolf Steiner Taschenbücher aus dem Gesamtwerk, Fist German Edition published 1919

Steiner, R. (date unknown, 1977, 2019) *Basic Issues of the Social Question,*, or *Towards Social Renewal: Basic Issues of the Social Question*, or *Toward a Threefold Society: Basic Issues of the Social Question*. Translated by F.T. Smith. Rudolf Steiner Publications

Steiner, R., (1966, 1972) *The Threefold Social Order*. Translated by F. C. Heckel. London: Rudolf Steiner

In the original German, *Die Kernpunkte der sozialen Frage in den Lebensnotwendigkeiten der Gegenwart und der Zukunft*
http://anthroposophie.byu.edu/schriften/023.pdf

GA 24

Steiner, R., *Aufsätze über die Dreigliederung des sozialen Organismus und zur Zeitlage 1915-1921*. First German Edition published 1961

Steiner R., (1985) *The Renewal of the Social Organism*. Translated by E. Bowen-Wedgewood and Ruth Mariott, revised by Frederick Amrine, Anthroposophic Press

GA 34

LUCIFER- GNOSIS 1903-1908 GRUNDLEGENDE AUFSÄTZE ZUR ANTHROPOSOPHIE UND BERICHTE. April 1904, translated by Nesta Carsten-Krüger; first German edition published 1960, (see p. 453, "und die Schattenseite…")
http://fvn-archiv.net/PDF/GA/GA034.pdf#page=453

GA 34

Steiner, R., "Anthroposophy and the Social Question," essay in three parts translated by Harry Collison: originally published in *LUCIFER-GNOSIS 1903-1908 GRUNDLEGENDE AUFSÄTZE ZUR ANTHROPOSOPHIE UND BERICHTE* in 1906/1906 as "Geisteswissenschaft und der soziale Frage;" p. 191
https://www.rudolfsteinerelib.org/Articles/GA034/ (whole volume)
https://wn.rudolfsteinerelib.org/Articles/GA034/English/MP1982/AnSoQu_index.html (the essay)

GA 68d (Note: this GA number contains a disparate collection of lectures)
"The Social Question and Theosophy," lecture given by Rudolf Steiner on October 26, 1905, Berlin, translated by John Root, Sr.
https://rsarchive.org/Lectures/SQ1157_index.html

GA 141

Steiner, R., *Das Leben zwischen dem Tode und der neuen Geburt im Verhältnis zu den kosmischen Tatsachen.* Ten private lectures given to the Members of the Anthroposophical Society between 11/5/1912 and 4/1/1913. First German Edition published 1916
Steiner, R., (1975) *Life between Death and Rebirth: The Active Connection between the Living and the Dead.* SteinerBooks; 1st edition, Translated by René M. Querido

GA 146

Steiner, R., *Die okkulten Grundlagen der Bhagavad Gita*, 1961
Steiner, R., (1968). *The Occult Significance of the Bhagavad Gita*, SteinerBooks, Translated by George and Mary Adams

GA 186

Steiner, R. *Die soziale Grundforderung unserer Zeit - In geänderter Zeitlage.* First German Edition published 1963

Steiner, R ,(1979). *The Challenge of the Times.* Translated by O. D. Wannamaker. SteinerBooks, first edition

Note that the online version has many more lectures in it than the book does.

GA 189

Steiner, R,. *Die soziale Frage als Bewußtseinsfrage. Die geistigen Hintergründe deer sozialen Frage - Band I.* Eight lectures given between 2/15/1919 and 3/16/1919. First German Edition published 1946

Steiner, R,. Lecture II, *Threefolding. The Intellectual, Political and Economic Life in its Relation to Prenatal, Present, and the Life after Death. The Twofold Way to the Christ.* February 16, 1919

GA 191

Steiner, R., *Soziales Verstandnis aus geisteswissenschaftlichen Erkentnis Die Geistige Hintergründe der Sozialen Frage - Band III.* Fifteen lectures given between 10/3/1919 and 11/15/1919. First German Edition published in 1972.

Steiner, R., *Social Understanding Through Spiritual Scientific Knowledge.* Lecture, October 4, 1919

GA 193

The Esoteric Aspect of the Social Question, GA 193, three lectures given by Rudolf Steiner in February and March, 1919, translated by Charles Davy, Anthroposophical Press, 1950, Rudolf Steiner Press, London, 1974; also published as The Inner Aspect of the Social Question

GA 332a

Steiner, R., *Soziale Zukunft.* First German Edition published in 1950. Six lectures given between 10/24/1919 and 10/30/1919

Steiner, R., (2013) *The Social Future.* Revised by Henry B. Monges. SteinerBooks

(online edition appears to be from 1945 and translation differs)

GA 340

Steiner, R., *Aufgaben einer neuen Wirtschaftswissenschaft, Bd.1, Nationalökonomischer Kurs.* First German Edition published in 1922. Fourteen lectures given between 7/24/1922 and 8/6/1922

Steiner, R., (1990) *World Economy.* Rudolf Steiner Press; 3rd edition, No translator cited.

Andrew Brogan, Steiner Shorts

#2: https://www.academia.edu/62166396/Steiner_Shorts_2_The_ Threefold_Social_Organism_An_Introduction

#3: https://www.academia.edu/67073076/Steiner_Shorts_3_The_ Social_Problem

ABOUT *the* AUTHOR *and* CONTRIBUTOR

MARC CLIFTON

Marc enjoys a career in software development and technical writing, having published over 250 articles on software development and four e-books. Marc has blogged about Goethean Conversation as described by Marjorie Spock and in general the spiritual concepts described by Rudolf Steiner as well as developing an experiential workshop on the practice of Goethean Conversation. Besides software development, he publishes a (mostly) monthly newsletter, The Philmonter, which always includes an interview of a Philmont NY resident to emphasize his passion regarding Community, Collaboration and Conversation.

Contact: marc.clifton@gmail.com

KATE REESE HURD

Kate Reese Hurd is a resident of Philmont NY, long-time anthroposophist and graduated eurythmist with a background in music and literature, reciter of poetry since 2015 and writer of articles and reports on eurythmy and a manual of speech work exercises (alliterations and assonance) in relation to eurythmy. In her library for many years has been the work of Rudolf Steiner on the three domains of the social organism. One reason for her long-standing interest in the 'social question' is not just what she has perceived as unhealthy arrangements within the body-social generally, but also what she experienced personally as someone inclined toward working in several of the arts. One of her parents actively blocked her efforts to gain appropriate training. Why was this? – for fear that she might not be able to 'support' herself as a musician, artist or eurythmist. And this worry is quite right when facing social arrangements as they stand! But one thing her parent failed to grasp is Kate's desire to work and to be productive no matter what – a healthy trait, artist or not!

Contact: sweatermender@gmail.com

Milton Keynes UK
Ingram Content Group UK Ltd.
UKHW022049240823
427459UK00013B/176/J

9 781960 090256